The genesis of literature in Islam

The New Edinburgh Islamic Surveys
Series Editor: Carole Hillenbrand

TITLES AVAILABLE OR FORTHCOMING

Contemporary Issues in Islam Asma Asfaruddin
The New Islamic Dynasties Clifford Edmund Bosworth
Media Arabic Julia Ashtiany Bray
An Introduction to the Hadith John Burton
A History of Islamic Law Noel Coulson
Medieval Islamic Political Thought Patricia Crone
A Short History of the Ismailis Farhad Daftary
Islam: An Historical Introduction (2nd Edition) Gerhard Endress
A History of Christian–Muslim Relations Hugh Goddard
Medieval Islamic Science Robert Hall
Shi'ism (2nd Edition) Heinz Halm
Islamic Science and Engineering Donald Hill
Islamic Law: From Historical Foundations to Contemporary Practice Mawil Izzi Dien
Sufism: The Formative Period Ahmet T. Karamustafa
Islamic Aesthetics Oliver Leaman
Persian Historiography Julie Scott Meisami
Pilgrims and Pilgrimage Josef Meri
The Muslims of Medieval Italy Alex Metcalfe
The Archaeology of the Islamic World Marcus Milwright
Twelver Shi'ism: Unity and Diversity in the Life of Islam Andrew Newman
Muslims in Western Europe (3rd Edition) Jørgen Nielsen
Medieval Islamic Medicine Peter E. Pormann and Emilie Savage-Smith
Islamic Names Annemarie Schimmel
The Genesis of Literature in Islam Gregor Schoeler
Modern Arabic Literature Paul Starkey
Islamic Medicine Manfred Ullman
Islam and Economics Ibrahim Warde
A History of Islamic Spain W. Montgomery Watt and Pierre Cachia
Introduction to the Qur'an W. Montgomery Watt
Islamic Creeds W. Montgomery Watt
Islamic Philosophy and Theology W. Montgomery Watt
Islamic Political Thought W. Montgomery Watt
The Influence of Islam on Medieval Europe W. Montgomery Watt

The genesis of literature in Islam

From the aural to the read

REVISED EDITION

GREGOR SCHOELER

in collaboration with and translated by

SHAWKAT M. TOORAWA

EDINBURGH UNIVERSITY PRESS

First published in France by
Presses Universitaires de France,
6 avenue Reille, 75014 Paris, in 2002 as
Écrire et transmettre dans les débuts de l'islam

Edinburgh University Press Ltd
22 George Square, Edinburgh
www.euppublishing.com

Typeset in Goudy by
Koinonia, Manchester, and
printed and bound in Great Britain by
CPI Antony Rowe, Chippenham, Wilts

A CIP Record for this book is available from the British Library

ISBN 978 0 7486 2467 6 (hardback)
ISBN 978 0 7486 2468 3 (paperback)

Ouvrage publié avec le concours du Ministère français chargé
de la culture – Centre national du livre.

Published with the assistance of the French Ministry of Culture –
National Book Centre.

Published with the support of the Edinburgh University Scholarly
Publishing Initiatives Fund.

Contents

Author's preface

This is a revised edition and English translation of my French book, *Écrire et transmettre dans les débuts de l'islam*. The text for this new edition has been carefully revised, corrected and enlarged. The most important revision is the addition of Chapter 7, 'Books and their readership in the ninth century', dealing essentially with al-Jāḥiẓ, to whose work I had devoted only a few pages in the first French edition. For this new chapter, I have made use of ideas I first put into words for a paper I presented at the International Conference, 'Al-Jahiz: A Muslim Humanist for our Time', held in Beirut in January of 2005. Another important modification is the conclusion, which I have significantly rewritten.

I am deeply indebted to Professor Shawkat Toorawa, the *spiritus auctor* of the project to translate my book into English, and also the editor of this work. Thanks to his expert knowledge in the field, Professor Toorawa has mastered the difficult task of translating my work with consummate skill. In addition, he suggested many corrections to the text and contributed many ideas of his own to the book.

In a word, he was not only the work's ideal translator but also the best collaborator I could wish for. What is more, our collaboration was a wonderful experience: during our common labour a deep mutual sympathy and friendship developed: I shall remember our collaboration with great pleasure and deep gratitude.

My thanks go to all those who have contributed to this project and brought it to fruition. I am in particular much obliged to Professor Carole Hillenbrand at the University of Edinburgh for her willingness to include this book in the New Edinburgh Islamic Surveys Series, and to our editor at Edinburgh University Press, Nicola Ramsey.

Basel, Switzerland

Translator's preface

At the annual meeting of the American Oriental Society in San Diego in 2004, Beatrice Gruendler mentioned Professor Gregor Schoeler's *Écrire et transmettre dans les débuts de l'Islam* (Paris, 2002) during a presentation. I had not yet seen the work but immediately bought and read it. That summer I travelled to Edinburgh and proposed to Professor Carole Hillenbrand that the book be included in the New Edinburgh Islamic Surveys Series. To my delight, Edinburgh University Press subsequently acquired the rights to the book, and invited me to translate it. I am grateful to the outside referees who endorsed me as a translator, and to Carole Hillenbrand, Nicola Ramsey and Eddie Clark at the Press for their confidence, limitless patience and goodwill.

I began translating in Delhi in mid-2006, and continued in 2007 in Oxford, while on a leave supported by a New Directions Fellowship from the Mellon Foundation. I am grateful to Chase Robinson and Jeremy Johns for sponsoring me as a Visiting Scholar at Wolfson College, and to Farhan Nizami for providing me with an office at the Oxford Centre for Islamic Studies. I completed the translation upon my return to Cornell University. I am especially grateful to my chair, Kim Haines-Eitzen, and to Maude Rith, Chrissy Capalongo, Julie Graham and Shelly Marino, for making the Department of Near Eastern Studies such a conducive and wonderful place to work.

I thank the members of RRAALL (www.rraall.org) for their *ṣuḥbah*; James Montgomery for very kindly sharing a pre-publication copy of the English translations of Professor Schoeler's German articles, published together in 2006 as *The Oral and the Written in Early Islam*; Joseph Lowry for nuancing my understanding of German and much else besides; Michael Carter for generous and expert assistance with the English rendering of Sībawayhi's chapter headings; and my wife Parvine Bahemia for bringing to bear her intuitive knowledge of French. As always, the support and indulgence of my family – Parvine, our children, Maryam and Asiya-Tanveer Jahan, and my late father, Mahmood, who eagerly awaited the appearance of this translation, but passed away a few weeks before it was completed – cannot be quantified or repaid.

Professor Schoeler and I corresponded regularly as we attempted to convey precisely his ideas as originally expressed, as they have been refined in light of the development of his thinking in the six years since the original French appeared, and as we re-ordered sections within chapters, and even added a chapter. Our conversations meant that I was able to engage, learn from, collaborate with, and befriend a formidable scholar. For this opportunity and pleasure, I reserve my greatest thanks.

Ithaca, New York

Introduction

Literature, as it is understood in this book, is the body of finalised, published written works belonging to a language or people – for our purposes, the Arabic language or the Arabic-speaking Muslim community. 'Finalised' means that those written works constituting 'literature' were definitively redacted and edited by their authors, and 'published' means that they were produced with a public readership in mind. Taken in this wider sense, literature perforce includes scholarly works, documents, official letters and the like, i.e. works serving practical needs. Besides contracts, official letters and so on, for more than a century after the appearance of Islam, there existed only one piece of literature in Arabic: the Qur'ān. But even this exceptional work – the very first work of Arabic literature – needed some twenty-five years to become an actual 'book', an actual 'literary work'. The Ḥadīth, the reports of the words and deeds of the Prophet Muḥammad disseminated and transmitted soon after his death, needed up to 250 years to become 'literature'; as for Arabic poetry, which had been in existence since long before the rise of Islam, it needed up to 300 years to become 'literature'. What was the nature of this early material? What form did it take and under what circumstances did it subsequently become actual literature? In what ways were the materials of this literature transmitted? And how did it go on to become one of the largest and most multifaceted of all the world's literatures? These are questions this book attempts to answer.

Since the matter of the genesis of Arabic literature is closely bound up with the nature and character of its transmission, and since this has been difficult for scholars to appreciate, I deal with this in the first part of this Introduction. In the second part, I briefly describe my methodology, in particular my attitude toward the sources. This account is necessary because incorrect recent assessments of both the nature and reliability of the sources we have available – even the historicity of Muḥammad, for instance, has been called into question – are having a truly damaging effect on the value accorded these sources and the events they report.

The problematic of the 'oral' and the 'written'

The relationship, in the early stages of Arabic literature, in particular during the first two centuries of Islam (ca. 600–800 CE), between the oral and the written is complex. Because of its complexity, this relationship has been difficult for scholars to grasp fully. This applies first and foremost to the Qur'ān. The Prophet Muḥammad (d. 11/632) is said to have dictated several Qur'ānic surahs, or parts of surahs; indeed, several of his Companions are reported to have had complete copies in their possession shortly after his death. Yet, in order to produce the first 'collection' of the Qur'ān under Abū Bakr (d. 13/634) or 'Umar (d. 25/644), the compiler, Zayd ibn Thābit (d. ca. 45/666), is said to have relied on notes written on various materials (pieces of papyrus, flat stones, palm leaves and so on) as well as on oral transmission. According to Muslim tradition, it was not until twenty-five years after Muḥammad's death, under 'Uthmān, that the Qur'ān acquired its definitive written form.

The relationship between the oral and the written is even more difficult to assess when it comes to Ḥadīth, the corpus of traditions (*aḥādīth*, sing. *ḥadīth*) relating Muḥammad's words and deeds. Although some Companions of Muḥammad who knew how to read and write appear initially to have made it a practice to write down some of his words and to display no scruples about doing so, Ḥadīth scholars argued throughout the eighth century, and indeed in the subsequent century too, about the permissibility of writing down ḥadīths. Many were of the opinion that it was forbidden, averring that the Qur'ān should remain Islam's one and only book. This argument presupposed, of course, that a significant amount of material had already been put into writing, an undertaking that had its own active supporters and whose slogan was 'Shackle knowledge' (*qayyidū al-'ilm*).[1] Moreover, biographical literature frequently makes mention of the 'books' (*kutub*) that Ḥadīth scholars had in their possession, and the claim is made that the leading scholar al-Zuhrī (d. 124/742) undertook to collect and write down ḥadīths on a large scale (*tadwīn*) under official impetus – this in spite of the fact that he is portrayed as an opponent of writing in several accounts. Yet, after his death only one or two notebooks were found among the things he left behind.

According to the information in the biographical literature, it was around the middle of the eighth century that works that can be classified as *muṣannafāt*, 'compilations systematically arranged according to content', first appeared in the various fields of Islamic scholarship. Nevertheless, the sources state about some of the compilers of these works that they 'possessed no book but rather reported (everything) from memory (*lam yakun lahu kitāb, innamā kāna yaḥfaẓu*)'. Even in the ninth century, at a time when the production of literary works had begun on a truly large scale, several scholars are said to have recited their teachings from memory without ever having used a book – the ninth-century compiler, Ibn Abī Shaybah (d. 235/849), for example, states at the beginning of several chapters in his magnum opus, 'This is what I know by heart from the Prophet'. And yet, we are told that a number of these very same scholars had in their homes a large number of 'books'.

If we turn to poetry and its transmission, we find that the situation is almost as complex. It is undeniable that for ancient Arabic poetry, composition, recitation and also transmission were all oral, whence the hapless attempts by American scholars of the late twentieth century to transpose onto ancient Arabic odes (*qaṣīdah*, pl. *qaṣā'id*) the 'theory of oral formulaic composition' developed by Milman Parry and Albert Lord.[2] This theory proposes that epics and other poetic texts preserved only in writing – but which supposedly first existed in popular oral forms – must have been improvised during recitation because of their use of recurrent formulae, a feature termed 'formulaic diction' or 'formularity'. The famous ninth-century poets Abu Tammām, al-Buḥturī and Ibn al-Rūmī did not find it necessary to produce editions of their own poetry. Indeed, most of the modernist 'Abbāsid poets (*muḥdathūn*) of the ninth and tenth centuries left it to later generations to compile their poems and to edit them in *dīwāns*, but we know for a fact that they used written notes and even had written collections. Specific references to written poetic collections appear very early, at the latest in the middle of the Umayyad period (ca. 700), in particular in poems of undeniable authenticity, such as one flyting (*naqīḍah*, pl. *naqā'iḍ*) by al-Farazdaq (d. ca. 110/728).[3] Certainly, poetic compositions were always intended for oral recitation.

This confusing and often contradictory picture has led both modern Western and modern Arab scholarship to an understanding of the relationship between the oral and the written that is only partly tenable – if it is tenable at all – notwithstanding the research undertaken by two formidable scholars, Nāṣir al-dīn al-Asad in poetry and 'Abd al-'Azīz al-Dūrī in historiography. Western scholarly interest in this thorny issue dates from the nineteenth century. Surprisingly, Aloys Sprenger, the very first scholar to have given serious thought to this question, is also the one to have proposed one of the most satisfactory answers. All credit is due to him for having pointed out a fundamental distinction that was almost completely forgotten by the second half of the twentieth century, when the debate around this question intensified, a distinction that has had to be rediscovered. In his monumental study of the Prophet Muḥammad, Sprenger pointed out that 'We have to distinguish between aides-mémoire, lecture notebooks, and published books'.[4] An earlier article by Sprenger on Ḥadīth is similarly replete with apposite observations about this question; he pointed out, for example, that the oldest notes in the domain of Ḥadīth were intended as aides-mémoire and not as actual books.[5]

After Sprenger, Ignaz Goldziher published an overview of the historical development of Ḥadīth, one that is still correct in the fundamentals and which to this day still elicits admiration.[6] Goldziher, following Sprenger, accurately qualified the ḥadīths written down in the earliest period and mentioned in the biographical sources as 'notebooks, perhaps collections of individual sayings ... for private use'.[7] He also described with great precision the debate among Ḥadīth scholars about recording ḥadīths in writing.[8] On the other hand, he failed correctly to appreciate two decisive stages of development,[9] that of *tadwīn*, the movement to collect material on a large scale often under official impetus, and that of *taṣnīf*,[10] the movement systematically to arrange material into thematic chapters. Thus, Goldziher was convinced that one had to reject as pure fiction any information about the large collections of ḥadīths systematically arranged into thematic chapters that are said to have existed in the eighth century. In order to support his denial of the existence of such collections a century before those of al-Bukhārī (d. 256/870) and Muslim (d. 261/875), even when biographical sources make repeated mention of them, Goldziher relied on statements which he gleaned from the very same sources, according to which many of these compilers are said to have 'possessed no book' and to have been 'committed to transmitting from memory'.[11] At most, he was willing to accept that certain juridical collections of that period (but which he did not qualify as Ḥadīth collections) were systematically organised, a position he had to adopt because of the existence of such works as the *Muwaṭṭa'* (The Well-Trodden [Path]) of Mālik ibn Anas (d. 179/796).

Goldziher's views prevailed virtually unchanged in Western scholarship until the 1960s. Joseph Schacht, for example, accepted Goldziher's views as self-evident in several of his works, including *The Origins of Muhammadan Jurisprudence*, a work that had no real stake in the question of the oral or written transmission of ḥadīths.[12] Goldziher's propositions were even enlisted to explain the appearance of other kinds of literature – history,[13] literary history, Qur'ānic commentary, and so on – which, in terms of the transmission of knowledge, followed the procedure customary in ḥadīth transmission of relying on a chain of authorities (*isnād*, pl. *asānīd*). This led, among other things, to an incorrect and contradictory evaluation of the sources of the great compilations of the ninth and tenth centuries. Jean Sauvaget consequently termed the sources upon which al-Ṭabarī relied for his monumental universal history 'oral' ones,[14] whereas Rudi Paret, author of the article on al-Ṭabarī in the first *Encyclopaedia of Islam*, divided these sources into 'oral transmission' and 'written sources', taking the latter to mean actual books.[15]

Martin Hartmann, a contemporary of Goldziher's, had already disputed the validity of the latter's views about the late beginning of the *taṣnīf* movement (i.e. not until the ninth century), but his objections fell on deaf ears.[16] Hartmann had invoked the existence of a part of the *Muṣannaf* (The Systematically Arranged [Collection]) of 'Abd Allāh ibn al-Mubārak (d. 181/797) preserved in later recensions. Even Goldziher's revision of his own original position has not received the attention it deserves: in a later study, he would subsequently recognise the existence of at least *one* Ḥadīth work of the eighth century organised into thematic chapters, namely the *Muṣannaf* of Wakīʿ ibn al-Jarrāḥ (d. 197/812), cited in the *Musnad* (The [Collection] Organised according to the Last Transmitter before the Prophet) of Aḥmad Ibn Ḥanbal (d. 241/855), the subject of Goldziher's study in question.[17] Consequently, Goldziher felt compelled to reject the information on which he had himself relied earlier, according to which Wakīʿ made it a practice always to transmit orally, without any book. As we shall see, the apparently contradictory accounts concerning this particular Ḥadīth scholar of Basra are in no way mutually exclusive if we take into account the methods of scholarly transmission in use at the time in his city.

In studies of the transmission of early Arabic poetry, the relationship between the oral and the written has not been properly understood either. This is especially true for the second half of the eighth century, what for Ḥadīth is the *taṣnīf* period. In Régis Blachère's view, the 'great transmitters' of that period, Abū 'Amr ibn al-'Alā' (d. ca. 154/770–1 or 157/774), Ḥammād al-Rāwiyah (d. ca. 156/773) and others, did not record in writing the poems and accounts they knew,[18] and it would only be in the next generation, the generation of scholars such as al-Aṣmaʿī (d. 213/826) and Abū 'Ubaydah (d. 207/822), that the materials they transmitted would find their way into 'written texts'; their students would then, in turn, orally explain and transmit these written works to compilers such as Abū al-Faraj al-Iṣbahānī (d. 356/967).[19] But as we shall see, one of these 'great transmitters', Ḥammād al-Rāwiyah, though he always transmitted his material orally, is nevertheless said to have recorded information about various tribes and their poetic output in 'writings' (*kutub*) that he used exclusively at home in order to help bolster his memory.

Since the 1960s Islamic Studies has had to reorient itself to, and sometimes engage in, a debate over an entirely different perspective on the question of the oral and the written. This was a direct result of the publication of two monumental works, Nabia Abbot's *Studies in Arabic Literary Papyri* on the one hand, and Fuat Sezgin's *Geschichte des arabischen Schrifttums* on the other.[20] These two scholars argued that Arabic authors had used writing on an occasional basis to note down poetry ever since pre-Islamic times. According to them, Arabs produced an ever-burgeoning literature right from the very beginnings of Islam and continued to do so during the Umayyad period, i.e. between 630 and 750; they also argued that several disciplines in Islamic scholarship were already fully developed as early as the eighth century.

Sezgin followed traditional scholars in maintaining that Ḥadīth and most of the other Islamic disciplines had developed more or less simultaneously and organically according to the following model:

kitābah (writing down ḥadīths, exegetical traditions, accounts etc.)
> *tadwīn* (collecting scattered material)
> *taṣnīf* (systematically arranging material in written works, with titles indicating the subject matter).[21]

According to Sezgin, whose reasoning deserves close scrutiny, actual books were composed not only during the *taṣnīf* phase, but in earlier times too. Thus ʿAbd Allāh ibn al-ʿAbbās (d. 68/687), for example, a cousin of the Prophet and the alleged founder of Qur'ānic exegesis, can be said to have 'himself written' a Qur'ān commentary.[22] The works of this early period, for the most part lost, as Sezgin himself conceded, could however be reconstructed, often word for word, and sometimes even in their entirety, by relying on the later compilations of the ninth and tenth centuries. This was possible thanks to the *isnāds*, or chains of authorities, provided by the transmitters and thanks also to a specific method developed by Sezgin, one he described in considerable detail.[23] Sezgin subsequently announced the discovery of a series of early texts, among them the *Tafsīr* (Qur'ān Commentary) of Mujāhid (d. 104/722) and the *Kitāb al-Ghārāt* (Book of Raids) of Abū Mikhnaf (d. 157/774), i.e. works that he assumed were sources for later compilations (e.g. the *Tafsīr* and *Ta'rīkh* of al-Ṭabarī [d. 310/926], respectively).[24]

With the introduction of this innovative hypothesis into the debate and the announcement of the discovery of source works dating from the seventh and eighth centuries, the way was now open for a series of studies designed to put this theory to the test. The outcome of these subsequent studies only partially confirmed what was being proposed. These studies made it even clearer that the transmission of knowledge in the Islamic disciplines had depended on written notes from an early date. And they showed that it was true that these disciplines developed more or less contemporaneously, even if that development did not occur in quite as schematic a way as Sezgin had imagined. In any event, there did exist, at the time of Mālik ibn Anas, and even before, early Ḥadīth works of the *muṣannaf* type, systematically organised into chapters: the *Jāmiʿ* (The Compilation) and the *Tafsīr* (Qur'ān Commentary) of Maʿmar ibn Rāshid (d. 154/770), and two parts of the *Muṣannaf* (The Systematically Arranged [Collection]) of ʿAbd Allāh ibn Mubārak (d. 181/797), namely the 'Kitāb al-Zuhd' (Book of Renunciation) and the 'Kitāb al-Jihād' (Book of Struggle), for example, which have survived in later recensions. On this question, therefore, Goldziher's initial position that there were no such works must be regarded as obsolete. On the other hand, by comparing several versions of the same report in the works of the compilers of the ninth and tenth centuries, considerable divergences emerged. Sezgin's notion that texts were transcribed word for word from actual books must therefore be regarded as mistaken.

What these studies underscored above all was that the alleged early works discovered by Sezgin were nothing of the sort: at best they were later recensions of these works, transmitted and often reworked by subsequent generations of disciples. This can be seen clearly with the Qur'ān commentary attributed to Mujāhid. In their careful analysis Georg Stauth and Fred Leemhuis have shown that it is categorically not the *original* (and frequently cited) work by this early commentator, but rather a ninth-century compilation in which numerous exegetical traditions attributed to Mujāhid are combined with other exegetical material not originating with him. The Mujāhid traditions it contains correspond not at all, or only partially, to those contained in well-known later compilations (e.g. al-Ṭabarī's *Tafsīr*).[25] As for the historian Abū Mikhnaf's *Kitāb al-Ghārāt* (Book of Raids), it turns out to be the *section* on *ghārāt* in the *Kitāb al-Futūḥ* (Book of Conquests) of Ibn A'tham al-Kūfī (d. after 204/819) in which the latter exclusively quotes reports originating with Abū Mikhnaf.[26]

Curiously, it was Rudolf Sellheim, an Arabist at Frankfurt University, the very same institution as Sezgin's, who set himself the task of refuting his colleague's hypothesis regarding the purported early literacy of the Islamic tradition and the alleged existence of early written works. Sellheim's own studies, but especially the doctoral and habilitation theses of his students, set out to show that the late compilations of al-Ṭabarī or of Ibn 'Abd Rabbihi (d. 328/940) cited information that had reached these authors exclusively through *oral* transmission.[27] The results of these studies, too, have proven only parts of the hypotheses that occasioned them. Once again it turns out that late compilations almost never transcribed word for word from the earlier sources as Sezgin had supposed. Thus, Sadun M. Al-Samuk was able to show that it was impossible to reconstruct word for word and in its original form the *Kitāb al-Maghāzī* (The Book of the Campaigns) of Muḥammad Ibn Isḥāq (d. 150/767), an eighth-century work surviving only in later recensions, preserved notably in Ibn Hishām and al-Ṭabarī.[28] When parallel Ibn Isḥāq accounts in these later compilations are taken one by one and compared, they often turn out to have significant divergences. In another study, Stefan Leder showed that some of the 'books' attributed to al-Haytham ibn 'Adī (d. 207/822) in later compilations (al-Balādhurī [d. 279/892], al-Ṭabarī and others) actually consist of material marshalled by al-Haytham for his teaching sessions and passed on in his lectures, and which was only later, during the process of transmission, or as a result of it, gathered together into written works.[29] On the other hand, these studies uncovered more and more evidence that written works, too, could be counted among the sources of these later compilations: thus, side by side with materials passed on in teaching sessions there also existed numerous works organised by al-Haytham himself and 'published' by him, not as books for readers, it is true, but as works to be recited orally as part of his teaching.[30] And Walter Werkmeister showed that the encyclopaedic compilation of Ibn 'Abd Rabbihi, the *Kitāb al-'Iqd al-farīd* (Book of the Unique Necklace) depended at least partly on written books and that writing had played a role even in the 'oral' tradition of the teaching sessions.[31]

Important research undertaken at other universities (and not as a direct outgrowth of this debate) includes Heribert Horst's study on the sources of al-Ṭabarī's Qur'ān commentary at the University of Bonn,[32] and two studies at the University of Halle-Wittenberg on works by Abū al-Faraj al-Iṣbahānī (d. 356/967): Manfred Fleischhammer's study on the sources of the *Kitāb al-Aghānī* (Book of Songs) and Sebastian Günther's study of the *Kitāb Maqātil al-Ṭālibiyyīn* (The Book of the Murders of the Descendants of Abū Ṭālib).[33] Günther has observed in later research on the same subject that some of the sources of the *Kitāb Maqātil al-Ṭālibiyyīn* occupy an intermediate position, between 'class notes' and 'actual books'.[34]

In these studies, as in those of Leder and Werkmeister, one conclusion emerges quite clearly, that the specificities of the transmission of Islamic scholarship in the first four centuries of Islam (ca. 600–1000) cannot be conceived of through the dichotomy oral/written. It is worth mentioning, in this context, that we never find the terms *shifāhan* or *al-riwāyah al-shafahiyyah* in our texts, terms that would be the exact equivalents of 'orally (transmitted)' and 'oral transmission'. What we do find, however, are *samā'an* and *al-riwāyah al-masmū'ah*, i.e. '(transmitted by) audition' and 'aural transmission' or 'audited transmission'.[35]

We are in fact in the presence of a unique phenomenon, one that requires careful characterisation and equally careful analysis. I have myself, in research spanning some twenty-five years, tried to identify this phenomenon and comprehensively to characterise it. As my research progressed little by little, and as I critically examined and re-evaluated earlier studies, it became clear to me that, in order to find a satisfactory answer to the question about the relationship between the oral and the written, the opposition between oral and written had to be rejected; it also became clear to me that we had to return to Sprenger's original conclusions. In a 1985 article, I accordingly adopted his distinction between aides-mémoire, lecture notebooks and actual books, placing that insight in the context of Muslim scholars' repeated emphasis on the importance of 'aural' or 'audited' transmission (which applies to all three of Sprenger's categories).[36] I then published a study in 1989 in which I focused on the very first book in Islamic scholarship, Sībawayhi's *al-Kitāb* (The Book) and in which I also introduced the terms *syngramma* (written composition, systematic work) and *hypomnēma* (written reminder, notes), a pair borrowed from the Greek.[37] Another 1989 article, one on the debate between Ḥadīth scholars about the permissibility of writing down ḥadīths, provided me with the opportunity to examine the reasons adduced by eighth-century and later scholars in opposing the use of writing.[38] In a fourth study, which appeared in 1992, I commented on two discrete concepts: on the one hand, 'writing', which does not necessarily imply a piece of *published* writing; and on the other 'publishing', which for a long time was only undertaken *orally*.[39] In a 1996 book-length study on the biography of Muḥammad, I addressed both the question of the modifications undergone by ḥadīths in the course of transmission, and also the question of the very authenticity of that transmission.[40] In the present work, I present in detail the conclusions I reached in those studies, and complement that presentation with an in-depth study of the ninth century: it is during the ninth century that actual books, properly speaking – that is, written works that are definitively redacted and edited – first made their appearance in significant numbers, signalling a shift in Islamic scholarship away from aural transmission toward the written book, culminating, as it were, in the preparation in the thirteenth century of a 'critical edition' of al-Bukhārī's *(al-Jāmi')* *al-Ṣaḥīḥ* (The Sound [Compilation]).

Methodological considerations

A word about my methodology, in particular regarding the nature of the sources I use and my attitude toward these sources, is in order.[41] None of the accounts we have about any event in the seventh century – the words and deeds of the Prophet Muḥammad, or the collection of the Qur'ān, for example – are in any way contemporary with the events they describe. The same holds true for most of the events of the eighth century. These accounts are all exclusively *reports*, transmitted according to established protocols in something like lecture courses, termed 'sessions' (*majālis*) or '[scholarly] circles' (*ḥalaqāt*) in Arabic. Their definitive redaction did not take place until the ninth and tenth centuries. There is, therefore, often an interval of one to two hundred years, sometimes more, between the time when these accounts first appear and the time when they are definitively written down. Take for example, the definitive recension of the Qur'ānic text, said to have taken place during the caliphate of 'Uthmān (ruled 23/644–35/656). The oldest source, as far as we know, is the eighth-century *Kitāb al-Riddah wal-futūḥ* (Book of Apostasy [Wars] and Conquests) of Sayf ibn 'Umar (d. ca. 184/800);[42] and the source most often cited in later works discussing this key event is later still, namely the *Ṣaḥīḥ* of al-Bukhārī.[43] In relating their accounts, both rely on witnesses, following the procedure customary in ḥadīth transmission, viz. listing a chain of authorities ('Sayf, on the authority of Muḥammad and Ṭalḥah, reports ...'). But we do not have any manuscripts reproducing the original version of Sayf's text; all we have is a later recension, which was only put together three generations after the author's version,[44] and which is therefore not even earlier than al-Bukhārī's *Ṣaḥīḥ*.[45]

Can we, therefore, believe what the later sources report? Western research has yielded two quite different answers to this question. Some scholars totally reject Muslim tradition, or almost totally. To justify this critical or hypercritical approach they cite the considerable span of time during which ḥadīths were transmitted and the absence of any mechanism to control transmission. They also adduce the accounts' numerous divergences and contradictions, the occurrence of serious misunderstanding and obvious errors, and the presence of legends and unbelievable stories.[46] As for the material in the tradition that relates to historical events, Leone Caetani and Henri Lammens both suggested at the beginning of the twentieth century that the very historicity of even this material was extremely doubtful.[47] In the mid-twentieth century, Joseph Schacht and Régis Blachère took a similar position,[48] one that has more recently been adopted by John Wansbrough, Michael Cook and Patricia Crone.[49] Wansbrough, for example, questions the historicity of the accounts transmitted in Muslim tradition regarding the recension of the Qur'ān and suggests that the Qur'ānic text did not take definitive shape until the end of the eighth century or even the beginning of the ninth century.

There are Western scholars, however, who believe that it is possible to subject the tradition to close critical examination in an attempt to discriminate between credible elements and accounts on the one hand and material that cannot be accepted on the other. The difficulty is establishing appropriate criteria. Evidence of obvious religio-political bias can provide one such criterion for the evaluation of a given report: one would reject or, at the very least, use with great caution a report in which one detected a pro-'Abbāsid or pro-'Alid bias for instance. This was the method adopted by most of the great German positivist scholars of the nineteenth century and by their twentieth-century successors; indeed, this was the method used in the early twentieth century by Theodor Nöldeke, Gotthelf Begsträsser and Otto Pretzl, the authors of the fundamentally important *Geschichte des Qorāns*.[50] In more recent times, William Montgomery Watt and Robert B. Sergeant formulated a methodological principle that they believed could validly be applied to historical inquiry. Their position is as follows: a report or tradition should be considered authentic, and its content considered trustworthy, as long as no reasons are found to reject it wholly or in part, reasons such as the inclusion of apocryphal material, or of contradictions.[51] Michael Cook, a representative of the hypercritical school, invoking the special character of the Islamic tradition, has countered this view with the following proposition, 'Yet it may equally be the case that we are nearer the mark in rejecting whatever we do not have specific reason to accept, and that what is usually to be taken for bedrock is no more than shifting sand.'[52]

The method I have followed in my research is essentially that of Nöldeke and his successors.[53] Generally speaking, no inference or conclusion is dependent on the historicity of any single report. It is true that a single report might well be altered, or even be false or fabricated, but we can, to my mind, be sure that the totality of the accounts at least accurately describes the essential outlines of events or prevailing practices even if it does not preserve the details. By way of illustration, let us return to my earlier example, the definitive recension of the Qur'ānic text. Many reports *praise* the caliph 'Uthmān for this undertaking, others *criticise* him for it; the latter characterise him as 'the one who burned/tore the Qur'ānic text' (*ḥarrāq/kharrāq al-maṣāḥif*), that is, the non-'Uthmānic codices.[54] But these accounts – evidently often quite divergent – all revolve around the figure and role of 'Uthmān in such a way as to make it impossible, in my opinion, to deny either his role in the recension of the Qur'ān or the fact of its occurrence. One independent fact confirms this. We now have fragments of a Qur'ān manuscript from Sanaa (Yemen) reliably dated by art historians to the second half of the first Islamic century, specifically to 710–15, during the reign of the caliph al-Walīd (ruled 86/705–96/715); an analysis using carbon dating has even suggested an earlier date, 'between 657 and 690'.[55] These fragments show the 'Uthmānic text (*rasm*) with orthographic variants, but no textual ones, and even include the first and last surahs, absent from some non-'Uthmānic codices. The definitive recension of the Qur'ānic text must therefore have taken place earlier than the date of these fragments, effectively setting aside Wansbrough's hypothesis that the recension was not produced until the end of the eighth century/beginning of the ninth century. Even if we had no reports whatsoever describing 'Uthmān's initiative, we would have to postulate a recension of the Qur'ān at approximately the time of 'Uthmān.

When it comes to our knowledge of teaching and learning practices, indeed of anything having to do with the methods of scholarly transmission in the first two centuries of Islam (ca. 670–800), we have no documents contemporary with the events on which to depend – our only recourse is to reports preserved in later biographical sources. In this case, though, the time lag between the occurrence of a particular event and the appearance of an account that reports the event is far shorter than the time lag between the collection of the Qur'ān and the reports that document it. Thus, Ibn Sa'd (ca. 168/784–230/845), who in his biography of Ibn Isḥāq (ca. 85/704–150/767) provides us with information about the origin and transmission of the latter's work on the life of the Prophet, lived only some decades after Ibn Isḥāq. Moreover, the essential points of earlier teaching practices and methods of transmission that can be gleaned from ninth-century accounts describing them are confirmed by their clear influence on subsequent practices.

Indeed, later circumstances often cannot properly be understood unless we also rely on corresponding accounts dealing with an earlier period. At the beginning of various chapters of his *Muṣannaf*, Ibn Abī Shaybah (d. 235/849) writes, 'Here is what I know by heart from the Prophet ...', illustrating that in his milieu in Kufa at the time, it was still normative, indeed required, to represent Ḥadīth collections as aides-mémoire, and not as actual books. This underscores the plausibility of everything the biographical literature recounts about the refusal to commit Ḥadīth to writing in Kufa one and two generations before Ibn Abī Shaybah. Indeed, if the later literature did not report anything about an eighth-century debate among the Ḥadīth scholars on this matter, we would have to postulate its existence. And if we did not know, thanks to information provided by biographers, that Ibn Isḥāq had produced a definitive recension of his *Kitāb al-Maghāzī*, we would in this case too have to postulate its existence. In fact, the various forms of this work as transmitted by later authors, even taking into consideration the variants and often quite stark divergences, nevertheless permit us to discern a systematically organised book, one markedly different from other *muṣannaf* works of the same period.

In sum, our sources, which for a long time are exclusively transmitted reports, can indeed be used systematically. To be sure, we cannot expect that these sources will provide information that is as accurate and as precise as the information we might glean from sources contemporary with the events they describe. But, if we examine them judiciously, always keeping in mind their individual specificities, we will find that they can often provide us with evidence or strong indications about matters that would otherwise remain nothing more than postulations or mere speculation.

Notes

1 al-Khaṭīb al-Baghdādī, *Taqyīd al-'ilm*, ed. Y. al-'Ishsh (n.p., ²1975), pp. 68 ff., 88, 89 ff., 92, 96 ff.

2 See J. T. Monroe, 'Oral Composition in Pre-Islamic Poetry', *JAL* 3 (1972), pp. 1–53; M. Zwettler, *The Oral Tradition of Classical Arabic Poetry: Its Character and Implications* (Columbus, Ohio, 1978); *cf.* G. Schoeler, 'Die Anwendung der oral poetry-Theorie auf die arabische Literatur', *Der Islam* 66 (1989), pp. 205–36 = 'Oral Poetry Theory and Arabic Literature' in Schoeler, *The Oral and the Written in Early Islam*, tr. U. Vagelpohl, ed. J. E. Montgomery (London, 2006), pp. 87–110.

3 *The Naḳā'iḍ of Jarīr and al-Farazdaq*, 3 vols, ed. A. A. Bevan (Leiden, 1905–12), vol. 1, no. 39, verses 57 and 61.

4 A. Sprenger, *Das Leben und die Lehre des Mohammed* (Berlin, ²1869), vol. 3, pp. xciii and ff.

5 'Ueber das Traditionswesen bei den Arabern', *ZDMG* 10 (1856), pp. 5–6 and ff.

6 I. Goldziher, 'Ueber die Entwickelung des Ḥadīth', in *Muhammedanische Studien*, vol. 2, pp. 1–274 (Halle, 1890) = *Muslim Studies*, ed. S. M. Stern, tr. C. R. Barber and S. M. Stern (London, 1971), vol. 2, pp. 17–251.

7 Ibid., p. 196 = *Muslim Studies*, vol. 2, p. 182.

8 Ibid., pp. 196 ff. = *Muslim Studies*, vol. 2, p. 182 ff.

9 Ibid., pp. 210 ff. = *Muslim Studies*, vol. 2, pp. 195 ff.

10 Ibid., pp. 210 ff. = *Muslim Studies*, vol. 2, pp. 195 ff.

11 Ibid., pp. 212 ff. = *Muslim Studies*, vol. 2, p. 196 ff.
12 J. Schacht, 'A Revaluation of Islamic Traditions', *JRAS* (1949), pp. 143–54; Schacht, 'On Mūsā ibn 'Uqba's *Kitāb al-Maghāzī*', *Acta Orientalia* 21 (1953), pp. 290 ff.
13 E.g. Schacht, 'On Mūsā'.
14 J. Sauvaget, *Introduction à l'histoire de l'Orient musulman. Eléments de bibliographie*, rev. Cl. Cahen (Paris, 1961), p. 29.
15 We can now be certain that al-Ṭabarī's sources were for the most part (a) lecture notes, and (b) works falling under the rubric of 'works of the school, for the school, intended for recitation'.
16 M. Hartmann, 'Die arabisch-islamischen Handschriften der Universitätsbibliothek zu Leipzig und die Sammlungen Hartmann und Haupt', *Zeitschrift für Assyriologie* 23 (1909), pp. 240 ff.
17 I. Goldziher, 'Neue Materialen zur Literatur des Ueberlieferungswesens bei den Muhammedanern', *ZDMG* 50 (1896), pp. 469 ff., and p. 500, esp. n. 1.
18 R. Blachère, *Histoire de la littérature arabe* (Paris, 1952–66), pp. 100 ff., 136.
19 Ibid., p. 136.
20 N. Abbott, *Studies in Arabic Literary Papyri*, 3 vols (Chicago, 1957–72); Fuat Sezgin, *Geschichte des arabischen Schrifttums*, 13 vols (Leiden, 1967–2007).
21 GAS, vol. 1, pp. 55 ff.
22 Ibid., vol. 1, p. 27.
23 Ibid., vol. 1, pp. 82 ff.
24 Ibid., vol. 1, pp. 19 ff., 29.
25 G. Stauth, 'Die Überlieferung des Korankommentars Muǧāhid b. Ǧabrs', doctoral thesis, Giessen, 1969; F. Leemhuis, 'Ms. 1075 Tafsīr of the Cairene Dār al-kutub and Mujāhid's Tafsīr', in *Proceedings of the Ninth Congress of the Union européenne des arabisants et islamisants*, ed. R. Peeters (Leiden, 1981).
26 See U. Sezgin, 'Abu Miḫnaf, Ibrāhīm b. Hilāl al-Ṯaqafī and Muḥammad b. A'ṯam al-Kūfī über *ǵārāt*', *ZDMG* 131 (1981), pp. *1*–*3*.
27 See e.g., R. Sellheim, *Materialien zu arabischen Literaturgeschichte*, 2 vols (Wiesbaden, 1976), vol. 1, pp. 33 ff.; Sellheim, 'Abū 'Alī al-Qālī. Zum Problem mündlicher und schriftlicher Überlieferung am Beispiel von Sprichwörtersammlungen', in *Studien zur Geschichte und Kultur des Vorderen Orients. Festschrift für Bertold Spuler zum siebzigsten Geburtstag*, ed. H. R. Roemer and A. Noth (Leiden, 1981), pp. 362–74; Sellheim, 'Muhammeds erstes Offenbarungserlebnis. Zum Problem mündlicher und schriftlicher Überlieferung im 1./7. und 2./8. Jahrhundert', *JSAI* 10 (1987), pp. 1–16.
28 S. M. Al-Samuk, 'Die historischen Überlieferungen nach Ibn Isḥāq', doctoral thesis, Frankfurt a.M., 1978.
29 St. Leder, *Das Korpus al-Haiṯam ibn 'Adī (st. 207/822). Herkunft, Überlieferung, Gestalt früher Texte der aḫbār Literatur* (Frankurt, 1991), p. 245.
30 Ibid., pp. 146, 176, 198, 234.
31 W. Werkmeister, *Quellenuntersuchungen zum Kitāb al-'Iqd al-farīd des Andalusiers Ibn 'Abdrabbih (246/860–328/940). Ein Beitrag zur arabischen Literaturgeschichte* (Berlin, 1983), pp. 348, 465 ff.
32 H. Horst, 'Zur Überlieferung im Korankommentar aṭ-Ṭabarīs', *ZDMG* 103 (1953), pp. 290–307, in which he notes about al-Ṭabarī's sources that 'in most cases, we are in the definite presence of lecture notes composed as aides-mémoire' (p. 307).
33 M. Fleischhammer, *Die Quellen des Kitāb al-Aǵānī* (Wiesbaden, 2004); S. Günther,

Quellenuntersuchungen zu den «Maqātil aṭ-Ṭālibiyyīn» des Abū l-Farağ al-Iṣfahānī (gest. 356/967) (Hildesheim, 1991).

34 S. Günther, 'Maqātil Literature in Medieval Islam', *JAL* 25 (1994), pp. 192–212, esp. pp. 197–9.

35 *Cf.* G. Schoeler, 'Die Frage der schriftlichen oder mündlichen Überlieferung der Wissenschaften im frühen Islam', *Der Islam* 62 (1985), p. 226 = 'The Transmission of the Sciences in Early Islam: Oral or Written', in Schoeler, *The Oral and the Written*, p. 41.

36 Ibid., pp. 201–30 = 'The Transmission of the Sciences in Early Islam', pp. 31–53.

37 G. Schoeler, 'Weiteres zur Frage der schriftlichen oder mündlichen Überlieferung der Wissenschaften im Islam', *Der Islam* 66 (1989), pp. 38–67 = 'The Transmission of the Sciences in Early Islam Revisited', in Schoeler, *The Oral and the Written*, pp. 55–78.

38 G. Schoeler, 'Mündliche Thora und Ḥadīṯ: Überlieferung, Schreibverbot, Redaktion', *Der Islam* 66 (1989), pp. 213–51 = 'Oral Torah and *Ḥadīṯ*: Transmission, Prohibition of Writing, Redaction', in Schoeler, *The Oral and the Written*, pp. 141–78.

39 G. Schoeler, 'Schreiben und Veröffentlichen. Zu Verwendung und Funktion der Schrift in den ersten islamischen Jahrhunderten', *Der Islam* 69 (1992), pp. 1–43 = 'Writing and Publishing: On the Use and Function of Writing in Early Islam', in Schoeler, *The Oral and the Written*, pp. 79–110; *cf.* Schoeler, 'Writing and Publishing. On the Use and Function of Writing in the First Centuries of Islam', *Arabica* 44 (1997), pp. 423–35, a shortened and translated version, introduced by Cl. Gilliot.

40 G. Schoeler, *Charakter und Authentie der muslimischen Überlieferung über das Leben Mohammeds* (Berlin, New York, 1996).

41 See the introduction to Schoeler, *Charakter und Authentie*.

42 Sayf ibn 'Umar, *Kitāb al-Riddah wal-futūḥ wa-Kitāb al-Jamal wa-sayr 'Ā'ishah wa-'Alī*, ed. Q. al-Sāmarrā'ī (Leiden, 1995), pp. 48 ff. (nos. 50, 52).

43 al-Bukhārī, *al-Jāmi' al-ṣaḥīḥ, Kitāb Faḍā'il al-Qur'ān, bāb Jam' al-Qur'ān* = Ibn Ḥajar al-'Asqalānī, *Fatḥ al-bārī bi-sharḥ Ṣaḥīḥ al-Bukhārī*, ed. Ṭ. 'A. Sa'd and M. M. al-Hawārī (Cairo, 1978), vol. 19, pp. 12 ff.

44 In this compilation of accounts attributed to Sayf, each account is introduced by the following chain of authorities: 'al-Sarī told us: Shu'ayb told us: Sayf told us, on the authority of …' This is in fact the *isnād* with which al-Ṭabarī introduces material emanating from Sayf ibn 'Umar, *cf.* GAS, vol. 1, pp. 311 ff. Al-Ṭabarī does not, however, narrate the account of the collection of the Qur'ān.

45 I do also on occasion cite much later biographical works, such as the *Siyar* of al-Dhahabī (14th c.) and the *Tahdhīb* of Ibn Ḥajar al-'Asqalānī (15th c.). Typically, these sources reprise what earlier authors have written, Ibn Sa'd, al-Fasawī and others, for example; in corresponding passages, variants do naturally appear. If I do not avoid using these works, it is because they very conveniently synthesise a mass of much earlier, scattered information.

46 *Cf.* P. Crone, *Slaves on Horses: The Evolution of the Islamic Polity* (Cambridge, 1980), pp. 4, 11 ff.

47 L. Caetani, *Annali dell'Islam*, 2 vols (Milan, 1905–7), vol. 1, pp. 28 ff. and 57 ('Introduzione'); H. Lammens, 'Qoran et tradition. Comment fut composée la vie de Mahomet?', *Recherches des sciences religieuses* 1 (1910), pp. 27–51.

48 For historiography, see Schacht, 'On Mūsā'; for law, see Schacht, *The Origins of*

Muhammadan Jurisprudence (Oxford, 1950); and for the life of Muḥammad, see R. Blachère, *Le problème de Mahomet. Essai de biographie critique du fondateur de l'Islam* (Paris, 1952).

49 For accounts about the collation of the Qur'ānic text, see J. Wansbrough, *Quranic Studies. Sources and Methods of Scriptural Interpretation* (Oxford, 1977), and Wansbrough, *The Sectarian Milieu. Content and Compositionof Islamic Salvation History* (Oxford, 1978); see also M. Cook, *Muhammad* (Oxford, 1983), pp. 61 ff.; Cook, *Early Muslim Dogma: a Source-critical Study* (Cambridge, 1981); P. Crone and M. Cook, *Hagarism. The Making of the Islamic World* (Cambridge, 1977); P. Crone, *Slaves on Horses*; Crone, *Meccan Trade and the Rise of Islam* (Princeton, 1987).

50 Th. Nöldeke, *Geschichte des Qorāns*, 3 vols, vols 1–2, ed. F. Schwally, vol. 3, ed. G. Begsträsser and O. Pretzl (Leipzig, 1919–38, repr. Hildesheim, 1981). For Nöldeke, see esp. his article, 'Die Tradition über das Leben Muhammeds', *Der Islam* 5 (1914), pp. 160–70, and his review of Caetani's *Annali dell'Islam* in *WZKM* 21 (1907), pp. 297–312.

51 W. M. Watt, 'The Reliability of Ibn Isḥāq's Sources' in *La vie du prophète Mahomet: colloque de Strasbourg, octobre 1980*, preface by T. Fahd (Paris, 1983), p. 32; R. B. Sergeant, 'Meccan Trade and the Rise of the Islam: Misconceptions and Flawed Polemics', *JAOS* 110 (1967), pp. 472–86 and esp. pp. 472 and ff.

52 Cook, *Muhammad*, p. 67.

53 See Schoeler, *Charakter und Authentie*, pp. 19 ff. and esp. pp. 22 ff.

54 See e.g. Sayf ibn 'Umar, *Kitāb al-Riddah*, p. 51 (no. 52).

55 *Cf.* H.-C. von Bothmer et al., 'Neue Wege der Koranforschung', *Magazin Forschung, Universität des Saarlandes* 1 (1999), p. 46. François Déroche dates another old codex, the 'Codex Parisino-Petropolitanus', to the third quarter of the first century of the Hijrah; *cf.* F. Déroche, *La transmission écrite du Coran dans les débuts de l'Islam. Le codex Parisino-Petropolitanus* (Leiden, in press).

1

The oral and the written during the Jāhiliyyah and early Islam

Contracts, treaties, letters

The Qur'ān is the very first book of Islam and also the very first book of Arabic literature. This does not mean, however, that writing was not used before the appearance of Islam. The use of writing in ancient Arabia to record contracts, treaties, letters and so on must date from the Jāhiliyyah, the so-called 'time of ignorance [before Islam]'. As for written treaties, letters and other documents in early Islam, their existence is undeniable. Since it is extremely unlikely that the use of writing for these purposes was introduced suddenly at the time of the Prophet, we can be certain that such documents were already in existence one or two generations before the appearance of Islam, at least in urban centres of Arabia such as Mecca and Medina.

Arab tradition also confirms for us the existence of written contracts during the Jāhiliyyah. It would certainly be unreasonable to insist that all the accounts describing them are reliable, but these accounts nevertheless constitute a valuable source of information about the practices and customs of early Arabia. Muḥammad ibn Ḥabīb (d. 245/860) preserves information about a pact of confederation (*ḥilf*) between the Khuzā'ah tribe and 'Abd al-Muṭṭalib, the grandfather of Muḥammad. He writes:[1]

> They entered the house of council [in Mecca] and resolved to draft between them a document in writing (*an yaktubū baynahum kitāban*) ... and suspended the document (*kitāb*) inside the Ka'bah.

The *Sīrah* ([The Prophet's] Biography) mentions a contract made two generations later, also in Mecca – while Islam was gaining ground, the Quraysh resolved not to contract marriages with members of the Banū Hāshim and Banū Muṭṭalib tribes:[2]

> They met and deliberated on drawing up a document (*an yaktubū kitāban*) ... When they had decided on this, they wrote it on a sheet (or: sheets) (*katabūhu fī ṣaḥīfah*) ... then they suspended the sheet(s) inside the Ka'bah.

The Qur'ān itself recommends using a scribe to record debts in writing:

> O you who believe! When you deal with each other in contracting a debt for a fixed term, then write it down! And have a scribe write it down between you faithfully! Let no scribe refuse to write, as it is God Who has taught him. Let him write, and let the debtor dictate ... (Baqarah 2: 282).

The famous 'Constitution of Medina', was known at the time of the Prophet Muḥammad simply as 'kitāb' ('writing').[3] It opens as follows:[4]

> This is an [agreement in] writing by Muḥammad the Prophet (*kitāb min Muḥammad al-nabī*) – God bless and honour him – between the believers and Muslims of Quraysh and Yathrib, and those who follow them ...

In his biography of the Prophet, Ibn Isḥāq uses the same term: 'The [agreement in] writing (*kitāb*) which the Messenger of God contracted between those who had left Mecca and the 'Helpers' of Medina'.[5] Other evidence of writing includes the famous Treaty of al-Ḥudaybiyah (6/628) between Muḥammad and the Meccans, and the numerous letters sent by Muḥammad to various Arab tribes.[6] Written treaties are also attested in contemporary poetry, such as the following verse from one of the poems of the Medinan poet Qays ibn al-Khaṭīm (d. 2 BH/620):[7]

> When, in the early morning, their battle lines appeared
> The relatives and leaves (*ṣuḥuf*, i.e. the treaty) called for us

The treaty concluded between the two tribes was recorded on the leaves (*ṣuḥuf*) mentioned in the verse. From the point of view of their function, official letters, safe-conducts and legal regulations from early Islam, or earlier still, can be likened to treaties and contracts.[8]

The 'publication' of official documents

In the absence of archives or a place specifically set aside for the preservation of documents in ancient Arabia, the respective parties customarily kept such documents in their homes or carried them on their person. The letters of the Prophet to the Arab tribes containing the conditions under which they were admitted into the Islamic community were apparently kept by notable families.[9] Very often we are told that a document was tied to someone's sword, or kept in its sheath; on the death of the owner of the sword or sheath, the document was passed on to family members.[10] There is a persistent ḥadīth that 'the Prophet wrote out the *ma'āqil*', that is, the provisions of the blood-wite.[11] According to one version of the ḥadīth, Muḥammad wrote the text on a leaf (*ṣaḥīfah*);[12] and in the version cited by al-Ṭabarī among the events of the second year of the Hijrah (623–4), the place the Prophet kept this document is also mentioned, namely 'attached to his sword'.[13]

According to our sources, significant contracts – at least those concluded in Mecca – were suspended or stored inside the Kaʿbah in order to underscore their weight and importance. A similar situation seems to have recurred in the early ʿAbbāsid period: al-Masʿūdī reports that Hārūn al-Rashīd (ruled 170/786–193/809) deposited the contract he made between his sons al-Amīn and al-Maʾmūn in the Kaʿbah.[14]

The practice of keeping official documents and other important texts in special places – temples, archives, libraries – was very widespread in Antiquity, in both East and West.[15] In Egypt, legal documents were preserved in temples and later in the libraries of Coptic monasteries.[16] In Samuel I 10: 25 we read:

> Then Samuel told the people the manner of the kingdom, and wrote it in a book, and laid it up before the Lord.

Heraclitus is said to have placed three *logoi* (orally delivered teachings), edited and collected into a book, in the temple of a deity.[17] Tacitus says of Caesar and Brutus 'For they did write poems and deposited them in libraries.'[18] And, according to H. S. Nyberg, the written Avesta, which was codified by the Sasanians but never accepted by the Zoroastrian priests in this written form, existed in only a few copies kept in the most important political and religious centres of the empire. This was done so that the texts could serve as a model.[19] For their part, the priests had meticulously transmitted the text orally for centuries with the utmost scrupulousness.

The purpose of depositing an important document in a temple or in any other revered site is clear: it draws attention to the nature and character of its content and, more importantly, it confers on the document the status of an authentic, perdurable, reproducible original, one that can be consulted by anyone, at any time. This is evidently a form of publication, or at least 'something that anticipates publication'.[20]

Poetry and tribal accounts: oral dissemination and the role of writing

That personal letters and other private documents were written is undeniable;[21] these would have included promissory notes (*sukūk*), redemptions of slaves (*mukātabāt*), land grants (*iqtāʿ*) and so on from early Islam, and maybe even from the Jāhiliyyah. The question is whether the *poetry* of the period, and of the period immediately following, was put into writing. Nāṣir al-dīn al-Asad and Fuat Sezgin have argued that it was and have suggested that this writing down of poetry dates to a very early time.[22]

There is no doubt that ancient Arabic poetry was intended to be recited and to be disseminated orally – the same was true of genealogies (*nasab*), of proverbs (*amthāl*), and of tribal narratives, both the legendary material that came to be known as *ayyām al-ʿArab*, 'the (battle-) days of the Arabs', and the historico-biographical material that came to be known as *akhbār*, 'accounts'. The act of recitation incorporated both the place of transmission and the place of publication. The process of publication for poetry, therefore, was utterly different from the process of publication for contracts, and recitation remained the regular method for the publication of poetry for a very long time, even after written collections began to be compiled. While a poet was alive, he or his transmitter(s) (*rāwī*, pl. *ruwāt*) recited and disseminated the poems.[23] After the death of the poet, recitation and dissemination were exclusively the task of the transmitter(s). When the transmitter(s) died, wider circles of individuals, starting with those in the poet's tribe, undertook to learn and disseminate the poems.[24] According to the sources, Bedouin (*a'rāb*), in particular the tribal elders or chiefs (*shaykh*, pl. *ashyākh*), played a role in this transmission, but so too did other male and female members of the poet's tribe.[25] And just as tribal chiefs and other Bedouin transmitted verses to subsequent generations, so too did the poet's descendants – a grandson of Jarīr is mentioned in one account, for example.[26] Moreover, poets themselves often transmitted the poetry of others. Dhū al-Rummah (d. 117/735), Jarīr (d. ca. 111/729) and al-Farazdaq (d. ca. 110/728), are representative of this category of 'transmitter-poets'.[27]

From about the second quarter of the eighth century, a new kind of transmitter appeared, in particular in southern Iraq – the learned *rāwī*, or *rāwiyah* (pl. *ruwāt*).[28] Prominent learned *ruwāt* included Abū 'Amr ibn al-'Alā' (d. ca. 154/770–1 or 157/774), Ḥammād al-Rāwiyah (d. ca. 156/773), Khalaf al-Aḥmar (d. ca. 180/796), and al-Mufaḍḍal al-Ḍabbī (d. ca. 164/780). These transmitters, some of whom were of non-Arab, typically Persian, origin (*mawlā*, pl. *mawālī*), played an important role, producing collections on a large scale and not confining themselves to material from a single tribe. As Régis Blachère has noted of this virtually academic enterprise:[29]

> They preserved every work in verse, provided it was noteworthy. In this way, these works acquired almost limitless diffusion after having initially enjoyed only local circulation.

The aim of the transmitters and the learned transmitters alike was not simply to preserve the material they had undertaken to disseminate, but also to preserve the quality of that material, sometimes even improving upon it when possible. One famous poet and transmitter, al-Huṭay'ah (d. ca. middle of the 2nd/7th century), is said to have exclaimed shortly before he died, 'Woe be to poetry which falls into the hands of a bad transmitter!'[30]

Several other testimonies confirm this state of affairs in early Islam. The poet Ibn Muqbil (d. after 35/656 or 70/690) is reported to have said:[31]

> 'I send the verses out crooked then the transmitters straighten them out [i.e. correct them and then recite them in an improved form].'

As for the great Umayyad poets Jarīr (d. ca. 111/729) and al-Farazdaq (d. ca. 110/728), they used to have their transmitters polish their poems. The *Kitāb al-Aghānī* (Book of Songs) preserves very interesting details about the methods of the transmitters in a long account recounted by Abū al-Faraj on the authority of al-Farazdaq's uncle:[32]

> Then I came to al-Farazdaq … and went to his transmitters. I found them straightening out whatever was 'crooked' in his poetry … I then came to Jarīr … When I went to his transmitters, I found them putting right whatever was 'crooked' in his poetry and correcting the occurrences of impure rhyme (*sinād*).

This account shows *inter alia* that the transmitters corrected faults in rhyme.

Khalaf al-Aḥmar, one of the most prominent learned transmitters, is said to have told his student, the philologist al-Aṣmaʿī, 'In the past, transmitters were wont to improve the poems of the ancients,'[33] and to have ordered al-Aṣmaʿī to correct a verse by Jarīr, even though there was no question that Jarīr had composed it that way, and no question that al-Aṣmaʿī had correctly recited it back in the presence of the transmitter Abū al-ʿAlāʾ. The correction involved the substitution of a preposition. Jarīr is reported to have said:[34]

> What a memorable day, the good fortune of which appeared *before* its misfortune (*khayruhu* qabla *sharrihi*), when the slanderer was still far and the abuser still quiet.

Khalaf thought *dūna* ('far less') would work better than *qabla* ('before'), giving:

> What a memorable day, the good fortune of which was *far less* than its misfortune (*khayruhu* dūna *sharrihi*) …

According to Khalaf, such situations occurred because 'Jarīr was not in the habit of polishing (his poetry), and his expressions were not apposite.'[35] Al-Aṣmaʿī is also reported to have corrected a line of Imruʾ al-Qays by replacing an expression he thought ill-chosen with one he thought was more appropriate.[36] Transmitters sometimes also corrected mistakes in language, i.e. in the use of pure Arabic (*ʿarabiyyah*).[37] The saying 'The transmitter is a poet (too)' reveals that the transmitters would often independently intervene in the material they transmitted.[38]

In this period, then, the emphasis was not on textual accuracy or on faithful transmission of the original but, rather, on the preservation and even improvement of the artistic and linguistic qualities of the poetry. This concept of transmission is, of course, incompatible with the idea of a definitive written redaction that will then form the basis for the literary publication of a text. In the case of documents such as contracts, the idea was indeed to make public a definitively redacted written text. With poetry, on the other hand, publication was inseparable from personal and oral transmission and dissemination. In the case of documents, there is a strong desire to preserve and to fix the content of a given text and to make sure it remains unambiguous and perdurable. In the case of poetry, however, the text perforce remains flexible; there is a desire to keep what is good, but there is no desire to preserve what has not yet fully matured, or what has not yet been perfected. The mechanism for such improvement cannot be a written text, no matter how well crafted: only a qualified individual will do.

It is essential to keep in mind that this is in no way meant to suggest that the use of writing is excluded in the transmission of poetry. In fact, we have a great deal of textual evidence for the Umayyad period proving that poets and transmitters had in their possession written notes, indeed even substantial collections of poems, and we can safely assume that this practice started earlier, probably with the poets and transmitters of the preceding generation. The written texts used by the transmitters were, however, intended neither for public dissemination nor for literary publication: they were meant to serve as aides-mémoire. The function of writing in this context was therefore completely different from its function in the drawing up of a contract or safe-conduct, and naturally completely different also from the function it would have in connection with actual books intended for publication. For contracts, safe-conducts and books proper, writing had a fundamental and intrinsic role to play, but in the case of poetry its role was purely auxiliary.

The Arabic word *kitāb* denotes all forms of writing, from notes and drafts to contracts, from epigraphic inscriptions to books proper.[39] By turning to the two Greek terms *hypomnēma* and *syngramma*, however, we can introduce an accurate conceptual and terminological distinction: *hypomnēma* (pl. *hypomnēmata*) describes private written records intended as a mnemonic aid for a lecture or discussion, and draft notes and notebooks. *Syngramma* (pl. *syngrammata*) describes actual books, composed and redacted according to the canon of stylistic rules, and intended for literary publication (*ekdosis*).[40] This distinction between *hypomnēma* and *syngramma* is useful in distinguishing between various kinds of writing and, though borrowed from a Greek context, can fruitfully be applied to the Arabic context.

In one of his *naqā'iḍ* (flytings), al-Farazdaq enumerates many earlier poets whose verses he transmits. In one line about Labīd and Bishr ibn Abī Khāzim, he says:[41]

> Of al-Ja'fari and Bishr before him, I have a written compilation (*al-kitāb al-mujmal*) of their poems.

A few verses later he adds:[42]

> They left me their 'book' (*kitābahum*) as an inheritance.

It is clear from these passages that al-Farazdaq had in his possession 'books', or rather draft notebooks, containing large collections of poems. The private character of these is underscored by the poet's remark that he acquired them through inheritance. Even poets and transmitters alive (at least) one generation before al-Farazdaq must have possessed such notebooks or else he could not have said that they had left him 'their' notebooks. In the case of one of al-Farazdaq's *rāwīs*, Ibn Mattawayhi, it is explicitly stated that he wrote down al-Farazdaq's poems.[43] As for Jarīr, when he resolved to compose a lampoon of the Banū Numayr, he instructed his *rāwī* Ḥusayn as follows:[44]

> Put more oil in the lamp tonight, and make ready the (writing) tablets (*alwāḥ*) and ink!

In the same period, 'books' containing tribal accounts already existed, as is attested in the following verse by the poet al-Ṭirimmāḥ (d. ca. 112/730), in which he describes a dictum he found in a certain *Kitāb Banī Tamīm*:[45]

> In 'The Book of the Tamīm tribe' we found: 'The best horse for a race is a borrowed one.'

In an anecdote reported in the *Kitāb al-Muwashshaḥ* (The Adorned) of al-Marzubānī (d. 384/994), Ḥammād al-Rāwiyah reads back Dhū al-Rummah's poems to him (*qara'a 'ala*), and Dhū al-Rummah, who evidently knows how to read, proceeds himself to verify and correct the notes that Ḥammād has taken.[46]

The above examples show that the use of writing as an aide-mémoire is attested among poets and transmitters in the first quarter of the eighth century and earlier. What is more, these accounts shed some light on the methodology of the learned transmitters who in this period were beginning to collect poetry on a large scale. Their method, known in Arabic as *qirā'ah*, was to write down the poems for their own personal use, then recite what they had written back to the poets and transmitters; if necessary, the latter corrected the text. Therefore, the notes which the transmitters kept at home for their personal use, and which they consulted when the need arose, have nothing to do with actual books. The reciting of poetry – which for the learned transmitters often became a form of scholarly lecture[47] – remained oral, in keeping with the custom of the Bedouin poets and transmitters. The learned transmitters recited the poems they collected from memory – just as the Bedouin poets and their transmitters had always done, and just as their Ḥadīth scholar contemporaries in Basra and Kufa were doing – and they left no written, edited materials intended for publication.

In his entry on Ḥammād al-Rāwiyah, Ibn al-Nadīm notes:[48]

> No-one had ever seen a book by Ḥammād. People did transmit (material) from him. The books (attributed to him) were composed after his death.

As is clear from the exchange with Dhū al-Rummah cited earlier, however, Ḥammād did have 'books' – or, rather, written notes or drafts – in his possession, but he only used them in a private capacity. According to an account in the *Kitāb al-Aghānī* reported on the authority of Ḥammād himself, he was once summoned by the caliph al-Walīd ibn Yazīd (ruled 125/743–126/744). Before presenting himself to the caliph, he refreshed his memory by consulting two of his 'books', the *Kitāb Quraysh* and *Kitab Thaqīf*, thinking (mistakenly, as it turned out) that the caliph would question him about the Quraysh and Thaqīf tribes; but al-Walīd questioned him instead about the Balī tribe.[49] Ḥammād evidently conducted himself in his private audience with the caliph the way he would have conducted himself during a scholarly lecture, that is, by leaving his books at home – he did not need the help of writing, or, at least, that is the impression he wanted to give.

This report also shows that Ḥammād, and no doubt other transmitters too, organised their compilations according to tribe and confirms the hypothesis of Goldziher and Bräu that such tribal collections were the original form of poetical collections and that they preceded the later *dīwāns* of individual poets.[50] But we must be careful not to equate these aides-mémoire with the tribal collections redacted by philologists in the ninth century (such as the *Dīwān* of the Hudhaylites, the only such collection still extant); they are at most precursors to these later compilations. Moreover, such eighth-century collections as these were very likely not only anthologies of poetry, but may well have included historical and biographical material about the tribe, proverbs (as is apparently the case with the *Kitāb Banī Tamīm* mentioned in the verse by al-Ṭirimmāḥ cited above), and much else besides.

In an elegy, the poet Abū Nuwās (d. ca. 200/815) praises his teacher Khalaf al-Aḥmar as follows:[51]

> He was not given to making the meaning of words abstruse (i.e. by shrouding them in obscure expressions), nor to reciting with the help of notebooks (*variant*: by relying on notebooks).

And al-Jāḥiẓ (d. 255/868–9) reports on the authority of Abū 'Ubaydah (d. 207/822 or slightly later) as follows about the *rāwiyah* Abū 'Amr ibn al-'Alā':[52]

> The books he had written, recorded from Bedouin of pure and correct speech (*fuṣaḥā' al-'arab*), filled one of his rooms almost to the ceiling.

Even if Abū 'Amr had not later burned his 'books', as al-Jāḥiẓ notes in a subsequent passage, these written notes would not have been transmitted to posterity: they were written through dictation and were thus akin to lecture notes for private use, not actual books. In keeping with contemporary practice, Abū 'Amr had acquired his knowledge through 'audited' transmission (*samā'*).[53]

The philologists of Kufa and Basra, like the Ḥadīth scholars in those cities, continued to teach orally until the ninth century, when, everywhere else in the Muslim world, literary works, i.e. actual books, had begun to circulate. The philologist Ibn al-A'rabī (d. 231/846) is said to have taught for years without written notes (*kitāb*), relying solely on his memory, or so reports his student Tha'lab in evident praise of the extraordinary memory of his teacher:[54]

> He would be asked questions, and would have material read back to him; he would then answer without (consulting) a book. I was his disciple for more than ten years and never once saw a book in his hands.

And yet, we learn from a fairly typical anecdote that Ibn al-'Arabī had a large number of draft notes and notebooks; at one gathering, he is said to have declared that there were Bedouin in his home, suggesting that he was asking them all manner of linguistic questions, but it turns out that there were no Bedouin in attendance at all and that he had in fact been consulting his 'books' (*kutub*).[55]

This anecdote illustrates a difference that existed at that time (and earlier) between ideal and reality, between the theory and the practice of philological and religious instruction, namely that scholars continued to maintain the fiction that they had acquired all their knowledge through audition and in direct personal contact with their teachers because this was still the most highly regarded method of transmission. In reality, they very often copied the notebooks (*kutub*, *ṣuḥuf*) that circulated; these were either the teacher's draft lecture notes (or a copy of them) or notes that auditors had taken during the teacher's instruction. This method of transmission was called *kitābah* or *kitāb* and was never recognised as equivalent to the methods that depended on audition and personal contact with the teacher, namely *samā'* or *qirā'ah*. We will see this again when we broach the question of Ḥadīth transmission and compilation.

Was there a Christian literature in Arabic before Islam?

Although this primacy of the Qur'ān as the very first book of both Islam and Arabic literature is very widely accepted, Anton Baumstark, an eminent specialist of Syriac literature, has advanced an alternative theory. He proposes that the Qur'ān is predated by the existence of Arabic liturgical books such as Gospels (especially of Palestinian origin)[56] – he is therefore postulating at least a partial translation of the Bible into Arabic *before* Islam. His main argument rests on the fact that the Church's attested practice was to use vernacular languages for the liturgy whenever it proselytised, thus Syriac, Coptic, Georgian and Ethiopic, for instance, in the East, and Gothic in the West. Why not suppose, then, Baumstark asks, that the Church would have followed the same practice with Arab populations? Baumstark's argument depends on an analogy which is admittedly defensible up to a point. He goes on to adduce various other points in support of his theory,[57] including the following Qur'ānic verse (Anbiyā' 21: 105):

> Before this We wrote in the Psalms, after the Message (given to Moses): My servants, the righteous, shall inherit the land.

The above verse includes an almost verbatim passage from Psalm 37(36), verse 29:

> The righteous shall inherit the land, and dwell in it forever.

Georg Graf, the author of a voluminous history of Christian Arabic literature, has advanced an entirely opposite theory to Baumstark's. For Graf, the very fact that the majority of the Arab Bedouin before Islam were illiterate argues against the possibility of an Arabic liturgy or any sort of literary production in Arabic for that matter; the only Christian literature in Arabia before Islam would perforce have to have been written in Greek or Syriac.[58] Whereas the liturgy would admittedly have been in one of these two foreign languages, religious instruction and, closely related to it, the reading of Bible passages, would have been done in Arabic. The texts were translated orally, as they were being used. In addition, Graf adduces four arguments in support of his position:[59]

1. In the first place, the oldest extant versions of the Bible in Arabic can be dated to no earlier that the ninth century.
2. Second, when it comes to the numerous Biblical echoes in the Qur'ān, in spite of some almost literal citations (such as the Anbiyā' 21: 105 passage cited above), the divergences between the Qur'ānic and Biblical versions are usually considerable. This suggests that the Christians of Mecca with whom the Prophet Muḥammad may have had contact had only oral traditions to draw upon.
3. Third, the most important Muslim author to cite passages from the Bible was the apostate 'Alī ibn Rabban al-Ṭabarī (d. ca. 250/864), who used his own Arabic translation of a Syriac text for his apologetic work, the *Kitāb al-dīn wal-dawlah* (Book of Religion and the State).[60] The assumption that he had relied on an Arabic translation possibly datable to the pre-Islamic period is thus groundless.
4. Finally, the passages of Scripture that appear in the writings of the earliest Arab Christian authors who cite the Bible – Theodore Abū Qurrah (d. after 204/820) for the Melkites, 'Abd al-Masīḥ al-Kindī (d. 3rd/9th c. [?]) for the Nestorians, and Severus ibn al-Muqaffa' (fl. 4th/10th c.) for the Copts – do not all emanate from a single Arabic translation: each has taken it upon himself to produce an Arabic version based on a text in another language. We are forced to conclude, therefore, that no common or widely recognised Arabic version of the Bible existed when they were writing, neither among Christian Arabs in general, nor within the respective churches in particular.

> The existence of an Arabic translation of the Bible dating from pre-Islamic times, then, is even more improbable and, consequently, one must conclude that there was no Arabic literature before Islam.

Graf's arguments are, it must be said, stronger than Baumstark's and tip the balance in his favour. If nothing else, the absence of an Arabic *literature* before Islam seems all but irrefutable. But could religious instruction and the reading of passages from the Bible – done in Arabic, as Graf himself recognises – really be accomplished without written translations? Was it really an exclusively oral tradition? Some clues suggest that this was not the case, at least in early Islam. In fact, clerics at that time may well have used translations and notes in Arabic as aides-mémoire. The strongest evidence in support of this view comes from the Qur'ān, where in Furqān 25: 5, we read:

> [The unbelievers] say [also]: '(These are the) tales of preceding generations (*asāṭīr al-awwalīn*), which he [i.e. the Prophet] has caused to be written and which are dictated to him morning and evening.'

Asāṭīr al-awwalīn here may refer to religious accounts. This reference has certainly generated much debate,[61] but what is important is the fact that Muḥammad's religious opponents in Mecca regarded the use of writing in this context as perfectly normal. It is not unreasonable to surmise that it was from Christian monks and missionaries recounting the life of Jesus in Arabic that they got their idea that someone could, for his own personal purposes, write *asaṭīr* and have them dictated to him.[62]

Muslim tradition too assumes that the Arabic-speaking 'People of the Book' (that is, those to whom God had revealed a Scripture) were in possession of religious texts in Arabic in the early days of Islam. It is reported several times that such and such a person had copied a book of this type for personal use. According to one account 'Umar is said to have copied 'one of the books of the 'People of the Book'' and shown it to the Prophet.[63] The latter is said to have become angry, in keeping with the position 'No book, except the Qur'ān.' 'Umar, for his part, is said to have struck one of the members of the 'Abd al-Qays tribe who had copied *Kitāb Dāniyāl* (The Book of Daniel) and then ordered him to erase it (it was apparently on parchment). A contemporary of the Prophet is also said to have had in his possession a book titled *Majallat Luqmān*, 'meaning a book containing the wisdom (*ḥikmah*) of Luqmān'.[64] The Prophet is said to have asked this man to recite this 'book' to him and to have recognised some merit in it.

Graf does not dispute that 'particular churches, and especially monasteries, had Biblical texts in Arabic in their possession and used these texts in different ways',[65] but Graf's observation applies to a slightly later period. Whatever the case may be, in every instance in the accounts quoted above, the texts which people copied were for personal use, notebooks intended for presentation orally, i.e. for *recitation* (*'arḍ*, *qirā'ah*): these copies did not circulate.[66] In no case can these be thought of as literary works intended to be disseminated in written form. They are therefore not actual books but, rather, private writings. The same observation will hold true when we look closely in the next chapter at the first phase of the writing down and 'fixing' of the Qur'ān.

Notes

1 Ibn Ḥabīb, *Kitāb al-Munammaq fī akhbār Quraysh* (Hyderabad, Deccan, 1964), pp. 88–91, citation at p. 89; *cf.* R. B. Sergeant, 'Early Arabic Prose', in *Arabic Literature to the End of the Umayyad Period*, ed. A. F. L. Beeston et al. (Cambridge, 1983), pp. 129 ff.; and N. al-Asad, *Maṣādir al-shi'r al-jāhilī wa-qīmatuhā al-ta'rīkhiyyah* (Cairo, [5]1978), p. 171.

2 *Sīrah*, vol. 1, p. 350; *cf.* Sergeant, 'Early Arabic Prose', p. 131; al-Asad, *Maṣādir*, p. 171.

3 *Sīrah*, vol. 1, pp. 501–4; *cf.* R. B. Sergeant, 'Early Arabic Prose', pp. 134–9 (English translation), and, for the best study, see M. Lecker, *The 'Constitution of Medina': Muḥammad's First Legal Document* (Princeton, 2004), text and English translation, pp. 10–39. See also Rubin, 'The 'Constitution of Medina', Some Notes', *Studia Islamica* 62 (1985), pp. 5–23.

4 *Sīrah*, vol. 1, pp. 501, lines 21–2. Translation based on Sergeant, 'Early Arabic Prose', p. 135.

5 *Sīrah*, vol. 1, pp. 501, lines 18–19.

6 Ibid., vol. 2, pp. 317–18; for Muḥammad's letters, see Ibn Sa'd, *Kitāb aṭ-Ṭabaqāt al-kabīr. Biographien Muhammeds, seiner Gefährten und der späteren Träger des Islams bis zum Jahre* 230, 9 vols, ed. E. Sachau, C. Brockelmann et al. (Leiden, 1904–40), vol. 1b, pp. 15–38; *cf.* J. Wellhausen, 'Ibn Sa'd: Die Schreiben Muhammads und die Gesandtschaften an ihn', in Wellhausen, *Skizzen und Vorarbeiten*, vol. 4 (Berlin, 1899), pp. 85–194 (German), 1–78 (Arabic).

7 Qays ibn al-Khaṭīm, *Dīwān*, ed. N. al-Asad (Cairo, 1962), p. 64, verse 23; *cf.* Schoeler, *The Oral and the Written*, p. 62.

8 See al-Jāḥiẓ, *Kitāb al-Ḥayawān*, ed. 'A. M. Hārūn (Cairo, [2]1965), vol. 1, p. 69.

9 Ibn Sa'd, *Ṭabaqāt*, vol. 1b, p. 30, lines 3 ff., p. 36, lines 18 ff., p. 37, lines 20 ff.; *cf.* Wellhausen, 'Ibn Sa'd', pp. 87, 89.

10 See Lecker, *The 'Constitution of Medina'*, pp. 194–203, esp. 194, 197, 199; GAS, vol. 1, pp. 394 ff., and below.

11 *Cf.* I. Goldziher, 'Kämpfe um die Stellung des Ḥadīth', *ZDMG* 61 (1907), p. 862 = 'Disputes over the Status of *Ḥadīth* in Islam', tr. G. Goldbloom, in H. Motzki (ed.), *Ḥadīth: Origins and Developments* (Aldershot; Burlington, VT, 2004), p. 57. Goldziher rightly recognised this an early complement to the Qur'ānic pronouncement regarding it. See also Sergeant, 'Early Arabic Prose', p. 138.

12 'Abd al-Razzāq, *al-Muṣannaf*, ed. H. al-A'ẓamī, 10 vols (Beirut, 1970–2), vol. 10, no. 18847; vol. 9, no. 16154.

13 al-Ṭabarī, *Ta'rīkh al-rusul wal-mulūk (Annales)*, Series 1–3, ed. M. J. de Goeje et al. (Leiden, 1879–1901), vol. 1, p. 1367 = *The Foundation of the Community*, The

History of al-Ṭabarī, vol. 7 (Albany, 1987), p. 92.
14 al-Mas'ūdī, *Murūj al-dhahab wa-ma'ādin al-jawhar*, 7 vols, ed. Ch. Pellat (Beirut, 1965–79), vol. 4, p. 270, § 2639 [VI, 635]; *cf.* al-Asad, *Maṣādir*, p. 171.
15 E. Peterson, *Heis Theos* (Göttingen, 1926), pp. 217–19; W. W. Jaeger, *Studien zur Entstehungsgeschichte der Metaphysik des Aristoteles* (Berlin, 1912), p. 138; S. Lieberman, *Hellenism in Jewish Palestine* (New York, 1950), p. 85; E. Pöhlmann, 'Zur Überlieferung grieschischer Literatur vom 8. bis 4. Jh', in *Der Übergang von der Mündlichkeit zur Literatur bei den Griechen* (Tübingen, 1990) [= *Scriptoralia* 30], pp. 21 and 23 (citing other examples too).
16 Peterson, *Heis Theos*, p. 219.
17 Jaeger, *Studien*, p. 138; Pöhlmann, 'Zur Überlieferung', p. 23.
18 Lieberman, *Hellenism*, p. 85, n. 16 (citing Tacitus, *Dial.* XXI.6).
19 Nyberg, *Die Religionen des alten Iran* (Leipzig, 1939), pp. 9 ff., *cf.* pp. 13–14.
20 Jaeger, *Studien*, p. 138.
21 See al-Asad, *Maṣādir*, pp. 68 ff.
22 Ibid.; GAS, vol. 2, pp. 14 ff.
23 See GAS, vol. 2, pp. 22 ff.; al-Asad, *Maṣādir*, pp. 222–254; Blachère, *Histoire*, pp. 91 ff.
24 See GAS, vol. 1, p. 33; al-Asad, *Maṣādir*, pp. 233 ff.
25 Abū Ḥātim, *Kitāb al-Mu'ammarīn* = *Das Kitāb al-Mu'ammarīn des Abū Ḥātim al-Siğistānī*, ed. I. Goldziher (Leiden, 1899) p. 25 (no. 20), line 15; p. 28 (no. 20), line 4; p. 39 (no. 37), line 19. *Cf.* al-Asad, *Maṣādir*, pp. 233 ff.
26 *al-Naqā'iḍ* = *The Naḳā'iḍ*, vol. 2, p. 647, lines 8–9.
27 GAS, vol. 2, p. 394 (Dhū al-Rummah), p. 356 (Jarīr), p. 359 (al-Farazdaq). On the learned transmitters, see al-Asad, *Maṣādir*, pp. 222–44; *cf.* GAS, vol. 2, p. 25.
28 See al-Asad, *Maṣādir*, pp. 267 ff.; GAS, vol. 2, pp. 26 ff.; Blachère, *Histoire*, pp. 96 ff.; E. Wagner, *Grundzüge der klassischen arabischen Dichtung*, 2 vols (Darmstadt, 1987–8), vol. 1, pp. 12 ff. Note that the distinction between *rāwī* and *rāwiyah* is an artificial one, introduced by European scholars. The sources use the two words interchangeably.
29 Blachère, *Histoire*, p. 99.
30 GAS, vol. 2, p. 236; *Aghānī*, vol. 2, p. 59. Al-Ḥuṭay'a was the *rāwī* of Zuhayr and Zuhayr's family: see *Aghānī*, vol. 15, p. 147; *cf.* Schoeler, *The Oral and the Written*, p. 84.
31 Tha'lab, *Majālis*, ed. 'A. M. Hārūn (Cairo, ²1957), p. 413.
32 *Aghānī*, vol. 4, p. 54.
33 al-Marzubānī, *al-Muwashshaḥ*, p. 199; *cf.* al-Asad, *Maṣādir*, p. 242.
34 al-Marzubānī, *al-Muwashshaḥ*, p. 199.
35 Ibid.
36 Ibid., pp. 27 ff.
37 Ibid., p. 150.
38 A. Spitaler, *al-Qalamu aḥadu l-lisānaini* (Munich, 1989), no. 98.
39 See *WKAS*, s.v. *Kitāb*; R. Sellheim, *EI²*, s.v. Kitāb.
40 H. von Arnim, *Leben und Werke des Dio von Prusa* (Berlin, 1898), p. 175. See also K. Praechter, 'Die griechischen Aristoteleskommentare', *Byzantinische Zeitschrift* 18 (1909), pp. 516–38, and Lieberman, *Hellenism*.
41 *al-Naqā'iḍ* = *The Naḳā'iḍ*, vol. 1, no. 39, verse 57 (p. 201).

42 Ibid., vol. 1, no. 39, verse 61 (p. 201).
43 Ibid., vol. 2, p. 908, line 1.
44 Ibid., vol. 1, p. 430, line 12.
45 al-Mufaḍḍal al-Ḍabbī, *al-Mufaḍḍaliyyāt* = *The Mufaḍḍalīyāt. An Anthology of Ancient Arabic Odes Compiled by al-Mufaḍḍal Son of Muḥammad*, ed. Ch. J. Lyall (Oxford, 1921), p. 676, line 9.
46 al-Marzubānī, *al-Muwashshaḥ*, p. 280.
47 See Ch. Pellat, *Le milieu baṣrien et la formation de Ǧāḥiẓ* (Paris, 1953), p. 135–7.
48 *Fihrist*[1], vol. 1, p. 92 = *Fihrist*[2], p. 104.
49 *Aghānī*, vol. 5, p. 174.
50. Goldziher, 'Some Notes on the Dīwāns of the Arabic Tribes', *JRAS* (1897), pp. 126 ff.; Bräu, 'Die alte Einteilung der arabischen Dichter und das 'Amr-Buch des Ibn al-Jarrāḥ (= supplement to) R. Geyer, *Die Mukāṭara von aṭ-Ṭayālisī* (Vienna and Leipzig, 1927), p. 10 ff.
51 Abū Nuwās, *Dīwān*, 6 vols, ed. E. Wagner and G. Schoeler (Wiesbaden, 1958–2006), vol. 1, p. 316, line 3.
52 al-Jāḥiẓ, *al-Bayān wal-tabyīn*, 4 vols, ed. 'A. M. Hārūn ([2]Cairo, n.d.), vol. 1, p. 321.
53 Ibid., vol. 1, p. 320.
54 *Fihrist*[1], p. 69 = *Fihrist*[2], p. 75.
55 Yāqūt, *Irshād al-arīb ilā ma'rifat al-adīb*, 7 vols, ed. D. S. Margoliouth ([2]Cairo, 1923–30), vol. 7, p. 8.
56 A. Baumstark, 'Das Problem eines vorislamischen christlich-arabischen Schrifttums in arabischer Sprache,' *Islamica* 4 (1931), p. 562 ff.
57 Ibid., p. 566.
58 S. Graf, *Geschichte der christlichen arabischen Literatur*, vol. 1, *Die Übersetzungen* (Vatican City, 1944), vol. 1, p. 36 ff.
59 Ibid., vol. 1, pp. 39–52.
60 GAS, vol. 3, pp. 236–40.
61 See GdQ, vol. 1, pp. 16 ff.; R. Paret (tr.), *Der Koran, Kommentar und Konkordanz* (Stuttgart, [2]1980), p. 137 (commentary on Q An'ām 6: 25, with bibliography). On Muḥammad's 'informants', see Cl. Gilliot, 'Les «informateurs» juifs et chrétiens de Muḥammad. Reprise d'un problème traité par Aloys Sprenger et Theodor Nöldeke', *JSAI* 22 (1998), pp. 84–126, and *idem*, 'Muḥammad, le Coran et les «contraintes de l'histoire»', in S. Wild (ed.), *The Qur'ān as Text* (Leiden, 1996), pp. 19 ff.
62 *Cf.* GdQ, vol. 1, pp. 10 ff.
62 al-Khaṭīb al-Baghdādī, *Taqyīd*, p. 51.
64 *Sīrah*, vol. 1, p. 427; al-Ṭabarī, *Ta'rīkh*, vol. 1, p. 1208. Luqmān is a legendary figure, celebrated for his wisdom.
65 Graf, *Geschichte*, vol. 1, p. 52.
66 This also holds true for what is regarded as the oldest surviving manuscript of a portion of the Bible in Arabic, a fragment of Psalm 77 (*cf.* Graf, *Geschichte*, vol. 1, p. 114). This two-folio parchment fragment discovered in Damascus is supposed to date to the end of the eighth century. It consists of the text in uncial Greek and an interlinear Arabic version transcribed in Greek characters. It is doubtless a translation for personal use, and therefore a written document that we can characterise as something like a *hypomnēma*.

2

The Qur'ān and Qur'ān 'readers' (*qurrā'*)

The Qur'ān

Even though the Qur'ān was Islam's first real book, it did not exist in that form during the lifetime of the Prophet Muḥammad: it was only as a result of a process that lasted some twenty-five years after Muḥammad's death that the Qur'ān acquired the form in which we know it today.[1]

According to the dominant opinion in Muslim tradition, the first revelation received by the Prophet was 'Alaq 96: 1–5, which opens with an invitation to recite:

> Recite in the name of your Lord (*iqra' bismi rabbika*) …

Other surahs dating from early in Muḥammad's mission begin with the almost synonymous imperative 'Say' (*qul*) (Kāfirūn 109, Ikhlāṣ 112, Falaq 113, Nās 114). This means that the Prophet first recited the surahs, or parts of them, and then had his audience repeat them. Initially, when the revelations were still short, there was probably no need to write them down. This situation changed, however, when the Qur'ānic proclamations became longer and more frequent. It is most probable that Muḥammad began to have revelations put into writing early on, during the so-called second Meccan period (615–20);[2] the tradition provides numerous details regarding this process of writing, including the names of the various individuals to whom Muḥammad dictated Qur'ānic passages.[3] Suffice to mention here the most important 'scribe of the revelation' (*kātib al-waḥy*), Zayd ibn Thābit (d. ca. 45/666).[4] These writings were, however, nothing more than mnemonic aids to help the faithful with their recitation.[5]

We do not know precisely when the project of producing a 'Book', a veritable 'Scripture', became a priority. The fact, however, that within the Qur'ān itself the term *kitāb* began to be used in increasing measure to describe the sum total of the revelation, effectively replacing the term *qur'ān*, shows that the idea of a 'Scripture' in book form like those possessed by Christians and Jews, the 'people of the Book', gained more and more prominence.[6] This development need not be seen as contradictory since the earlier term, *qur'ān*, means both 'recitation' (the infinitive of the verb *qara'a*) and 'lectionary' (borrowed from the Syriac *qəryānā*);[7] indeed, 'recitation' by no means excludes the possibility of a written text, and 'lectionary' actually presupposes one.

Yet, no 'Scripture' or compiled 'Book' existed at the time of Muḥammad's death – Muslim tradition and the majority of modern scholars are in agreement on this point.[8] According to Muslim tradition, all that existed at the time, besides oral tradition, were scattered writings on various materials, such as fragments of parchment and papyrus, slates, pieces of leather, shoulder blades, palm stalks and so on.[9] There were also *ṣuḥuf*, sheets, 'containing the Book' (*fīhī al-kitāb*),[10] but the sources do not tell us enough to establish whether any longer and continuous text was written on these sheets.[11]

According to the dominant opinion in Muslim tradition, the first recension of the Qur'ān was ordered by Abū Bakr on 'Umar's advice, a task then undertaken by the 'scribe of the revelation', Zayd ibn Thābit: this resulted in the compilation of a copy on sheets of the same shape and dimension.[12] A book 'between two covers' (*bayna al-lawḥayn*), an actual codex, thus came into existence.[13] Even though a number of statements in the tradition suggest otherwise, this collection could not yet have been an official 'state copy'[14] or else, when 'Umar died, it would have devolved to his successor, rather than being inherited by a family member, his daughter Ḥafṣah. This collection, called *ṣuḥuf* ('sheets') in the sources (and only rarely *muṣḥaf*, 'codex'),[15] was thus a personal copy that the caliph wanted to have available for his private use. This explains why there appears to have been no opposition to it – it was not, after all, an official copy and consequently laid no claim to being a definitive recension of the Qur'ānic text.

The Qur'ānic verse, 'We have sent down the Book (*al-kitāb*) to you that it be recited to them' ('Ankabūt 29: 51), makes clear that writing was only one of the methods used for the preservation and transmission of Revelation. After the idea of a written Revelation gained prominence, the original idea of an oral recitation of the sacred text was by no means lost. 'Recitation' and 'Book', i.e. oral and written transmission, were two aspects of a single Revelation. Already, during the Prophet's lifetime, recitation and oral transmission of the Qur'ān had been vouchsafed to 'readers', or rather 'reciters' (*qāri'*, pl. *qurrā'*).[16] They recited from memory the passages of Revelation out loud in public; as for those who could read and write, they relied on written notes recorded on various materials which they kept at home as aides-mémoire. Their methods were thus the same as those of the transmitters of ancient poetry. Edmund Beck was the first to recognise and carefully describe the close relation between *qāri'* and *rāwī*, noting that 'both recite the words of a predecessor, the *rāwī* the words of his poet, the *qāri'* the words of Revelation as given to Muḥammad'.[17]

The caliph and his family were not the only ones to have in their possession a copy of the Qur'ān for their own private use. According to Muslim tradition, there also existed other collections, initiated by various individuals who were contemporary with the Abū Bakr/'Umar collection.[18] Tradition credits numerous prominent individuals with copies, the most well known of whom are the reciters Ubayy ibn Ka'b (d. 19/640 or later) and 'Abd Allāh ibn Mas'ūd (d. 32/652–3 or later), who are said to have had in their possession complete copies based on their own collections.[19] In the absence of an official 'edition', however, marked variants became the object of disputes about the 'correct' form of the sacred text.[20] Such disagreements had already arisen during the lifetime of Muḥammad,[21] but he was of course able to resolve them. After his death, there was no longer an authority capable of deciding such matters.

In the field of poetry the varying and flexible character of a text was considered normal and sometimes even welcome since, due to this flexibility, the poetic text was open to improvements; but when it came to the revealed word of God, such a notion eventually came to be seen as scandalous. When disputes regarding the correct text of the sacred book arose in the army, threatening the sense of Muslim unity, the caliph 'Uthmān (ruled 23/644–35/656) decided to commission an official edition of the Qur'ānic text, on the advice of Ḥudhayfah, one of his generals.[22] That recension came to be known as the 'Uthmānic codex.

The task of collecting and editing the revelations fell once again to Zayd ibn Thābit, this time with the help of a commission. On this point, Muslim tradition is unanimous. The majority of accounts agree on another point too, namely that Zayd and those who assisted him based themselves on the collection (*ṣuḥuf*) in the possession of Hafṣah, 'Umar's daughter. According to Friedrich Schwally, the caliph was content to have Zayd rely upon this collection alone, located in Medina, the capital of the empire.[23] According to some isolated reports, the commission also made use of the sparse notations on slates, shoulder blades and so on which were brought from different areas.[24] The caliph gave the edition he had commissioned official status by ordering that copies be sent to all the provincial capitals of the empire, where they were to serve as authoritative exemplars. In addition, he ordered that all collections not conforming to the new official edition be destroyed.[25]

The Qur'ān had now become in reality what it had only been in theory in the time of the Prophet: a book of (almost) definitive form and configuration, a codex (*muṣḥaf*). What is more, it was, in the minds of the central authority, a 'published book', the text of which was binding on every single Muslim. It was 'published' in the sense that exemplar copies had been sent to the provincial capitals. This method of publication was, of course, not new: as we saw in Chapter 1 above, a similar procedure was followed for contracts and treaties in the pre-Islamic and early Islamic period. As Bergsträsser and Pretzl have noted, 'With the 'Uthmānic recension, the main emphasis in Qur'ānic transmission shifted toward the written book.'[26] Indeed. from now on, poetry and the Qur'ān differed in an important way: in poetry, free oral publication and dissemination continued without any restrictions; but for the dissemination of the Qur'ān, a single text became the basis for its transmission.

One pro-'Uthmān account shows that some welcomed this development. Supporters of the 'Uthmānic codex maintained that[27]

> If 'Uthmān had not ordered the Qur'ān to be written down, we would have found people reciting poetry [i.e. we would have thought that those people were reciting poetry when they were in fact reciting the Qur'ān].

According to them, there was a real risk that the Qur'ān transmitters would manipulate the sacred text in the same way that poets and transmitters (*ruwāt*) had the habit of manipulating the texts of the poems they transmitted. But 'Uthmān's initiative also had its detractors. For the Qur'ān reciters, the establishment of an official edition of the sacred text disrupted their way of doing things. They had always published the way the transmitters of poetry published, by reciting the texts, relying only on written versions as aides-mémoire. The indignation of these detractors is echoed in the following later reproach of 'Uthmān by political rebels:[28]

> The Qur'ān was (several) books; you discarded them except for one
> (*Kāna al-qur'ān kutuban fa-taraktahā illā wāḥidan*)

The reciters (*qurrā'*) and their supporters were simply not willing to accept the 'Uthmānic codex as the single authoritative text of the Qur'ān; for them, that recension was nothing more than one version among many. One emblematic figure in this group, Ibn Mas'ūd, even succeeded in imposing 'his' Qur'ān for a short time in Kufa (where he was then qadi and treasurer).[29] This is a reflection of the considerable freedom enjoyed by poetry transmitters, a freedom they regarded as quite normal. In fact, in the pre-'Uthmānic period, certain reciters regarded transmission of only the meaning of the sacred text as sufficient.[30] They deemed it legitimate, for example, to replace certain terms by their synonyms or to change the order of words. One reciter, Anas ibn Mālik, a contemporary and a Companion of Muḥammad, is said to have recited *aṣwabu* ('more accurate') instead of *aqwamu* ('firmest') in Q Muzzammil 73: 6 ('Surely the rising by night is the firmest way [*aqwamu*] to tread and the the most suitable for recitation') and to have justified this substitution by declaring, '*aqwamu, aṣwabu, ahya'u*, it's all the same thing!'[31] Disputes among Qur'ān reciters in the pre-'Uthmānic period about the correct transmission of the sacred text were precursors, therefore, of later discussions among traditionists about whether transmission faithful to *meaning* (*riwāyah bil-ma'nā*) was sufficient, or whether it was necessary to transmit the text *verbatim* (*riwāyah bil-lafẓ*).[32]

The reciters had not, to be sure, lost all their prerogatives. The Qur'ān was after all the *word* of God, which it was necessary to present *orally*, through *recitation*. True, there was now an official text, but it was still only a consonantal structure (*rasm*) without any diacritical marks or vowels, which allowed for different readings since some consonant marks could be read in different ways; and the fact that vocalisation was not initially marked allowed for even further permutations. Moreover, the exemplar copies 'Uthmān sent to the provincial capitals included variants and also dialectal forms that had slipped into the text and that consequently needed to be studied to determine whether they needed to be corrected according to the *'arabiyyah*, or pure Arabic,[33] which was the norm in matters of proper usage. The reciters continued for a time to enjoy vestiges of the freedom they had known before, but the standardisation of the 'Uthmānic codex and its dissemination in writing marked the end of 'the great freedom enjoyed by the *qāri'* regarding the Qur'ānic text during the pre-'Uthmānic period'.[34] The almost definitive consonantal text of the 'Uthmānic codex (*muṣḥaf*) had shackled that freedom.

The seven 'readers' and the 'Science of Readings'

In the tenth century, seven methods of reciting the Qur'ān were elevated to the status of canonical readings and were the only ones deemed acceptable by the political and religious authorities. These readings derived from seven 'readers' (i.e. reciters) of the eighth century who gained followings in different cities of the empire, namely Nāfi' in Medina, Ibn Kathīr in Mecca, Abū 'Amr ibn al-'Alā' in Basra, Ibn 'Āmir in Damascus, and 'Āṣim, Ḥamzah ibn Ḥabīb and al-Kisā'ī in Kufa. Some of these men were of the same generation as the learned transmitters (*rāwiyahs*) of ancient poetry; one, Abū 'Amr ibn al-'Alā', was both Qur'ān reciter and transmitter. As Beck notes, 'It is not surprising, therefore, that the same forces were at work in the two areas [*qirā'ah* and *riwāyah*].'[35] Poetry transmitters claimed it was their right not only to transmit a poem, but also to improve upon it whenever possible. Certain reciters (*qurrā'*) active until about 750 claimed a similar prerogative, arguing that it was their right to follow their own linguistic knowledge rather than the dead letter of the consonantal *muṣḥaf*, in particular when it came to dialectal forms in the 'Uthmānic codex.[36] We thus find Abū 'Amr enlisting his knowledge of the pure *'arabiyyah* in favour of the reading *wa-inna hādhayni* (showing the expected accusative case) instead of the 'Uthmānic recension's *inna hādhāni* (not showing the accusative case) at Q Taḥrīm 66: 20.[37] He effectively deemed the 'Uthmānic recension's *wa-inna hādhāni* to be faulty Arabic and justified his move by citing a tradition in which the Prophet says:[38]

> 'In the *muṣḥaf* there are dialectal expressions (*laḥn*), but the Arabs will put them in order.'

Nevertheless, the later development of the 'Science of Readings' was characterised by two tendencies: an increasingly strong attachment to the 'Uthmānic codex on the one hand, and a growing weight of tradition on the other. The weight of tradition was so great that it ended up more or less arbitrarily legitimising the readings of certain reciters: in this way, the 'Seven Readings' became normative. By the tenth century, at the latest, the era of 'creative' readings was decidedly over: one was now constrained to read the text according to the traditions of the school of reading to which one was affiliated, such was the definitive victory of the principle of tradition.[39]

We know that the Qur'ānic text was read out loud or recited during lectures, the teacher indicating the correct 'reading' of a problematic word and explaining the difficult passages.[40] And, as Bergsträsser and Pretzl have shown, from the very beginning students noted down their teachers' explanations. The earliest such notes are attested from before the middle of the eighth century and thus originate with the younger canonical Qur'ān readers, or with the students of the older ones.[41] Ibn al-Jazarī and others expressly state that certain readers from the generation of Ḥamzah (d. 156/773), notably Nāfi' (d. 169/785) and Abū 'Amr ibn al-'Alā' (d. 154/770 or 157/774) used written notes:[42]

> He [the student] had a notebook (filled with notes taken during the lecture) from him [the teacher] [*lahu 'anhu nuskhah*].

Less often we find, 'He wrote down the reading from' (*kataba al-qirā'ah 'an*), and, in one instance, 'I read before Nāfi' his Qur'ān reading and wrote it down in my book' (*qara'tu 'alā Nāfi' qirā'atahu ... wa-katabtuhā fī kitābī*). Bergsträsser and Pretzl are right, therefore, in maintaining that these 'books' (*kutub*) or notebooks (*nusakh*) were not actual published books but in fact notes intended for private use. They do not constitute 'strictly speaking a 'Qur'ān readings' *literature* but rather its precursor'.[43] According to them, these notes contained only 'brief remarks about how the Imam in question read problematic passages'.

The *Kitāb* of Nāfi''s disciple was a notebook containing notes taken during the master's teaching; these notes concerned the readings themselves, of course, but probably also included Nāfi''s explanations about them. A number of other books bearing the title *Kitāb al-Qirā'ah* (Book of Qur'ān Reading) from the same period are likely to have been of the same type. Writings of this sort are attributed to Abū 'Amr ibn al-'Alā' (d. 154/770 or 157/774) and al-Kisā'ī (d. 189/905).[44] These evolved into such treatises as *Ikhtilāf Nāfi' wa-Ḥamzah* (The Difference/Disagreement between [the readings of] Nāfi' and Ḥamzah), containing the readings of the two named authorities.[45] Subsequently, authors began to compile books with titles such as *Kitāb al-Qirā'āt* (Book of Qur'ān Readings), comprising the readings of *several* authorities. According to Ibn al-Jazarī, the third/ninth-century authors Abū 'Ubayd (d. 224/838) and Abū

Ḥātim al-Sijistānī (d. 255/869) were the first to compile works of this type.[46] This progression is an exact parallel to the developments in Ḥadīth, philology and other disciplines of Islamic scholarship: that is, actual books were preceded by notes, taken for private purposes and intended as aides-mémoire, and by lecture notebooks. And, as in other domains, Abū 'Ubayd was the first to produce a manual in this field.

The primacy of the aural

The system of education in Islam required that every text to be studied – including the ones that existed as actual books – be 'heard' or 'read' in the presence of the author, or of an authorised transmitter, even if these texts were in fact often only disseminated through written copies. In the study of Ḥadīth and philology (which had their own specificities), but also in other disciplines, personal contact with the teacher was absolutely essential: transmission of a text by audition (*al-riwāyah al-masmū'ah*) was of paramount importance. If a scholar simply copied notebooks (*ṣuḥuf*), he was called a *ṣaḥafī* (or *ṣuḥufī*),[47] and the material he transmitted through (mere) copying (*kitāb, kitābah*) was deemed of low value (*ḍa'īf*, lit. 'weak'). If someone produced or possessed such a notebook, he was supposed to read it aloud in the presence of the author or of an authorised transmitter in order to check the text and correct it under the supervision of the teacher.

Statements such as 'People used to correct their Qur'ān copies (*maṣāḥifahum*) according to his reading', said of 'Aṭiyyah ibn Qays (d. 121/739),[48] show that what we have suggested about other kinds of texts also applied to copies of the Qur'ān. Qur'ān manuscripts copied without authorised control were only 'notes', the errors in which would only be corrected during instruction, under the direct supervision of the teacher, through audition (*samā'*) or by reading aloud (*qirā'ah*). Just as there were *ṣaḥafī*s in other areas of scholarship, in the discipline of Qur'ān readings there correspondingly were *muṣḥafiyyūn*, individuals whose knowledge of the readings derived solely from consulting *written* copies of the Qur'ān. This is why Abū Ḥātim al-Sijistānī and others strongly advised their students against basing their knowledge on manuscript copies of the Qur'ān:[49]

> 'Do not recite [i.e. learn] the Qur'ān from people who (merely) rely on Qur'ān codices (*muṣḥafiyyūn*), and do not convey knowledge (of the Ḥadīth obtained) from people who rely (only) on notebooks (*ṣaḥafiyyūn*).'

In conclusion, it seems that at no point did the 'Book' (*al-kitāb*) cease to be regarded as the orally recited word of God, not even after its definitive written canonisation in the 'Uthmānic codex. The Qur'ān itself underscores recitation: 'We have sent down the Book (*al-kitāb*) to you that it be recited to them' (Q

'Ankabūt 29: 51). From a very early period, the sacred text was simultaneously 'published' in two ways: on the one hand through recitation by 'readers', and on the other through exemplar written copies, which in turn were used as the model for written copies destined for further and much greater diffusion. Since there was no overlap between the people involved in these two modes of publication – transmitters of the Qur'ānic text on the one hand, and representatives of the state on the other – and since they anyway had very different ideas and interests, they were initially inevitably at odds with one another. It soon turned out, however, that a compromise would resolve the conflict. Besides the status of the written text, the readings of the *qurrā'* were also accorded the highest possible value, even in the matter of transmission; thus, copies of the written text were corrected against the *qurrā'*'s readings. Written transmission and oral transmission – more precisely, *aural* transmission – thus found a way to co-exist. This compromise anticipated the mode of transmission in all fields of Islamic scholarship: even in the presence of books, the knowledge they contained had (at least in theory) to be transmitted not only through written copies, but also in a more direct and personal way, namely *aurally*.

Notes

1 The following paragraphs are indebted to *GdQ*, vols 2 and 3; W. M. Watt, *Bell's Introduction to the Qur'ān* (Edinburgh, 1977); and A. Neuwirth, 'Koran', in *GAPh*, vol. 2, pp. 96–135.
2 *Cf.* Neuwirth, 'Koran', p. 102; Watt, *Bell's Introduction*, pp. 37, 136; and J. Bellamy, 'The Mysterious Letters of the Koran: Old Abbreviations of the Basmalah', *JAOS* 93 (1973), p. 271.
3 They are all named at *GdQ*, vol. 1, p. 46, n. 5.
4 M. Lecker, 'Zayd b. Thābit: 'A Jew with Two Sidelocks': Judaism and Literacy in Pre-Islamic Medina (Yathrib)', *Journal of Near Eastern Studies*, vol. 56/4 (1997), pp. 259–73.
5 Signalled by Sprenger, *Das Leben*, vol. 3, p. xxxv; Watt, *Bell's Introduction*, p. 136.
6 *Cf.* Watt, *Bell's Introduction*, pp. 137 ff., and especially T. Nagel, 'Vom «Qur'ān» zur «Schrift». Bells Hypothese aus religionsgeschichtlicher Sicht', *Der Islam* 60 (1983), pp. 143–65, and D. Madigan, in *EQ*, s.v. 'Book'.
7 *GdQ*, vol. 1, pp. 32 ff.; Welch, *EI*², s.v. al-Ḳur'ān, pp. 400 ff.; Watt, *Bell's Introduction*, pp. 135 ff.; Neuwirth, 'Koran', p. 102.
8 Wansbrough and Burton, whose theories contradict one another, are exceptions in this regard (see bibliography).
9 Respectively: *riqā'*, *likhāf*, *qita' 'adīm*, *aktāf* and *uṣub*: *GdQ*, vol. 2, p. 13; al-Dānī, *Kitāb al-Muqni' fī rasm maṣāḥif al-amṣār* (*Orthographie und Punktierung des Koran*), ed. O. Pretzl (Istanbul and Leipzig, 1932), p. 6; Ibn Abī Dāwūd, *Kitāb al-Maṣāḥif* = A. Jeffery, *Materials for the History of the Text of the Qur'ān. The Old Codices. The Kitāb al-Maṣāḥif of Ibn Abī Dāwūd* ... (Cairo, 1936, Leiden, 1937), pp. 7, 8, 10.
10 Ibn Abī Dāwūd, *Kitāb al-Maṣāḥif* = Jeffery, *Materials*, p. 24.

11 Ibid., pp. 7, 10.
12 al-Bukhārī, *al-Jāmiʿ al-Ṣaḥīḥ*, *kitāb Faḍāʾil al-Qurʾān*, *bāb Jamʿ al-Qurʾān* = Ibn Ḥajar, *Fatḥ al-bārī bi-sharḥ Ṣaḥīḥ al-Bukhārī*, 28 vols, *Muqaddimah*, ed. Ṭ. ʿA. Saʿd and M. M. al-Hawārī (Cairo, 1978), vol. 19, pp. 12 ff.; al-Dānī, *al-Muqniʿ*, pp. 3 ff.; Ibn Abī Dāwūd, *Kitāb al-Maṣāḥif* = Jeffery, *Materials*, pp. 5 ff.; *GdQ*, vol. 2, pp. 11 ff.; R. Sayed, *Die Revolte des Ibn al-Ašʿaṯ und die Koranleser* (Freiburg i Br., 1977), pp. 286 ff.
13 Ibn Abī Dāwūd, *Kitāb al-Maṣāḥif* = Jeffery, *Materials*, p. 5.
14 That is the opinion of the majority of scholars since Sprenger, *Leben*, vol. 3, pp. xlii ff.; *cf.* *GdQ*, vol. 2, p. 21; Watt, *Bell's Introduction*, pp. 41 ff.; Blachère, *Introduction au Coran* (Paris, ²1959), p. 34; Neuwirth, *'Koran'*, p. 103 ff.
15 *GdQ*, vol. 2, pp. 24 ff.
16 Ibid., vol. 2, pp. 5 ff.; Paret, *EI²*, s.v. Ḳirāʾa, and Sayed, *Die Revolte*, pp. 281 ff.
17 E. Beck, "Arabiyya, Sunna und ʿĀmma in der Koranlesung des zweiten Jahrhunderts', *Orientalia* N.S. 15 (1946), p. 209.
18 *GdQ*, vol. 2, pp. 27 ff.
19 Ibid.
20 Ibid., vol. 2, pp. 47 ff.
21 Ibid., vol. 2, pp. 48 ff.
22 Ibid.; Sayed, *Die Revolte*, pp. 292 ff.
23 *GdQ*, vol. 2, p. 62.
24 Ibn Abī Dāwūd, *Kitāb al-Maṣāḥif* = Jeffery, *Materials*, p. 24.
25 *GdQ*, vol. 2, p. 49; E. Beck, 'Die Kodizesvarianten der Amṣār', *Orientalia* N.S. 16 (1947), pp. 353–76.
26 *GDQ*, vol. 3, p. 119.
27 Ibn Abī Dāwūd, *Kitāb al-Maṣāḥif* = Jeffery, *Materials*, p. 13.
28 al-Ṭabarī, *Taʾrīkh*, vol. 1, p. 2952.
29 *GdQ*, vol. 2, pp. 92, 116 ff., vol. 3, pp. 95, 104 and ff., and 147; E. Beck, 'Der ʿuṯmānische Kodex in der Koranlesung des zweiten Jahrhunderts', *Orientalia* N.S. 14 (1945), pp. 355 ff. (contra *GdQ*, vol. 2, pp. 116 ff.).
30 *GdQ*, vol. 2, pp. 105 ff.
31 al-Ṭabarī, *Jāmiʿ al-bayān fī tafsīr al-Qurʾān*, vol. 1 (Būlāq, 1322 H [= 1904]), vol. 1, p. 17, line 8; *cf.* *GdQ*, vol. 3, p. 105; Beck, 'Der ʿuṯmānische Kodex', p. 372.
32 Cf. Juynboll, *Muslim Tradition* (Cambridge, 1983), vol. 1, p. 52.
33 *GdQ*, vol. 3, pp. 1 ff., 6ff., 121; Beck, 'Der ʿuṯmānische Kodex', esp. pp. 361 ff.; Beck, 'Die Kodizesvarianten'.
34 Beck, "Arabiyya', p. 208.
35 Ibid., p. 210.
36 See note 33 above.
37 al-Farrāʾ, *Maʿānī al-Qurʾān*, 3 vols, ed. A. Y. Najātī and M. ʿA. al-Najjār (Cairo, ²1980), vol. 2, pp. 183 ff.; cf. Beck, 'Der ʿuṯmānische Kodex', p. 360.
38 al-Farrāʾ, *Maʿānī*, vol. 2, pp. 183 ff.; cf. Beck, 'Der ʿuṯmānische Kodex', p. 360.
39 *GdQ*, vol. 3, pp. 127 ff.; Beck, "Arabiyya', esp. pp. 222 ff.
40 G. Bergsträsser, 'Die Koranlesung des Ḥasan von Basra', *Islamica* 2 (1926), p. 11: 'we are dealing with transmission that was oral in the first instance and only later fixed by writing'.
41 *GdQ*, vol. 3, p. 205.
42 Ibn al-Jazarī, *Ṭabaqāt* = *Ghāyat al-nihāya fī ṭabaqāt al-qurrāʾ* (*Das biographische Lexikon*

der Koranleser), 3 vols, ed. G. Bergsträsser (Cairo, Leipzig, 1932–5), vol. 1, no. 874, 22, 755, 1581, 1965, 1377. Cf. *GdQ*, vol. 3, p. 206, n. 1.

43 *GdQ*, vol. 3, p. 206.

44 *Fihrist*[1], p. 35 = *Fihrist*[2], 38; cf. *GdQ*, vol. 3, p. 206, n. 5.

45 It could be that writings of this type (and some others too) arising out of the *kutub al-qirā'ah/qirā'āt* belong to the category I am styling 'literature of the school, for the school intended for recitation': see Chapter 5 below.

46 Cf. *GdQ*, vol. 3, pp. 205–8.

47 See Chapter 7 below. *Cf.* Schoeler, 'Die Frage', pp. 227 ff. =Schoeler, 'The Transmission', 41 ff., and Schoeler, 'Weiteres', pp. 65 ff. = Schoeler, 'The Transmission … Revisited', pp. 59 ff.

48 Ibn al-Jazarī, *Ṭabaqāt*, vol. 1, p. 514 (no. 2125); cf. *GdQ*, vol. 3, p. 145, n. 8.

49 *GdQ*, vol. 3, p. 146, note 1; M. J. Kister, 'Lā taqra'ū l-qur'āna …', *JSAI* 22 (1988), pp. 127–62, especially pp. 133 ff.

3

The beginnings of religious scholarship in Islam: *Sīrah*, *Ḥadīth*, *Tafsīr*

The beginnings of 'academic instruction' in Islam

The history of the beginning of Islam coincides with the history of the life and work of its founder, the Prophet Muḥammad. The deliberate study of the history of early Islam and the collection of narratives describing the events of that time were first undertaken in Medina. Those who engaged in this activity belonged to the younger representatives of the first generation of Followers (*tābi'ūn*), that is, those who came just after the generation of Muḥammad and his Companions (*ṣaḥābā*).[1]

If Muslim tradition is to be believed, certain contemporaries or Companions of Muḥammad occasionally took notes in order to record his words and actions.[2] Muḥammad's cousin and the putative founder of Qur'ānic exegesis, Ibn al-'Abbās (d. ca. 68/687), for instance, is said to have had in his possession several writing tablets (*alwāḥ*) on which he is said to have written 'some of the deeds of the Messenger of God'. Another companion by the name of Abū Shāh is even said to have recorded in writing in its entirety the sermon delivered by the Prophet upon the conquest of Mecca.[3] It is, however, difficult to regard things being put into writing in such a haphazard way as a 'deliberate endeavour'.

The activity first undertaken in Medina by those individuals living in the last third of the seventh century and the early part of the eighth century, namely the Umayyad period, was completely different, since they had not themselves met Muḥammad. They began systematically to collect information about his words and deeds, grouped these accounts, and then transmitted them to their listeners following a method that we elaborate upon below.[4] They gathered this information from various informants, in particular from those Companions of Muḥammad who were still living. As Johann Fück has observed, the children and grandchildren of the very first believers, 'excluded, as things turned out, from participation in the political life of the times, and removed from the activities of the larger world, now devoted themselves to a study of the glorious past'.[5] Their narratives were designated by the term *ḥadīth*, a word initially used only in the singular, and which essentially meant 'narrative, account'; later, however, this word acquired a much more restricted accepted meaning.[6] These systematic activities were naturally not confined to matters historical; they also encompassed jurisprudence, questions about ritual obligations, Qur'ānic exegesis, and other matters.

Scholars transmitted their 'knowledge' (*'ilm* – the word often has the same meaning as Ḥadīth) to contemporaries with a thirst for learning, an activity that resulted in the development of a kind of 'academic instruction'. This transmission took place within *majālis* (sing. *majlis*) and *ḥalaqāt* (sing. *ḥalqāh*, or *ḥalaqah*), as the sessions and learned circles that formed around the scholars came to be known, especially in the Prophet's Mosque in Medina (but also in private homes). These took the form of classes, consisting on the one hand of the accounts and reports transmitted by the teacher, and on the other of replies to questions posed. From the very start, those who transmitted an account would on occasion name their informant, that is, the authority they invoked, as follows: '*qāla* A *ḥaddathanī* B '*an* C', 'A said, 'B told (or transmitted to) me from C'. This was the beginning of the notion of the *isnād* (or *sanad*), a term customarily used to describe the chain of authorities involved in the transmission of a given report. In time, this practice became very widespread.

Over the course of the following generations, several factors contributed to the development of this kind of academic instruction, in particular the influx of large numbers of Muslims from every part of the Islamic world first to Medina and Mecca, and subsequently to Basra and Kufa (and elsewhere), which like the holy cities of Mecca and Medina in their turn also became important centres of learning. Among the factors that contributed to this development were the end of the first wave of expansion through conquest, the fact that Medina lost political significance after the battle on the Ḥarrah in 63/683, and the end of the civil war that had lasted from 60/680 to 72/692.[7]

'Urwah ibn al-Zubayr, the first representative of the Medinese school of law and history

One of the first, and certainly the most important, of these early scholars was the 'historian' and jurist 'Urwah ibn al-Zubayr, who was born into a noble family in 23/643 or later and who probably died in 94/712.[8] His father, al-Zubayr ibn al-'Awwām, an eminent companion and cousin of the Prophet, had died during the Battle of the Camel in 36/656; his mother was the daughter of the caliph Abū Bakr; his brother was the famed anti-caliph 'Abd Allāh ibn al-Zubayr; and his maternal aunt was none other than 'Ā'ishah, Muḥammad's beloved wife. 'Urwah would have obtained much information from these leading personalities, especially 'Ā'ishah, but also from other Companions of the Prophet. As a result, Islamic tradition regards 'Urwah as an eminent authority on religious law and history, in particular on anything having to do with the life of Muḥammad.

'Urwah addressed most of his questions to 'Ā'ishah, her answers to which he is said to have recorded in writing.[9] We have a few other details about 'Urwah's activities as a collector of information:[10] for instance, he is reported to have one day sent a message to three of the Prophet's Companions, among them Jābir ibn 'Abd Allāh,[11] questioning them about an incident during the migration to Medina (the *Hijrah*). As for his teaching, on the other hand, we have very few details, which makes what little information we do have very precious, since it sheds light on the beginning of academic instruction in Medina, indeed on the beginning of academic instruction in the whole Islamic world. It is reported, for example, that:[12]

> People came together (to listen) to the ḥadīths of 'Urwah.

Indeed, 'Urwah taught publicly – in the Prophet's Mosque in Medina[13] – but also at home. During his public sessions, he forbade his sons from disturbing him with questions, though they were permitted to address him once he was alone.[14] He used to present the information he had collected on matters of religious law (*fiqh*) according to a systematic classification based on content: he began with the chapter on divorce (*ṭalāq*), then treated divorce requested by the wife (*khul'*), then the pilgrimage (*ḥajj*), and so on.[15] This was the precursor of *taṣnīf*, a method of presenting knowledge which consisted in classifying collected material systematically into 'books' (*kutub*) subdivided into chapters, a method that would take hold in the eighth century.[16] 'Urwah would then have his sons repeat the ḥadīths he had recited:[17] this clearly represents the beginnings of the method that would later come to be known as *mudhākarah*.[18]

It goes without saying that at this time recitation was done from memory; but Muslim tradition explicitly reports that 'Urwah had in his possession notes or draft notebooks which contained his legal ḥadīths and/or his juridical opinions (*kutub fiqh*). He is, however, reported to have burned these writings on the day of the battle on the Ḥarrah, i.e. during or immediately following the failed revolt of the Medinese against the Umayyads in 63/683, an act he was later to regret.[19] Another version of this report gives an alternative motivation for his act, namely that he erased his notes (on parchment, perhaps) because he was – temporarily – of the view that the only book in Islam ought to be the Qur'ān; according to this report too, he would later regret his hasty act.[20] The view that only the Qur'ān, i.e. Revelation, was worthy of being written down, was a fairly widely held view in the eighth century:[21] we shall have cause to mention this again on several occasions.

The historical reports transmitted by 'Urwah demonstrate that he collected information about all the significant events in the life of the Prophet. He thereby established the foundation for the specific historical discipline of *Maghāzī* (lit. 'campaigns', but in fact more generally, life of the Prophet).[22] The sources do not state explicitly whether he put into writing the accounts he collected on the Prophet's life, but he did respond, in writing, to specific questions posed, also in writing, by the caliph 'Abd al-Malik on this and other subjects; we shall return to 'Urwah's epistles (*rasā'il*) when we broach the question of the impetus given by the caliphal court to the birth of Arabic literature (in Chapter 4 below). 'Urwah thus composed written material which can be characterised as 'specialised treatises' on certain aspects of Islamic history; these treatises – in letter form – are therefore the Islamic world's first scholarly writings (*syngrammata*). It is true that these works had not originally been composed for a wider, public audience, but instead for a very limited circle consisting only of the caliph and his court; however, 'Urwah's son, Hishām, transmitted these epistles in the same way apparently that regular ḥadīths were transmitted, that is, in the course of public teaching. By virtue of this, 'Urwah's writings survived: they are, for instance, quoted in al-Ṭabarī and later historians.[23]

'Urwah did not put together and author a *Kitāb al-Maghāzī* (Book of Campaigns), notwithstanding the views expressed by certain much later authors such as Ibn Kathīr and Ḥājjī Khalīfah, who make statements such as:[24]

> He ['Urwah] was the first to compose (a book) on the *Maghāzī*, subdivided into chapters.

This contradicts the propositions of Western scholars about the level of Arabic literature's development in the first two centuries of Islam;[25] but it also contradicts the dominant view within the Arabic literary tradition itself, which maintains that works systematically subdivided into chapters (*muṣannafāt*) did not appear in all disciplines, including writings on the *Maghāzī*, until the middle of the eighth century, that is in the heyday of Ma'mar ibn Rāshid (d. 154/770), Ibn Jurayj (d. 150/767), Mālik ibn Anas (d. 179/796) and Ibn Isḥāq (d. 150/767), each in their respective discipline.[26]

That 'Urwah was, in later times, considered the author of a systematically organised *Kitāb al-Maghāzī* is perhaps due to the fact that his students had collected his historical accounts and collated them into books titled 'kutub Maghāzī (li-) 'Urwah ibn al-Zubayr' ('books of Campaigns by 'Urwah Ibn al-Zubayr'). 'Urwah's adopted son, Abū al-Aswad Yatīm 'Urwah (d. 131/748 or later),[27] for instance, transmitted a *Kitāb al-Maghāzī* in Egypt on the authority of his adopted father.[28] And in the tenth century, Ibn al-Nadīm refers in his bio-bibliographical *Fihrist* (Catalogue), to a *Kitāb Maghāzī 'Urwah ibn al-Zubayr* transmitted on the authority of another scholar, al-Ḥasan ibn 'Uthmān al-Ziyādī (d. 243/857).[29] It is often the case that the authorship of 'books' comprising material going back to early authorities, but collected together and compiled by later ones, is attributed to the earlier ones.[30]

If, on the other hand, we think of the *Kitāb al-Maghāzī* in this specific context as a rough draft, or a *hypomnēma* consisting of notes for private use, including the drafts or copies of the epistles, then it is entirely conceivable that 'Urwah wrote a *Kitāb al-Maghāzī*,[31] especially in light of the fact that he also had in his possession – or had had at one time – 'juridical notebooks' (*kutub fiqh*). It bears repeating that the sources are silent on this point. It is accordingly fruitless to speculate on the structure of this hypothetical draft notebook of 'Urwah's; it is, for instance, impossible to know if it was divided into chapters. It is, however, all but certain that it was not ordered chronologically since 'Urwah had no interest in chronology: the historical reports that he transmits almost never provide the dates of the events they describe.[32]

We are certainly entitled to think of 'Urwah as the founder and first head of a 'Medinese historical school'.[33] Besides his epistles (*rasā'il*), a significant number of ḥadīths survive, comprising, on the one hand, reports about the life of the Prophet and early Islam, and on the other, information on various legal and religious matters. These include instructions about ritual matters, especially questions of ritual purity and prayer, and information relating to the Qur'ān and Qur'ānic exegesis, especially details about the circumstances around the revelation of a particular verse of the Qur'ān and information about the meaning of particular words.[34] 'Urwah often names his informants, but not unfailingly: his use of *isnāds*, therefore, is sometimes inconsistent. To judge from those occasions when he does name his source, in two-thirds of the cases his aunt, 'Ā'ishah, is the origin of the information he reports.[35]

The historical reports and legal ḥadīths collected by 'Urwah were used in instruction by 'Urwah himself, then by his students, and then by his students' students, and so on. 'Urwah had numerous students who transmitted these historical and legal ḥadīths. One of these was his son Hishām (d. 146/763),[36] another his above-mentioned adopted son Abū al-Aswad Yatīm 'Urwah (d. 131/748 or later).[37] The most famous of his students, however, was al-Zuhrī (d. 124/742), discussed below. Reports were transmitted in this way for generations; it was only in the ninth and tenth centuries that they found their way into the compilations that have come down to us, such as the *Sīrah* of Ibn Hishām, or the canonical and non-canonical Ḥadīth collections (e.g. the *Muṣannaf* of 'Abd al-Razzāq or the *Ṣaḥīḥ*s of al-Bukhārī and Muslim). In the present day, a few scholars have devoted themselves to collecting the scattered reports transmitted by 'Urwah about the life of the Prophet with the aim of collecting them into a single corpus.[38] Modern scholars and medieval scholars alike collected and published his reports as a book proper, the *Kitāb al-Maghāzī li-'Urwah ibn al-Zubayr* – posterity has thus been able to do what 'Urwah himself never did.

Mujāhid ibn Jabr, representative of the Meccan School, and of Qur'ānic exegesis

To understand better the developments in Islamic scholarship in 'Urwah's time, we can turn to the figure of Mujāhid ibn Jabr,[39] an illustrious representative of the Meccan school, which flowered at the same time as the Medinese school, or shortly thereafter. Mujāhid was born in Mecca in 21/643 and died there in 104/722. He was a Qur'ān reciter (*qāri'*) and had his own recitation (*ikhtiyār*), though he was not one of the 'Seven Qur'ān readers'.[40] He was also a scholar learned in law and Ḥadīth, making him both a *faqīh* (jurist) and *muḥaddith* (Ḥadīth scholar). His principal area of expertise, however, was exegesis of the Qur'ān.

In Qur'ānic exegesis, Mujāhid's most important teacher was the celebrated Ibn al-'Abbās, in whose presence he had recited the Qur'ān several times – according to one version, as many as thirty times.[41] According to another version of the account, Mujāhid is said to have remarked as follows:[42]

> I recited the Qur'ān three times in the presence of Ibn al-'Abbās, breaking after every *āyah* [verse division] to ask him why and under what circumstances it (the *āyah*) was revealed.

Many of Mujāhid's students transmitted from him, and the exegetical ḥadīths he transmitted can be found in almost all later exegetes; the *Tafsīr* of al-Ṭabarī, for instance, is replete with such ḥadīths.[43] Like 'Urwah, his Medinese contemporary, Mujāhid recited and transmitted his material in the context of his teaching. His students are reported to have taken down in writing his *tafsīr* while studying with him,[44] but the transmission of the exegetical information he had collected seems to have been undertaken slightly differently from the way in which 'Urwah's information was transmitted. According to the famous critic, Ibn Ḥibbān (d. 354/965):[45]

> al-Qāsim (ibn Abī Bazzah)[46] was the only (student) who heard the *tafsīr* (directly in its entirety) from Mujāhid. [...] Ibn Abī Najīḥ,[47] Ibn Jurayj and Ibn 'Uyaynah [and others] relied on the 'book' (*kitāb*) of al-Qāsim ibn Abī Bazzah and did not hear it (directly) from Mujāhid.

This would mean that only one of Mujāhid's students, al-Qāsim ibn Abī Bazzah, received the *Tafsīr* (in its entirety) through 'aural/audited' transmission (*samā'*); he would have put into writing the entire exegesis of his teacher and would thus have found himself in possession of a *kitāb*, in the sense of a 'notebook' or 'draft notes', which included the whole *Tafsīr*. According to Ibn Ḥibbān, all the other transmitters simply copied this *kitāb* of al-Qāsim's. This method of transmission, *kitābah*, though, in theory, never fully recognised, was in practice frequently employed. In fact, transmitters were obliged to indicate in their *isnād*s precisely how they came to be in possession of their teachers' learning; if transmitters copied a 'book' without having personally heard its contents delivered, they were in principle required to make this explicit.[48] Transmitters often concealed the fact, however, that they had relied on this method of transmission, and it turns out that this was the case with Mujāhid's students – not a single one makes it explicit, a dishonesty (*tadlīs*) remarked upon in traditional Islamic scholarship. Clearly, in the seventh and the first half of the eighth centuries, the transmission of ḥadīths through writing alone was strongly looked down upon in Mecca, but also in Medina and in the Muslim world generally, even if it seems that the writing down of ḥadīths for personal use enjoyed less disapproval in Mecca than in Medina.[49]

In this connection, an observation concerning the teaching system of a later period may be worth mentioning. From the eleventh century onward, certificates of audition (*ijāzāt al-samāʿ*, *samāʿāt*) appear in the manuscripts. Comparing the certificates of audition and the recorded chains of transmission in a given manuscript with its colophon, where the copyist provides his name and the date of the work's completion, reveals that sometimes students were in the habit of attending 'classes' of a particular teacher without taking any notes.[50] When such students subsequently wished to teach and transmit the material they had earlier heard, it sometimes happened that they had to borrow a copy of the work, that of the teacher himself or that of someone who had written down what the teacher had taught; they would then copy it for their own personal use, and that copy would then serve as the basis for their own teaching. Since they had indeed at some point received direct instruction from the teacher and had personally heard him say the words they were transmitting, they were consequently authorised to use the formulations in their *isnāds* that suggested direct audition (*ḥaddathanī x* or *samiʿtu ʿan x*). On the other hand, they do not include the name of the person whose notebook they copied in their *isnāds*.

Now, there does exist a relatively old *Tafsīr* attributed to Mujāhid.[51] Sezgin believed that this was veritably a book by Mujāhid, 'in the recension of Ibn Abī Najīḥ (d. 131/748)',[52] in spite of the fact that the exact title, *Tafsīr Warqāʾ ʿan Ibn Abī Najīḥ ʿan Mujāhid*, pointed to a work compiled by a later authority.[53] Two studies, one by Georg Stauth and another by Fred Leemhuis, have independently shown that a large number of exegetical ḥadīths originating with authorities other than Mujāhid were added not only by Mujāhid's student Ibn Abī Najīḥ and his student, Warqāʾ (d. 160/776), but also by Ādam Ibn Abī Iyās (d. 220/835), the transmitter of the *Tafsīr* from Warqāʾ.[54] The *Tafsīr* is not, therefore, a book by Mujāhid, but a ninth-century compilation by Ādam ibn Abī Iyās, consisting mainly, but not exclusively, of exegetical ḥadīths originating with Mujāhid.

Stauth and Leemhuis compared these ḥadīths with those al-Ṭabarī and other later exegetes describe as originating with Mujāhid:[55] this revealed that the material cited in the *Tafsīr Warqā'* was not identical to the material appearing in the *Tafsīr* of al-Ṭabarī. What we have, generally speaking, are on the one hand ḥadīths common to both texts, close scrutiny of which nevertheless reveals divergences and variants between parallel passages, and on the other ḥadīths originating with Mujāhid, but which are to be found in only one of the two compilers. We are once again led to the conclusion that, in this period, material was transmitted selectively, only 'conveying the meaning, or sense' (*al-riwāyah bil-ma'nā*), i.e. the gist, rather than 'conveying the wording' (*al-riwāyah bil-lafẓ*). This was so even when the transmitters were able to rely on draft notes written by one of them; indeed, this appears to have been the case with the *Tafsīr Warqā'*.

The surviving manuscript of the '*Tafsīr Warqā'*'' was copied in 544/1149; it includes a chain of transmission (*riwāyah*), certificates of audition (*samā'āt*), and a colophon.[56] What is more, the method of transmission we described above is clearly discernible: the copyist, one Ibn Ḥamdī, 'heard' the text of the *Tafsīr* without taking notes, and obtained permission to teach (*ijāzah*) from his teachers. In order to have a personal written copy, he later copied the teacher's 'book', which had passed to one of the latter's students when he died.

Al-Zuhrī and the writing down of ḥadīths

We turn now to the Medinese Ibn Shihāb al-Zuhrī (d. 124/742),[57] the most illustrious student of 'Urwah ibn al-Zubayr. Focusing on this scholar allows us to identify various developments that affected the second generation of Followers (*atbā' al-tābi'īn*). Like his teacher, al-Zuhrī was a Ḥadīth scholar, a jurist, and, last but by no means least, a major scholar of *maghāzī*. He was born in 50/670 or a little later and studied with 'Urwah and important scholars such as Sa'īd ibn al-Musayyab, Abān ibn 'Uthmān, and others. He also asked questions of informants who were not scholars, young and old alike: he would, for example, go to the homes of the *Anṣār* (Helpers) in Medina, even going so far as trying to obtain information from their wives.[58]

The reports describing al-Zuhrī's search for ḥadīths and his use of writing while he gathered his information appear to be contradictory. According to al-Zuhrī's student Mālik ibn Anas, an eminent scholar in his own right, when he asked al-Zuhrī whether he used to write down ḥadīths, al-Zuhrī replied that he did not.[59] It is reported in several other places, however, that al-Zuhrī did make it a habit of writing down ḥadīths in large numbers while collecting them. According to Ma'mar ibn Rāshid, another of al-Zuhrī's students, a companion of al-Zuhrī's called Ṣāliḥ ibn Kaysān (d. after 140/757–8) reported as follows:[60]

> al-Zuhrī and I met while collecting ḥadīths (*naṭlubu al-ʿilm*). We agreed to write down the practices of the Prophet (*sunan*). So we wrote down everything that we heard on the Prophet's authority. Then we wrote what we heard on the authority of his Companions.

According to another of al-Zuhrī's companions, al-Zuhrī always carried tablets and sheets with him and would write down everything that he heard.[61] The contradiction between these accounts can to a certain point be resolved if we accept that al-Zuhrī initially deemed unacceptable the writing down of ḥadīths, a widely held view during his time, especially in Medina. Much later, he may have changed his position and started to use writing more and more, as circumstances required. Other reports appear to confirm this. It would appear that in the beginning al-Zuhrī transmitted his learning exclusively through academic instruction. A small number of his many students, however, wanted to have easier access to the materials he had collected. One of them, al-Layth ibn Saʿd (d. 161/778), is said to have asked his teacher to compile a book containing all the ḥadīths he knew, proposing as follows:[62]

> O Abu Bakr, if you would only organise and compile these 'books' [sc. notebooks] for people's benefit, you would be able to free yourself of all this work.

But al-Zuhrī is said to have refused and to have adopted a different method instead, one that was far more practical: he lent his notebooks to his students and had them copy them. A number of reports describing this procedure of al-Zuhrī's have come down to us, so it is reasonably certain that he is the originator of this new method of transmission, called *munāwalah*, never fully recognised, but which became significant from this time period on.[63] His illustrious student Mālik ibn Anas sometimes used this procedure to transmit his *Muwaṭṭa'*.[64]

Regarding al-Zuhrī's later scholarly activity, we also find two apparently contradictory accounts. On the one hand, we are told that several muleloads were required for the draft notes of the ḥadīths that al-Zuhrī had been ordered by the caliphal court to dictate to scribes (*kutub* or *dafātir*), and which were removed from the caliph's library after the assassination of al-Walīd II in 125/743.[65] On the other hand, two of al-Zuhrī's students report that their teacher had at his home only one book, or only two books, the one 'a book containing his family's genealogy',[66] the other 'something about his family's genealogy and some poems'.[67] The two accounts need not be incompatible: those who opposed the writing down of ḥadīths – among whom al-Zuhrī counted himself his whole life long – thought it worse to own and bequeath written materials, in particular ones relating to religious matters, than to dictate such materials to others. There was even a widely held view that if one owned any writings, these had to be destroyed, before, or even after, one died. This was justified by quoting the following ḥadīth of the Prophet transmitted by Abu Saʿīd al-Khudrī (d. 74/693 or later):[68]

> Write nothing from me except the Qur'ān. If anyone has (already) written down anything from me other than the Qur'ān, then let him erase it.

Al-Zuhrī's collections have not come down to us in their original form. What survives are a multitude of ḥadīths scattered in later works of Ḥadīth, of religious law (*fiqh*), and relating to the Prophet's campaigns (*maghāzī*). Thanks to a relatively early work, however, namely the *Muṣannaf* of 'Abd al-Razzāq (d. 211/827), we can get a general idea about the nature and basic shape of al-Zuhrī's collections relating to the life of the Prophet. The *Muṣannaf* contains in it a *Kitāb al-Maghāzī*, the bulk of the material for which 'Abd al-Razzāq obtained from his teacher Ma'mar ibn Rāshid (d. 154/770);[69] Ma'mar must therefore be considered the true compiler of this particular book. As for Ma'mar, he himself obtained approximately half of the material he cites from his teacher, al-Zuhrī. These narratives, which are typically quite long, invariably go by the name *ḥadīth*, in the singular. Frequently, but not in every case, these accounts include chains of authorities in which al-Zuhrī often names his teacher 'Urwah.[70] Sometimes, events of central importance, such as the Battles of Badr or Uḥud, are dated at the beginning of the ḥadīth text.

In light of the foregoing, it is nevertheless clear that al-Zuhrī's *Kitāb al-Maghāzī* was not yet a book proper, not yet one arranged systematically into thematic chapters, like the one which would be put together by Ibn Isḥāq, another of al-Zuhrī's students. Al-Zuhrī's 'book' was in all likelihood nothing more than a collection of historical ḥadīths about the life of the Prophet, loosely arranged, and thus similar to the *Kitāb al-Maghāzī* of 'Abd al-Razzāq/Ma'mar which survives. We therefore concur with Abd al-'Azīz al-Dūrī that, in going beyond the pioneering work of 'Urwah, al-Zuhrī 'gave the first definite frame of the *Sīrah* and that he drew its lines clearly, to be elaborated later, in details only'.[71]

In the first half of the eighth century, there were several different kinds of written texts: (1) simple notes, not always systematically arranged, intended for personal use; (2) detailed draft notes ('lecture notebooks'), containing the ḥadīths the teachers would teach during their 'classes' (sometimes handed over to others to be copied, but intended for use by the teacher in oral recitation); (3) official collections produced by order of the caliphal court, and for the exclusive use of the court.[72] Al-Zuhrī was not only unable to prevent the compilation and dissemination of written materials of the first type (simple notes), or indeed of the second (detailed draft notes), he even ended up *authorising* his draft notes. The difference between notes and draft notes or notebooks is, in reality, a minor one: in Greek, both are indistinguishably termed *hypomnēma*. What is more, al-Zuhrī found himself engaged in producing writings of the third type, compiling them himself, by order of the caliphal court. An oft-cited report describes the most celebrated of these compilations: a collection, or official recension, of the Ḥadīth, comparable to the Qur'ān recension undertaken during the reign of ʿUthmān.[73] Such large-scale collection was termed *tadwīn*, and al-Zuhrī is credited with originating the procedure:[74]

> The first person to have collected and written down knowledge [i.e. ḥadīths] (on a large scale) (*awwal man dawwana al-ʿilm wa-katabahu*) was Ibn Shihāb (al-Zuhrī).

In this way, a huge step was taken in extending the use of writing. But, it must be emphasised that in this period the readership for such compilations was extremely limited, effectively only the court, consisting of the caliph, princes and other dignitaries. We will return to the subject of al-Zuhrī's 'official' collections when we investigate the role of the court in providing the impetus for such works.

In any event, by compiling ḥadīth collections and other works intended for a public readership, al-Zuhrī broke a taboo that had been in force for decades and that had prevented the production of religious writings or, at least, the publishing of 'books' on religious matters, other than the Qur'ān (and in the generation after al-Zuhrī, opposition to the writing down of Ḥadīth came to an end, at least in Medina). But it appears that al-Zuhrī faced quite a few problems for having done so; he justified his move on many occasions, each time adducing new arguments. According to the best known justification, it was because of pressure from the Umayyad leadership that he began to write things down, and that he could no longer stop anyone from doing so:[75]

> We disapproved of writing down knowledge [i.e. ḥadīths] (*kunnā nakrahu kitābat al-ʿilm*) until these rulers compelled us to do it. Then we were [i.e. now we are] of the opinion that we should not prohibit any Muslim from doing so.

Notes

1 For what follows, *cf.* Schoeler, *Charakter*, pp. 27–37; E. Sachau, 'Introduction' to Ibn Saʿd, *Ṭabaqāt*, IIIa, pp. v and ff.; and J. Fück, 'Die Rolle des Traditionalismus im Islam', *ZDMG* 93 (1939), pp. 2 ff. See also GAS, vol. 1, pp. 237 ff., and esp. 251 ff.; W. M. Watt, *Muhammad at Medina* (Oxford, 1956), p. 338, and M. Lecker, 'The Death of the Prophet Muḥammad's Father: Did Wāqidī Invent Some of the Evidence?', *ZDMG* 145 (1995), pp. 11 ff.

2 al-Khaṭīb al-Baghdādī, *Taqyīd*, pp. 64 ff., 82 ff.; GAS, vol. 1, pp. 54 ff. and 84 ff.; Abbott, *Studies*, vol. 2, pp. 11 ff.; Juynboll, *Muslim Tradition*, p. 21; Schoeler, *The Oral and the Written*, pp. 117 and 127 ff.; Schoeler, *Charakter*, p. 27; Ibn Saʿd, *Ṭabaqāt*, II b, p. 123.

3 Ibn Ḥajar, *Fatḥ*, vol. 1, pp. 311 ff., no. 112; al-Khaṭīb al-Baghdādī, *Taqyīd*, p. 86; *cf.* Schoeler, *The Oral and the Written*, p. 138.

4 *Cf.* e.g. J. Horovitz, *The Earliest Biographies of the Prophet and their Authors*, ed. L. I. Conrad (Princeton, 2002), pp. 1 ff.; A. A. Duri, *The Rise of Historical Writing among the Arabs*, ed. and tr. L. I. Conrad, introd. F. M. Donner (Princeton, 1983), pp. 23 ff.; J. von Stülpnagel, ''Urwa Ibn az-Zubair. Sein Leben und seine Bedeutung als Quelle frühislamischer Überlieferung', unpublished doctoral thesis, Tübingen, 1956, p. 15.

5 J. Fück, 'Muḥammad Ibn Isḥāq. Literaturhistorische Untersuchungen', doctoral thesis, Frankurt a.M, 1925, p. 1; *cf.* Fück, 'Die Rolle', pp. 2 ff., and W. M. Watt, 'The Reliability of Ibn Isḥāq's Sources', in *La vie de prophète Mahomet: colloque de Strasbourg (octobre 1980)*, pref. T. Fahd (Paris, 1983), p. 41.

6 See e.g. (Pseudo-) al-Zuhrī, 'al-Maghāzī al-nabawiyyah', ed. S. Zakkār (Damascus, 1980), pp. 62, 71, 76, 78, 80; *cf.* von Stülpnagel, ''Urwa', p. 15, n. 1. *Cf.* Juynboll, *Muslim Tradition*, pp. 9 ff.

7 Fück, 'Die Rolle', pp. 2 ff.

8 On 'Urwah, see G. Schoeler, *EI*², s.v. 'Urwa b. al-Zubayr; GAS, vol. 2, pp. 278 ff.; Horovitz, *The Earliest Biographies*, pp. 15 ff.; Fück, 'Muḥammad Ibn Isḥāq', p. 7; Duri, *The Rise*, pp. 25 ff. and 76 ff.; W. M. Watt, *Muhammad at Mecca* (Oxford, 1953), pp. 180 ff.; F. Rosenthal, *A History of Muslim Historiography* (Leiden, ²1968), pp. 69 and 130 ff.; M. M. al-A'ẓamī, 'Introduction' to 'Urwah ibn al-Zubair, *Maghāzī rasūl Allāh bi-riwāyat Abī al-Aswad 'anhu*, ed. M. M. al-A'ẓamī (Riyadh, 1981), and esp. von Stülpnagel's fundamental ''Urwa', pp. 14 ff. For the production and evaluation of a complete corpus of 'Urwah's reports on the life of Muḥammad, see A. Görke and G. Schoeler, *Die ältesten Berichte über das Leben Muḥammads. Das Korpus 'Urwa ibn az-Zubair* (Princeton, 2008).

9 Ibn Ḥajar, *Fatḥ al-bārī*, vol. 17, p. 102, no. 4574; al-Khaṭīb al-Baghdādī, *Kitāb al-Kifāyah fī 'ilm al-riwāyah* (Hyderabad, Deccan, ²1970), p. 237.

10 Ibn Sa'd, *Ṭabaqāt*, vol. 8, p. 129, line 5; *cf.* von Stülpnagel, ''Urwa', pp. 14 ff.

11 Jābir dies in 73/692–3, or some years later; Ibn Ḥajar, *Tahdhīb al-tahdhīb*, 14 vols (Beirut, 1984–5), vol. 2, p. 37.

12 al-Fasawī, *Kitāb al-Ma'rifah wal-ta'rīkh*, 3 vols, ed. A. Ḍ. al-'Umarī (Beirut, ²1981), vol. 1, p. 552; Abū Nu'aym al-Iṣbahānī, *Ḥilyat al-awliyā' wa-ṭabaqāt al-aṣfiyā'*, 10 vols (Cairo, 1932–8), vol. 2, p. 176; Ibn Ḥajar, *Tahdhīb*, vol. 7, p. 164; al-Dhahabī, *Siyar a'lām al-nubalā'*, 25 vols, ed. S. al-Arna'ūṭ et al. (Beirut, ³1985), vol. 4, p. 431.

13 See al-Dhahabī, *Siyar*, vol 4, pp. 424 ff.

14 al-Fasawī, *Kitāb al-Ma'rifah*, vol. 1, p. 551.

15 Ibid.

16 See Chapter 5 below.

17 al-Fasawī, *Kitāb al-Ma'rifah*, vol. 1, p. 551.

18 *Cf.* M. Ahmed, 'The Institution of al-Mudhākara', ZDMG *Suppl.* I, part 2 (1969), pp. 595–603.

19 Ibn Sa'd, *Ṭabaqāt*, vol. 5, p. 133; 'Abd al-Razzāq, *al-Muṣannaf*, vol. 11, p. 425, no. 20902; al-Dhahabī, *Siyar*, vol. 4, p. 426; A. Fischer, *Biographien von Gewährsmännern des Ibn Isḥāq, hauptsählich aus aḏ-Ḏahabī* (Leiden, 1980), p. 41; Ibn Ḥajar, *Tahdhīb*, vol. 7, p. 165.

20 Ibn Ḥajar, *Tahdhīb*, vol. 7, p. 165; *Siyar*, vol. 4, p. 436; Fischer, *Biographien*, p. 47.

21 See Schoeler, *The Oral and the Written*, pp. 111–41 ('Oral Torah and *Ḥadīṯ*'), and Cook, 'The Opponents of Writing'.

22 *Cf.* Fück, 'Muḥammad Ibn Isḥāq', p. 7; von Stülpnagel, ''Urwa', p. 54.

23 See GAS, vol. 1, p. 279; *cf.* Horovitz, *The Earliest Biographies*, pp. 23 ff.; F. Buhl, *Das Leben Muhammeds*, tr. H. H. Schaeder (Leipzig, 1930), p. 306. Von Stülpnagel, ''Urwa', pp. 61 ff., has translated all of 'Urwah's epistles. See also Sprenger, *Das Leben*, vol. 1, pp. 356 ff., vol. 2, pp. 42 ff., and vol. 3, pp. 142 ff.

24 Ibn Kathīr, *al-Bidāyah wal-nihāyah*, 14 vols (Cairo, 1932–9), vol. 11, p. 101; Ḥājjī

Khalīfah, *Kashf al-ẓunūn ʿan asāmī al-kutub wal-funūn*, 2 vols, ed. S. Yaltakaya and K. R. Bilge (Istanbul, 1941– 3, repr. Baghdad, n.d. [ca. 1970]), vol. 2, p. 1747.

25 *Cf.* von Stülpnagel, ''Urwa', p. 116.

26 See Ibn Ḥajar, *Fatḥ*, 'Muqaddima', pp. 5 ff.; al-Kattānī, *al-Risālah al-mustaṭrafah li-bayān mashhūr kutub al-sunnah al-musharrafah* (Damascus, ^{3}1964), vol. 1, pp. 6 ff., esp. p. 9; Yāqūt, *Irshād al-arīb*, vol. 1, p. 399. *Cf.* Chapter 5 below.

27 See GAS, vol. 1, pp. 284 ff.

28 al-Dhahabī, *Siyar*, vol. 6, p. 150. Al-Aʿẓamī has attempted a reconstruction of this work: see 'Urwah ibn al-Zubayr, *Maghāzī*.

29 *Fihrist*^{1}, p. 110 = *Fihrist*^{2}, p. 123. On al-Ziyādī, see GAS, vol. 1, p. 316.

30 See Schoeler, *The Oral and the Written*, p. 37, and n. 145 (p. 179).

31 One of 'Urwah's contemporaries, Abān ibn 'Uthmān (d. 96/714–5 or later; see GAS, vol. 1, p. 277), another authority in the area of *maghāzī*, is reported to have compiled such a book; see al-Zubayr ibn Bakkār, *al-Akhbār al-Muwaffaqiyyāt*, ed. S. M. al-ʿĀnī (Baghdad, 1972), pp. 331 ff.; Schoeler, *The Oral and the Written*, p. 81, and n. 504 (p. 199).

32 *Cf.* von Stülpnagel, ''Urwa', p. 60; Schoeler, *Charakter*, p. 32, n. 47. Görke and Schoeler, *Die ältesten Berichte*, pp. 21, 272 ff.

33 O. Loth, *Das Classenbuch des Ibn Saʿd. Einleitende Untersuchungen über Authentie und Inhalt* (Leipzig, 1869), p. 43; Fück, 'Muḥammad Ibn Isḥāq', p. 7.

34 Von Stülpnagel, ''Urwa', pp. 54 ff.; Görke and Schoeler, *Die ältesten Berichte*, pp. 15 ff.

35 Von Stülpnagel, ''Urwa', p. 119; Görke and Schoeler, *Die ältesten Berichte*, pp. 255 ff.

36 GAS, vol. 1, pp. 88 ff.

37 Ibid., vol. 1, pp. 284 ff.

38 E.g. the corpus established in S. Mursī al-Ṭāhir, *Bidāyat al-kitābah al-ta'rīkhiyyah 'inda al-ʿArab, awwal sīrah fī al-Islām: 'Urwah ibn al-Zubayr ibn al-ʿAwwām* (Beirut, 1995); Görke and Schoeler, *Die ältesten Berichte*.

39 Ibn Ḥajar, *Tahdhīb*, vol. 10, pp. 38–40; al-Dhahabī, *Siyar*, vol. 4, pp. 449–52; GAS, vol. 1, p. 29; G. Stauth, 'Die Überlieferung des Korankommentars Muǧāhid b. Ǧabrs', doctoral thesis, Giessen, 1969; Cl. Gilliot, 'Les débuts de l'exégèse coranique', *Revue du Monde musulman et de la Méditerranée* 58 (1990), pp. 88 ff.

40 Ibn al-Jazarī, *Ṭabaqāt*, vol. 2, p. 41, no. 2659.

41 GAS, vol. 1, pp. 25 ff.; Cl. Gilliot, 'Portrait «mythique» d'Ibn 'Abbās', *Arabica* 32 (1985), pp. 127–84.

42 al-Dhahabī, *Siyar*, vol. 4, pp. 450; *cf.* Ibn Ḥajar, *Tahdhīb*, vol. 10, p. 40.

43 Approximately 700 reports according to GAS, vol. 1, p. 29.

44 al-Khaṭīb al-Baghdādī, *Taqyīd*, p. 105.

45 Ibn Ḥibbān, *Kitāb al-Thiqāt*, 9 vols (Hyderabad, Deccan, 1973–83, repr. Beirut, 1988), vol. 7, p. 331; Ibn Ḥajar, *Tahdhīb*, vol. 8, p. 279.

46 See Ibn Ḥajar, *Tahdhīb*, vol. 8, pp. 278 ff.

47 Mujāhid's principal transmitter.

48 Occasioning such formulations as *wajadtu fī kitāb x* or *kataba ilayya x*, and not *ḥaddathanī x* or *samiʿtu ʿan x*, for example.

49 al-Khaṭīb al-Baghdādī, *Taqyīd*, p. 105.

50 *Cf.* Stauth, 'Die Überlieferung', pp. 14 ff.; G. Schoeler, *Arabische Handschriften*, vol. 2 (Stuttgart, 1990), p. 40 (no. 30).

51 F. Leemhuis, 'Ms. 1075 Tafsīr of the Cairene Dār al-kutub and Muǧāhid's Tafsīr', in

Proceedings of the Ninth Congress of the Union européenne des arabisants et islamisants (Amsterdam, 1978), ed. R. Peters (Leiden, 1981), pp. 169–80. It was edited in 1989 under the title *Tafsīr Mujāhid* (see Bibliography).

52 GAS, vol. 1, p. 29.

53 The complete title is *Tafsīr [Ādam ibn Abī Iyās 'an] Warqā' 'an Ibn Abī Najīḥ 'an Mujāhid* (The Qur'ān commentary of Warqā' on the authority of Ibn Abī Najīḥ on the authority of Mujāhid).

54 Stauth, 'Die Überlieferung'; Leemhuis, 'Ms. 1075 Tafsīr'.

55 Stauth, 'Die Überlieferung', esp. pp. 190 ff.; Leemhuis, 'Ms. 1075, Tafsīr', pp. 172 ff.

56 *Cf.* Stauth, 'Die Überlieferung', pp. 2 and pp. 14 ff.

57 M. Lecker, in *EI*², s.v. al-Zuhrī; GAS, vol. 1, pp. 280–2; Horovitz, *The Earliest Biographies*, pp. 50 ff.; Fück, 'Muḥammad Ibn Isḥāq', pp. 9 ff.; Rosenthal, *A History*, pp. 130 ff.; A. A. Duri, 'Al-Zuhrī. A Study on the Beginnings of History Writing in Islam', *BSOAS* 19 (1957), pp. 1–12; Duri, *The Rise*, pp. 27 ff. and 95 ff.

58 al-Fasawī, *Kitāb al-Ma'rifah*, vol. 1, p. 622; al-Dhahabī, *Siyar*, vol. 5, p. 345; Ibn 'Asākir, *Ta'rīkh madīnat Dimashq: al-Zuhrī* ..., ed. Sh. Ibn N. Qawchānī (Beirut, 1982), pp. 77 ff. (hereafter Ibn 'Asākir, *al-Zuhrī*).

59 Fischer, *Biographien*, p. 69.

60 'Abd al-Razzāq, *al-Muṣannaf*, vol. 11, p. 258; al-Fasawī, *Kitāb al-Ma'rifah*, vol. 1, p. 637; Fischer, *Biographien*, p. 67; al-Khaṭīb al-Baghdādī, *Taqyīd*, pp. 106 ff. On Ṣāliḥ ibn Kaysān, see Ibn Ḥajar, *Tahdhīb*, vol. 4, p. 350.

61 al-Dhahabī, *Siyar*, vol. 5, p. 332; Fischer, *Biographien*, p. 67; al-Fasawī, *Kitāb al-Ma'rifah*, vol. 1, p. 639.

62 Fischer, *Biographien*, pp. 68 ff.; Ibn 'Asākir, *al-Zuhrī*; *cf.* Horovitz, *The Earliest Biographies*, p. 63; on Layth, see GAS, vol. 1, p. 518.

63 al-Dhahabī, *Siyar*, vol. 5, pp. 338 and 334; Fischer, *Biographien*, pp. 69 ff.; Ibn 'Asākir, *al-Zuhrī*, pp. 151 ff.; *cf.* Schoeler, *Charakter*, pp. 34 ff.

64 al-Khaṭīb al-Baghdādī, *al-Kifāyah*, p. 443; Goldziher, 'Ueber die Entwickelung', p. 221; GAS, vol. 1, p. 458.

65 al-Fasawī, *Kitāb al-Ma'rifah*, vol. 1, p. 638; al-Dhahabī, *Siyar*, vol. 5, p. 334; Fischer, *Biographien*, p. 71; Ibn 'Asākir, *al-Zuhrī*, pp. 91 ff.

66 al-Fasawī, *Kitāb al-Ma'rifah*, vol. 1, p. 641; Fischer, *Biographien*, p. 68; Ibn 'Asākir, *al-Zuhri*, pp. 86 ff.

67 al-Fasawī, *Kitāb al-Ma'rifah*, vol. 1, p. 643; Ibn 'Asākir, *al-Zuhrī*, pp. 87 ff.

68 al-Khaṭīb al-Baghdādī, *Taqyīd*, pp. 29–32; *cf.* Schoeler, *The Oral and the Written*, pp. 116, 124 ff.; on Abū Sa'īd al-Khudrī, see *Tahdhīb*, vol. 3, p. 417.

69 'Abd al-Razzāq, *al-Muṣannaf*, vol. 5, pp. 313 ff. = (Pseudo-) al-Zuhrī, 'al-Maghāzī al-nabawiyyah'.

70 This also applies to al-Zuhrī's juridical ḥadīths; see H. Motzki, 'Der Fiqh des -Zuhrī: Die Quellenproblematik', *Der Islam* 68 (1991), p. 6.

71 Duri, 'Al-Zuhrī', p. 7.

72 For a fourth type of writing, namely the epistle (*risālah*), see Chapter 4 below.

73 Ibn 'Abd al-Barr, *Jāmi' bayān al-'ilm wa-faḍlihi wa-mā yanbaghī fī riwāyatihi wa-ḥamalatihi*, 2 vols (Cairo, n.d.), vol. 1, p. 76. *Cf.* Schoeler, *The Oral and the Written*, pp. 123 ff.

74 Ibid., vol. 1, p. 73; Abū Nu'aym, *Ḥilyat al-awliyā'*, vol. 3, p. 363.

75 'Abd al-Razzāq, *al-Muṣannaf*, vol. 11, p. 258, no. 20486; Ibn Sa'd, *Ṭabaqāt*, vol. 2, p. 135.

4

Literature and the caliphal court

For Muslim scholars, the transmission and dissemination of their knowledge was initially accomplished orally, or, to be more precise, 'aurally'. It depended, in fact, on audition (*samā'*) and on personal instruction, which took place in scholarly sessions and circles; in some ways this was not unlike classes in present-day universities. In fact, there was opposition to any 'writing down of knowledge' (*taqyīd al-'ilm*), notably in Medina and in Iraq, especially Basra and Kufa, and the opposition was particularly strong when it came to legal opinions (*ārā'*) or any ḥadīths attributed to the Prophet.[1] In practice, however, this opposition was not particularly successful: the auditors took notes, either during the teacher's class or afterwards, by copying the notes of another auditor, or indeed those of the teacher himself. In either case, writing was always secondary in the transmission of knowledge. To put it in terms borrowed from Antiquity, only *hypomnēmata*, private written records intended as a mnemonic aid for a lecture (or a discussion) were used, as opposed to *syngrammata*, actual books, composed and redacted according to the canon of stylistic rules, and intended for literary publication (*ekdosis*). Those wishing to acquire knowledge (*'ilm*, Ḥadīth in this context) were thus, in principle, obliged personally to attend the teachers' classes and accordingly often had to undertake long journeys in order to do so (*riḥalāt fī ṭalab al-'ilm*), a practice that became common in the second half of the eighth century.

The demands of the courtly environment

It is not difficult to see why the Umayyad caliphs preferred to have knowledge accessible in their palace libraries.[2] There, they could easily consult not only the collections containing the traditions of Muḥammad and the accounts relating to his life, but also information about the Arab past. To accomplish this they initially (in the mid-seventh century) had scholars brought to the court, where scribes would then write down what these scholars reported. A little later (during the time of 'Urwah ibn al-Zubayr), we find the caliph asking a scholar questions by writing him a letter and receiving a reply also in writing. It is in the following generation (that of al-Zuhrī), that we first have evidence of large-scale collections and of actual books commissioned by the rulers and their governors.

Already, in the middle of the seventh century, the first Umayyad caliph, Mu'āwiyah (ruled 41/661–60/680), is said to have ordered that the (pseudo-) historical accounts about Arab antiquity, which the Yemeni 'Abīd ibn Sharyah (d. after 60/680) would recount at court, be written down.[3] When Zayd ibn Thābit (d. 45/666), Muḥammad's own scribe, came to Mu'āwiyah's court, the caliph is said to have asked him for accounts of what the Prophet said and did (ḥadīths) and to have ordered a scribe to write down these accounts, but Zayd is said to have then erased everything that had been written down.[4] While he was Governor of Medina, the future caliph Marwān (ruled 64/684–65/685) is reported to have expressed the desire to have a scribe write down the ḥadīths transmitted by the celebrated Companion Abū Hurayrah. But Abū Hurayrah is reported to have refused, saying 'Transmit them the way we have [i.e. orally].'[5] Ziyād ibn Abīhi (d. 53/673), Mu'āwiyah's governor in Iraq, is said to have been the first person to commission a *Kitāb al-Mathālib* (Book of the Evil Deeds [of the Arabs]), apparently because of the ignominies he suffered as a result of his modest and non-Arab origins. He is said to have given this book to his sons, saying: 'Seek this book's help against the Arabs, for then they will leave you alone.'[6] Later, the caliph al-Walīd II (ruled 125/743–126/744), is said to have 'collected the records (*dīwān*) of the Arabs, their poems, accounts, genealogies and dialectal expressions'.[7] To this end, he seems to have used material compiled by, and in the possession of, some learned transmitters; in any case, we learn that afterwards 'he gave back the records (*dīwān*) to Ḥammād (al-Rāwiyah) and Jannād'.[8]

The Umayyad rulers were also interested in the Prophet Muḥammad's life. Prince Sulaymān, who would rule as caliph between 96/715 and 99/717, is said to have ordered Abān ibn 'Uthmān (d. between 96/714 and 105/723–4) to write down the accounts relating to Muḥammad's life (*siyar*) and campaigns (*maghāzī*), and then to have handed the text to ten scribes who were charged with copying it.[9] But, according to this report, he later destroyed these parchments because he wished to consult his father, the caliph 'Abd al-Malik (probably because the latter had long been an opponent of such written accounts). According to another report, when 'Abd al-Malik saw a work titled *Hadīth al-Maghāzī* (Account of the Campaigns) in the hands of one his sons (Sulaymān, perhaps), he had it burned, and then counselled his son to devote himself to the recitation of the Qur'ān and to learning and following the Sunnah of the Prophet (rather than to the reading of such histories).[10] Evidently, 'Abd al-Malik was initially of the view that the Qur'ān should remain Islam's only book, but later seems to have changed his mind. At any rate, he showed great interest in the life of the Prophet, even going so far as sending 'Urwah ibn al-Zubayr letters with questions on the subject, to which 'Urwah responded in writing.

As we noted in Chapter 3, 'Urwah composed what might be termed specialised treatises on Islamic history, indeed the first scholarly writings in the Islamic world. 'Urwah's student al-Zuhrī is himself reported to have been charged by the Umayyad governor, Khālid al-Qasrī (d. 126/743–4), with compiling a book of genealogies; Khālid is then said to have ordered him to stop all work on the book of genealogies and to write a book on the *Sīrah*.[11] The report does not specify whether this book was ever completed. Al-Zuhrī is also reported to have edited annals on the history of the caliphate (*Asnān al-khulafā'*), the very first book of its kind, a small fragment of which is quoted by al-Ṭabarī.[12] Once he had started working for the Umayyads, al-Zuhrī was called upon several times to put his knowledge at their disposal by producing written collections of ḥadīths. Various reports describe him as either compiling these collections or dictating them. According to one report, it was for the Umayyad ruler, 'Umar II (ruled 99/717–101/720), that al-Zuhrī devoted himself to ḥadīth collection on a large scale,[13] and for the education of the princes at the court of another Umayyad ruler, Hishām ibn 'Abd al-Malik (ruled 105/724–125/743), that he dictated many ḥadīths. According to one source, he dictated ḥadīths for the princes to a scribe for a whole year (*sc.* entirely from memory).[14] According to another source, he twice dictated four hundred traditions a month apart (*sc.* without the help of notes), and the two dictations were identical in every way.[15] With the exception of 'Urwah's letters, all the above-mentioned books and compilations – inasmuch as their authors ever completed them – disappeared with the fall of the Umayyads. These were evidently works of which only a small number of copies were produced which were then deposited in the caliph's library and which were intended for the exclusive use of the caliph and court.

The state secretaries

In the meantime, a new social class, or scholarly cadre, had appeared on the scene and taken its place next to the scholars learned in the fields of religious and linguistic scholarship: these *kuttāb* (sing. *kātib*), literally 'scribes' or 'writers', but here meaning 'state secretaries', henceforth became an integral part of Arabic writerly culture.[16] Ever since the end of the Umayyad period, they had worked in the administrative offices of the state, specifically in the chanceries (sing. *dīwān al-rasā'il*) of the caliphs and governors, where their job was to draft the official correspondence of state. Of non-Arab descent – in Iraq recruited mainly from families of Persian origin – these new Muslims had ideas and ideals completely different from those of the Muslim scholars engaged in religious and linguistic scholarship; H. A. R. Gibb has described their relationship to the State as follows:[17]

> Their aim was not to destroy the Islamic empire but to remold its political institutions and values, which represented in their eyes the highest political wisdom.

As it turns out, this specific objective was completely in line with the aspirations of the early ʿAbbāsid caliphs.[18] The state secretaries borrowed their ideal cultural model and their material from the fallen Sasanid empire. They did this because no viable alternative presented itself: given their objective, Arab tradition had nothing to offer them.[19] Their works were therefore markedly different, in both spirit and content, from the works produced by Muslim scholars (traditionists, historians, exegetes, philologists, and so on); their literary output consisted in part of original works and in part of translations, or adaptations rather, of books from Middle Persian.

The original works composed by the state secretaries often took the form of epistles (*risālah*, pl. *rasā'il*) and were consequently addressed to a specific person, the caliph, a prince, other secretaries and the like. This holds true for all the works of ʿAbd al-Ḥamīd al-Kātib (d. 132/750), in all likelihood of Iranian origin, who was secretary to Marwān, the last Umayyad caliph (and holds true for at least one work of Ibn al-Muqaffaʿ too).[20] The titles of ʿAbd al-Ḥamīd's best known writings confirm this: 'Epistle to the Secretaries', 'Epistle to the Crown Prince', 'Epistle on Chess', and so on. 'It is with his name', Latham points out, ' ... that we most commonly associate the beginnings of Arabic prose as a written art – an art, that is to say, inspired by a conscious literary purpose and a desire to display the imaginative and creative talents of the writer.'[21] Indeed, the literary genre in which Arabic artistic prose had first manifested itself was the *risālah*, the epistle or letter. This genre had in a sense existed since the rise of Islam – we have seen that the Prophet Muḥammad addressed letters to the Arab tribes, and that ʿUrwah ibn al-Zubayr wrote to the caliph ʿAbd al-Malik, but these were not literary texts *per se*, but functional ones rather, specialised treatises as it were. Arabic artistic prose, properly speaking, came into being, therefore, in the chancery bureaux of state.

Translations and adaptations from Middle Persian do not seem to have been undertaken until the early ʿAbbāsid period. The most famous translator was Ibn al-Muqaffaʿ (d. 139/757), a secretary of Iranian origin.[22] Two of his books, *Siyar mulūk al-ʿAjam* (Lives of the Persian Kings) and *Kalīlah wa-Dimnah* (Kalilah and Dimnah), are of special importance. The former contained the national history of Iran from the beginning of creation up to the end of the Sasanid Empire. This translation – or adaptation – by Ibn al-Muqaffaʿ of the Middle Persian *Khwāday-Nāmag* (Book of Kings) does not survive in its entirety, though extracts are quoted in other works. Other adaptations, based on translations other than Ibn al-Muqaffaʿ's, do survive in Arabic and Persian, the most celebrated of which is Firdawsī's *Shāhnāma* (Book of Kings) the great Iranian national epic. Ibn al-Muqaffaʿ's *Kalīlah wa-Dimnah*, on the other hand, has come down to us. It is a 'mirror for princes' work, the original Indian version of which was translated into Middle Persian in the sixth century. Ibn al-Muqaffa' translated, that is, adapted and embellished, the Middle Persian version and in so doing gave the Arabic language its first prose masterpiece.

Ibn al-Muqaffa' (or perhaps a son of his) also translated an epitome on Aristotelian logic.[23] This work, which is extant and has been edited, must have depended on a Middle Persian version. This brings us to the question of the origins of the great movement to translate works of Greek thought into Arabic, an enterprise that began under the early 'Abbāsids. It is now generally accepted that Arabic translations of Greek works through the intermediary Syriac versions were preceded by translations of Middle Persian works inspired by Greek ones.[24] These Middle Persian works – prolegomena to works of logic or philosophy, for instance, or books of astrology – originated in the Sasanid court, notably that of the great Khusraw Anūshirwān (ruled 531–79), where Nestorian Christians had been given the task of translating and adapting Greek works. Ibn al-Muqaffa' (or his son) is thus to be placed also in the early history of translation into Arabic of Hellenistic material. After him, the most important translators were no longer Persians, but Aramean and Arab Christians, usually Nestorians: this explains why they would have recourse to Syriac versions of the works of Aristotle and other Greek thinkers when perfecting their translations.

Ibn al-Muqaffa' was clearly a gifted translator, but he was also the author of original works. One of the most celebrated of these is in the epistolary genre, the *Risālah fī al-Ṣaḥābā* (Epistle on Courtiers). This 'memorandum on the Caliph's entourage', no doubt composed for al-Manṣūr (ruled 136/754–158/775), is an administrative document that outlines the measures needed to ensure the stability of the empire.[25]

George Saliba has recently shown that the generation of state secretaries responsible for the Arabisation of government administration played an important role in the movement to translate scientific and philosophical texts. So too, according to Saliba, did their descendants, the following generation of state secretaries, and others tied to them in one way or another.[26] That said, as Dimitri Gutas has shown in some detail, it was the 'Abbāsid caliphs themselves who were the engine for this great movement: they considered themselves not only successors to the Prophet Muḥammad but also heirs of the Sasanid emperors and therefore deemed it their responsibility to continue the latter's 'cultural policy' of initiating the translation of Greek works for specific ideological reasons.[27]

Whether in the form of epistles or of adaptations of works in Persian, we have here literary prose – artistic prose, even – bearing the imprint of the authors' personalities. Moreover, these works by the state secretaries were books conceived of entirely with the prospect of written transmission in mind;[28] they were therefore intended for *readers*. It is true that, initially, this readership consisted exclusively of the caliph and his court, but subsequently a larger readership had access to such works; readers could actually lay their hands on them by getting hold of manuscript copies. These were, therefore, actual books.

It is worth recalling the specific nature of the 'books' produced by the traditional scholars and the way in which they were published. Those books can best be characterised as collections of traditions, acquired through audition in the presence of the teacher. They were written as notes or notebooks, and their publication by the scholar who had drafted those notes took place during a subsequent audition, without there being any formal redaction. These writings properly belong, therefore, to the category of aide-mémoire. The traditional scholars can consequently best be characterised as *transmitters*, whereas the state secretaries and authors of Persian origin are *men of letters* or *writers*. The historian al-Mas'ūdī (d. 345/956) tried to get to the heart of the difference between transmitters on the one hand and men of letters on the other – though there were admittedly examples of mixed and transitional ways of working.[29] Al-Mas'ūdī contrasts al-Jāḥiẓ (d. 255/868–9), illustrative of the secretarial class and an author of epistles and actual books, with his contemporary al-Madā'inī (d. 235/850), typical of the traditional scholars and a transmitter of historical reports (*akhbār*), noting:[30]

> None of the transmitters (*ruwāt*) nor any of the scholars (*ahl al-'ilm*) is known to have written more books than he [i.e. al-Jāḥiẓ]. It is true that Abu al-Ḥasan al-Madā'inī was a prolific writer (*qad kāna kathīr al-kutub*), but it was his practice to transmit what he had heard [to auditors, students] (*kāna yu'addī mā sami'a*), whereas the books of al-Jāḥiẓ (on the other hand) remove rust from the mind and bring clear proofs to light, because he has composed books according to the best arrangement (*naẓamahā aḥsan naẓm*).

A comparison of the beginning of any book or epistle of al-Jāḥiẓ, the *Kitāb fakhr al-sūdān 'alā al-bīḍān* (Epistle on Vaunting of Blacks over Whites), for instance, with the beginning of the *Kitāb al-Murdifāt min Quraysh* (Book on the Women of the Quraysh who were Married more than Once), one of al-Madā'inī's two extant works, supports al-Mas'ūdī's characterisation:

> May God protect and preserve you; may He bring you the joy of obeying Him and accept you among those who win His mercy.
>
> You mentioned … that you have read my essay on … and that I make no mention of the vaunts of the blacks. Know, may God protect you, that in fact I delayed doing so on purpose. You also mentioned that you wanted me to write for you about the vaunts of the blacks. Therefore, I have written down for you what comes to mind of their boastings.
>
> (al-Jāḥiẓ)[31]

> Abū al-Qāsim 'Abd Allāh ibn Muḥammad reported (*ḥaddathanā*) to us, saying: Abū Ja'far Aḥmad ibn al-Ḥārith al-Khazzār informed us (*anba'anā*): Abū al-Ḥasan 'Alī ibn Muḥammad [al-Madā'inī] informed us (*anba'anā*), saying: 'Umm Kulthūm was married …'
>
> (al-Madā'inī)[32]

Al-Jāḥiẓ opens by blessing his addressee and then reiterates a criticism of one of his books as expressed by the latter; the book transmitted on the authority of al-Madā'inī opens with no prefatory statement of introduction whatsoever, but with the chain of authorities, which indicates the transmission of the report that follows all the way back to al-Madā'inī. The text as we have it had evidently not been fixed until three generations after al-Madā'inī: he had originally presented the material in a lecture (as signalled by *anba'anā*), then one of his students (al-Khazzār) and a transmitter in each of the following two generations recorded it and passed it on. This first report is immediately followed in the text by an *isnād* leading back to al-Madā'inī, the report in question, and so on.

The different methods of transmission employed by al-Jāḥiẓ and al-Madā'inī explain another important fact about their respective works, namely that numerous works by al-Jāḥiẓ survive, whereas only very few of al-Madā'inī's *kutub* (i.e. lecture notes, notebooks, draft notes) are extant, and then only in the form of further transmitted texts, edited by a later generation of scholars. The material collected and passed on by al-Madā'inī is therefore not lost, but has found its way into later compilations.[33] The works of al-Jāḥiẓ, on the other hand, as writings always intended for a reading public, were from the very beginning 'passed on' through written transmission, through the copying of manuscripts.

The influence of the princely environment on traditional scholars

Did traditional scholars possibly modify the way they worked, either at the suggestion of the caliph, or, given their contact with the court, through the influence of works written by the state secretaries? Muslim scholars in the generation following al-Zuhrī, i.e. those active about the middle of the eighth century, had begun to classify their material into works systematically subdivided into thematic chapters. This method was called *taṣnīf*, and the works organised according to this method were called *muṣannafāt*. *Muṣannafāt* appeared in the fields of law, exegesis, Ḥadīth, history and philology – some modern scholars even go so far as to speak of a *taṣnīf* or *muṣannaf* 'movement'.[34] Can we discern in the traditional scholars' use of *taṣnīf* the influence of the state secretaries, or was this an independent internal development? We cannot be certain, but we do know this: traditional scholars continued to publish their *muṣannafāt* in the way which was familiar to them, namely by reciting them or by dictating them when they provided academic instruction in the sessions or scholarly circles they held. Their method of publication only changed under the impetus of the court, and even then only a few isolated works were affected.

According to an account preserved in *Ta'rīkh Baghdād* (History of Baghdad) the substance of which is confirmed by a parallel and slightly more elaborated account in Ibn Sa'd, the 'Abbāsid caliph al-Manṣūr asked Ibn Isḥāq (d. 150/767), an eminent authority on the life of Muḥammad, to compose for crown prince al-Mahdī a large book consisting of a summation of history, beginning with the creation of Adam and continuing to the present day.[35] Al-Manṣūr is said to have played a similar role in the genesis of the celebrated anthology of poetry that later came to be known as *al-Mufaḍḍaliyyāt*, commissioning the learned transmitter al-Mufaḍḍal al-Ḍabbī to put together the anthology for al-Mahdī.[36] (Al-Manṣūr was also the addressee of some of Ibn al-Muqaffa''s epistles.)

The 'great book' (*al-kitāb al-kabīr*) that Ibn Isḥāq compiled for the crown prince is said to have comprised three parts: a *Kitāb al-Mubtada'* (Book of the Beginning) on creation and the biblical prophets, a *Kitāb al-Mab'ath* (Book of the Mission [of Muḥammad]) on the Meccan period of Muḥammad's life, and a *Kitāb al-Maghāzī* (Book of Campaigns) on the Prophet Muḥammad's campaigns in the Medinese period of his life;[37] and it may be that the *Kitāb al-Khulafā'* (Book of Caliphs) is a continuation of the *Kitāb al-Maghāzī*, even though Ibn al-Nadīm identifies it as a separate work.[38] No definitive edition established by Ibn Isḥāq himself has come down to us. In any case, the 'great book', of which there were no doubt very few copies, is not preserved in its original form: what does survive of Ibn Isḥāq's works is what his students transmitted from him. The *Kitāb Sīrat rasūl Allāh* (Biography of the Messenger of God) by Ibn Hishām (d. 218/834) – a student of a student of Ibn Isḥāq – constitutes the most important recension of the information contained in Ibn Isḥāq's work. Ibn Hishām's book does not take into account the whole of the *Kitab al-Kabīr*, but relies, for the main part, on the information appearing in the two parts concerning the life of Muḥammad. Ibn Isḥāq's historical accounts appear in other transmissions too: suffice to mention here the numerous passages included in al-Ṭabarī's *Ta'rīkh* (History).

Recensions of the *Kitāb al-Maghāzī* and quotations from it – the only forms in which the book survives – do nonetheless suffice to reveal the literary and artistic character of the work. It is well thought out, it is divided into chapters, and events are arranged in chronological order, without precluding classification based on genealogical or practical considerations when the need arises.[39] Ibn Isḥāq frequently prefaces the different reports relating to a particular event with preliminary remarks summarising and dating the information he provides. He also frequently inserts transitional phrases between the various accounts. The principal outcome of this is a coherent narrative, but – and this is the crux – Ibn Isḥāq has above all put together his material in the service of a guiding principle, namely 'Plac[ing] the history of the Prophet and of the new faith into the history of divine revelation since the beginning of the world'.[40]

To see more clearly the uniqueness of Ibn Isḥāq as a *muṣannaf* author, we need only compare his *Kitāb al-Maghāzī* with another work of the same name by his contemporary, Maʿmar ibn Rāshid (d. 154/770). What we have of Maʿmar's work comes to us as transmitted by one of his students, ʿAbd al-Razzāq ibn Ḥammām (d. 211/827), in the latter's own *Kitāb al-Maghāzī*.[41] At first glance, it appears that in Maʿmar's work the events described proceed more or less chronologically.[42] Accounts devoted to earlier events (e.g. the digging of the well of Zamzam, or the history of the Prophet's grandfather, ʿAbd al-Muṭṭalib) are followed by events from Muḥammad's life in Mecca, then by events from his life in Medina; after describing Muḥammad's death, the author has also added some accounts about the first four ('rightly guided') caliphs. The sequence of Muḥammad's campaigns is to a certain extent respected: the Battle of Badr (2/624), the Battle of Uḥud (3/625), the Battle of the Trench (5/627), the execution of the Banū Qurayẓah (5/627), the conquest of Khaybar (7/628) and the conquest of Mecca (8/630). But on closer inspection, it becomes clear that the chronological sequence is not at all consistent: the pact of al-Ḥudaybiyah (6/628), for example, is reported separately, and before Badr (2/624); conversely, the Bi'r Maʿūnah incident (4/625) appears after the conquest of Mecca (8/630). Besides being only loosely chronological, the text is also arranged 'pragmatically', for want of a better term; thus, after presenting events in the life of the Prophet that pertain to the public sphere (and enumerated above), Maʿmar goes back in time and resumes his narrative about events before the Hijrah, namely the emigration of the early believers to Abyssinia. Then the author turns to slightly more private matters (such as the Hijrah, and the slandering of ʿĀ'ishah), but without any specific arrangement. Preliminary remarks and transitional phrases between different accounts are absent in what is effectively a collection consisting of scattered traditions belonging more or less together, in juxtaposition. Maʿmar's work lacks the coherent narration characteristic of Ibn Isḥāq's work. It goes without saying that Maʿmar's *Kitāb al-Maghāzī* does not have a guiding principle governing it, and can therefore not be described as a well-organised book, as is the case with Ibn Isḥāq's.

Traditional scholars certainly recognised the uniqueness of Ibn Isḥāq. The celebrated Ḥadīth critic, Ibn Ḥibbān (d. 354/965), said of him: 'He was one of those people who arranged the narratives in the best possible manner.'[43] Horovitz's assessment is similar, though more comprehensive and couched in the language of modern scholarship: 'The material in traditions transmitted to him by his teachers, which he enlarged with numerous statements collected by himself, Ibn Isḥāq compiled into a well-arranged presentation of the life of the Prophet.'[44] In short, we can consider the *Kitāb al-Maghāzī* of Ibn Isḥāq a *syngramma*, an actual book, composed and redacted according to the canon of stylistic rules, and intended for literary publication, rather than a *hypomnēma*, a private written record intended as a mnemonic aid for a lecture or a discussion. We do have to bear in mind, however, that the public this work addressed was an extremely restricted one – it was intended for the exclusive use of the caliph and his court.

Scholarly treatises taking the form of epistles

The impact of the caliphal court on the methods of the traditional scholars is clear. Whereas these scholars originally 'published' through the medium of oral instruction – which did not in any way preclude the use of written notes – now they composed their works by giving them a definitive shape, and with the reader in mind. Besides the court's wish to have at its disposal – i.e. in its libraries – works which the scholars ordinarily only disseminated through audition, we must take into account two additional motivations. In the first place, the state administration, both in the capital and in the provinces, felt a need to have the policies it was carrying out spelled out in writing. This need was the catalyst for the *Kitāb al-Kharāj* (Book of Land-Tax) of Abū Yūsuf Ya'qūb (d. 182/798), one of the very first actual books in the field of law to have survived. It is true that the *Muwaṭṭa'* of Mālik (d. 179/796), the founder of the Mālikī legal school, may predate it, but the *Muwaṭṭa'* is not an actual book; rather, it is a collection of legally relevant ḥadīths and legal opinions (*ārā'*) of the Followers (*tābi'ūn*), of which we have several recensions compiled by Mālik's students: its author did not give it a definitive shape. Like most of the *syngrammata* of the eighth century, Abū Yūsuf's work takes the form of an epistle, as Ibn al-Nadīm's characterisation of it in the *Fihrist* attests: *Kitāb risālatihi fī al-kharāj ilā al-Rashīd* (The Book of his Epistle on Land-Tax [addressed] to al-Rashīd).[45] This epistle, commissioned by Hārūn al-Rashīd, opens as follows:[46]

> This is what Abū Yūsuf [...] wrote to the Commander of the Faithful Hārūn al-Rashīd. May God prolong the life of the Commander of the Faithful and perpetuate his might in perfect happiness and in prestige endless (*fī tamāmīm min al-ni'mah wa-dawāmīm min al-karāmah*)! The Commander of the Faithful ... asked me to compose for him an all-inclusive book (*kitāban jāmi'an*) on the calculation of the land-tax ... to be consulted and to be followed when doing so.

The author's use of a style akin to rhythmic, rhyming prose in his prefatory remarks, particularly in the two parts of the eulogy, is tangible influence of the secretaries' literary *risālahs*. What is more, the book's immediate predecessor, a work also called *Kitāb al-Kharāj* (Book of Land-Tax), was also composed by a secretary, Ibn Yasār (d. 170/786), the first person to compose a work of this kind, in fact.[47]

The second factor that motivated traditional scholars to give their works a definitive shape was the conflict with sects and heterodox movements. Indeed, this is the impetus that occasioned the very earliest theological writings, works such as the *Risālah fī al-qadar* (Epistle on Destiny),[48] attributed to al-Ḥasan al-Baṣrī (d. 110/728) and addressed to the caliph 'Umar II,[49] the 'Anti-Qadarī Epistle' attributed to 'Umar II (d. 101/720),[50] and the *Kitāb al-Irjā'* (Book on the Postponement of Judgement),[51] said to have been written by al-Ḥasan ibn Muḥammad ibn al-Ḥanafiyyah (d. 99/717).[52] Although the authenticity of the extant works is doubtful, the fact remains that they are datable to relatively early – the first half of the eighth century, or the second half at the latest.[53] All of these 'books', including the *Kitāb al-Irjā'*, are epistles and are thus tied to the tradition of writing official letters, private letters and documents (which, as we have seen, was a practice already in existence in the beginning of Islam). The above-mentioned epistles were documents with a specific function, what we might term scholarly epistles.

The epistle, as a *literary* genre, originates with the state secretaries and is exemplified by the works of 'Abd al-Ḥamīd or Ibn al-Muqaffa'. The scholarly epistle, on the other hand, appears to be quite a bit older and may well have developed out of the earliest functional epistle. The transition between the two is almost seamless: to take again the example of 'Urwah ibn al-Zubayr's replies to the questions posed by the caliph 'Abd al-Malik, his letters are practically scholarly treatises. The developed character of the scholarly epistle, as is the case with Abū Yūsuf's *Kitāb al-Kharāj* and numerous later epistles, is nevertheless still heavily influenced by the literary *risālah*. As we saw earlier, the *Kitāb al-Kharāj* even has recourse in its preface to a literary feature, namely rhythmic, rhyming prose. It is therefore not surprising that the fully developed scholarly *risālah* of the scholars was modelled on the literary *risālah* of the secretaries.

The first works of Arabic literature conceived of as written works from the start, whether they were scholarly (such as the letters of 'Urwah and other Arab scholars) or literary (such as the epistles of 'Abd al-Ḥamīd and Ibn al-Muqaffa'), were the result of an impetus that came from the court. These works all took the form of *letters*, i.e. private communications intended for specific individuals, and not the form of *books* intended for a wider readership. It would seem that, until the end of the eighth century, a text composed as a personal communication was more easily accepted than one composed as a book from the very start and intended for a wider audience.

Notes

1 See Schoeler, *The Oral and The Written*, pp. 111–41 (ch. 5, 'Oral Torah and *Ḥadīṯ*'), and Cook, 'The Opponents'.
2 *Cf.* Schoeler, *Charakter*, pp. 46 ff.; Abbott, *Studies*, vol. 1, pp. 9 ff. and vol. 2, pp. 18 ff. On the libraries (*buyūt al-ḥikmah*) of the early Umayyad caliphs, see Y. Eche, *Les bibliothèques arabes publiques et sémi-publiques en Mésopotamie, en Syrie et en Egypte au Moyen Age* (Damascus, 1967), pp. 11 ff.
3 *Fihrist*[1], p. 89 = *Fihrist*[2], p. 102. On 'Abīd, see GAS, vol. 1, p. 260.
4 al-Khaṭīb al-Baghdādī, *Taqyīd*, p. 35. On Zayd, see GAS, vol. 1, p. 401.
5 Ibid., p. 41; al-Dārimī, *al-Sunan*, 2 vols, ed. 'A. H. Yamānī al-Madanī (Medina, 1966), vol. 1, p. 22.
6 *Fihrist*[1], p. 89 = *Fihrist*[2], p. 101; *cf.* GAS, vol. 1, p. 261.
7 *Fihrist*[1], p. 91 = *Fihrist*[2], p. 103; *cf.* GAS, vol. 1, p. 367. *Dīwān* may here mean 'lists of persons' (see S. Leder, *Das Korpus al-Haiṯam ibn 'Adī (st. 207/822). Herkunft, Überlieferung, Gestalt früher Texte der aḫbār Literatur* [Frankfurt, 1991], pp. 197 ff.). The content of such lists (which were often very specialised) are reflected in the titles of some of Muḥammad ibn Ḥabīb's works, e.g. *Asmā' al-mughtālīn min al-ashrāf fī al-Jāhiliyyah wa-fī al-Islām* (The Names of The Nobles [?] who were Murdered in Pre-Islamic Times and in Islam) and *Kitāb man nusiba ilā ummihi min al-shu'arā'* (Book on Poets who took their *nasabs* from their Mothers) (*cf.* I. Lichtenstädter, *EI*[2], s.v. Muḥammad b. Ḥabīb). I am indebted to Professor Wolfhart Heinrichs for this information.
8 *Fihrist*[1], p. 91 = *Fihrist*[2], p. 103.
9 al-Zubayr ibn Bakkār, *al-Akhbār al-Muwaffaqiyyāt*, pp. 331 ff. On Abān, see GAS, vol. 1, pp. 277 ff.
10 al-Balādhurī, *Ansāb al-ashrāf*, vol. 11 = *Anonyme arabische Chronik* ed. W. Ahlwardt (Greifswald, 1883), p. 172; cf. GAS, vol. 1, p. 255.
11 *Aghānī*, vol. 19, p. 59.
12 al-Ṭabarī, *Ta'rīkh*, vol. 2, p. 428.
13 Ibn 'Abd al-Barr, *Jāmi'*, pp. 73, 76; Abū Nu'aym, *Ḥilyat al-awliyā'*, vol. 3, p. 363; *cf.* Schoeler, 'Mündliche Thora', pp. 227–30 = Schoeler, *The Oral and the Written*, pp. 121–4.
14 al-Fasawī, *Kitāb al-Ma'rifah*, vol. 1, p. 632.
15 Ibid., vol. 1, p. 640; Fischer, *Biographien*, p. 69.
16 See R. Sellheim-D. Sourdel, *EI*[2], s.v. Kātib.
17 H. A. R. Gibb, 'The Social Significance of the Shuubiyya', in Gibb, *Studies on the Civilization of Islam*, ed. S. J. Shaw and W. R. Polk (London, 1962), p. 66.
18 See D. Gutas, *Greek Thought, Arabic Culture. The Graeco-Arabic Translation Movement in Baghdad and Early 'Abbāsid Society (2nd–4th/8th–10th centuries)* (London, 1998), and Gutas, *EI*[2], s.v. Tardjama.
19 W. Heinrichs, *Arabische Dichtung und griechische Poetik* (Beirut, 1969), pp. 40 ff.
20 On 'Abd al-Ḥamīd, see D. Latham, 'The Beginnings of Arabic Prose Literature: The Epistolary Genre', in Beeston et al., *Arabic Literature to the End of the Umayyad Period*, pp. 164–9; W. al-Qāḍī, 'Early Islamic State Letters: The Question of Authenticity', in *The Byzantine and Early Islamic Near East*, vol. 1, *Problems in the Literary Source Material*, ed. A. Cameron and L. I. Conrad (Princeton, 1992), pp. 215–75.

21 Latham, 'Beginnings', p. 165.

22 On Ibn al-Muqaffaʿ, see D. Latham, 'Ibn al-Muqaffaʿ and Early ʿAbbāsid Prose', in Beeston et al., *Arabic Literature to the End of the Umayyad Period*, pp. 48–77; F. Gabrieli, *EI*², s.v. Ibn al-Muqaffaʿ; J. van Ess, *Theologie und Gesellschaft im 2. und 3. Jahrhundert Hidschra. Eine Geschichte des religiösen Denkens im früher Islam*, 6 vols (Berlin, 1991–1995), vol. 2, pp. 22–36.

23 This text has been published under the title *al-Manṭiq li-Ibn al-Muqaffaʿ*. See P. Kraus, 'Zu Ibn al-Muqaffaʿ. I. Die angeblichen Aristoteles-Übersetzungen des Ibn al-Muqaffaʿ', *RSO* 14 (1933), pp. 1–14; van Ess, *Theologie und Gesellschaft*, vol. 2, p. 27.

24 *Cf.* P. Kunitzsch, 'Über die Frühstadium der arabischen Aneignung antiken Gutes', *Saeculum* 26 (1975), pp. 268–82; D. Gutas and F. de Blois, *EI*², s.v. Tardjama, sect. 2 and 3; G. Endress, 'Wissenschaftliche Literatur', *GAPh*, vol. 2, p. 420.

25 *Cf.* Latham, 'Ibn al-Muqaffaʿ', p. 64.

26 *Cf.* G. Saliba, *al-Fikr al-ʿilmī al-ʿarabī: nash'atuhu wa-taṭawwuruhu* (Beirut, 1998).

27 Gutas, *Greek Thought*, esp. pp. 34 ff.

28 *Cf.* al-Qāḍī, 'Early Islamic State Letters', p. 165.

29 See S. M. Toorawa, *Ibn Abī Ṭāhir Ṭayfūr and Arabic Writerly Culture: a Ninth-Century Bookman in Baghdad* (London, New York, 2005), esp. pp. 7–17, for a discussion of this transition, and pp. 123–7 for a description of al-Jāḥiẓ as transitional; *cf.* Toorawa, 'Ibn Abī Ṭāhir Ṭayfūr vs al-Jāḥiẓ', in *ʿAbbāsid Studies. Occasional Papers of the School of ʿAbbāsid Studies. Cambridge, 6–10 July 2002*, ed. J. E. Montgomery (Leuven, 2004), pp. 247–261; Toorawa, 'Defining *Adab* by (Re)defining the *Adīb*: Ibn Abī Ṭāhir and Storytelling', in *On Fiction and* Adab *in Medieval Arabic Literature*, ed. P. F. Kennedy (Wiesbaden, 2005), pp. 287–304.

30 al-Masʿūdī, *Murūj al-dhahab*, vol. 5, p. 104 (= VIII, 34). On al-Jāḥiẓ, see Ch. Pellat, *EI*², s.v. al-Djāḥiẓ; Pellat *Le milieu basrien*; Pellat *The Life and Works of Jahiz: Translations of Selected Texts*, tr. D. M. Hawke (Berkeley, 1969); and J. E. Montgomery, 'al-Jāḥiẓ', in *Arabic Literary Culture*, 500–925, ed. M. Cooperson and S. M. Toorawa (Detroit, 2004), pp. 231–42. On al-Madā'inī, see U. Sezgin, *EI*², s.v. al-Madā'inī.

31 al-Jāḥiẓ, *Rasā'il*, 2 vols, ed. ʿA. M. Hārūn (Cairo, 1964–1965), vol. 1, p. 177; *cf.* T. Khalidi, '"The Boasts of the Blacks over the Whites' (Jahiz)', *Islamic Quarterly* 25(1&2) (1981), p. 3.

32 In *Nawādir al-makhṭūṭāt*, 2 vols, ed. ʿA. M. Hārūn (Cairo, 1951), vol. 1, p. 57.

33 See *EI*², s.v. al-Madā'inī.

34 M. Abdul Rauf, '*Ḥadīth* Literature – I: The Development of the Science of *Ḥadīth*', in Beeston et al., *Arabic Literature to the End of the Umayyad Period*, p. 272: 'the *Muṣannaf* movement'. The term '*Taṣnīf* movement' is preferable, and is the one we adopt in Chapter 5 below.

35 al-Khaṭīb al-Baghdādī, *Ta'rīkh Baghdād*, 14 vols (Cairo, 1931), vol. 1, pp. 220 ff.; Ibn Saʿd, *Ṭabaqāt (al-qism al-mutammim)*, pp. 401 ff.; al-Dhahabī, *Siyar*, vol. 7, p. 48.

36 *Fihrist*¹, p. 68 = *Fihrist*², p. 75; al-Qālī, *Kitāb Dhayl al-Amālī wal-nawādir* (Cairo, 1344 H [= 1926]), pp. 130–2.

37 Ibn ʿAdī, *al-Kāmil fī ḍuʿafā' al-rijāl*, 8 vols, ed. S. Zakkār (Beirut, ³1988), vol. 6, p. 112; Ibn Ḥajar, *Tahdhīb*, vol. 9, p. 39; *cf.* GAS, vol. 1, p. 89. Although it is the title of only the third part of the work, from early on the whole work came to be known as *Kitāb al-Maghāzī*.

38 *Fihrist*[1], p. 92 = *Fihrist*[2], p. 105.
39 *Cf.* Fück, 'Muḥammad Ibn Isḥāq', p. 38.
40 Ibid., p. 37.
41 'Abd al-Razzāq, *al-Muṣannaf*, vol. 5, pp. 313–492.
42 See 'Abd al-Razzāq, *al-Muṣannaf*, vol. 5, pp. xii–xiii (table of contents).
43 Ibn Hibbān, *Kitāb al-Thiqāt*, vol. 7, p. 383 = Ibn Ḥajar, *Tahdhīb*, vol. 9, p. 40
44 Horovitz, *The Earliest Biographies*, p. 89; see also Fück, 'Muḥammad Ibn Isḥāq', pp. 38 ff.
45 *Fihrist*[1], p. 203 = *Fihrist*[2], p. 503
46 Abū Yūsuf, *Kitāb al-Kharāj* (Būlāq, 1302 H [= 1884–1885), p. 2.
47 GAS, vol. 1, p. 519.
48 Edited by H. Ritter: 'Studien zur Geschichte der islamischen Frömmigkeit I: Ḥasan al-Baṣrī', *Der Islam* 21 (1933), pp. 67–82.
49 GAS, vol. 1, pp. 591 ff.
50 Edited, translated and commented by J. van Ess in *Anfänge muslimischer Theologie. Zwei antiqadaritische Traktate aus dem ersten Jahrhundert der Hiğra* (Beirut, 1977), pp. 43–57 and 113 ff.; GAS, vol. 1, p. 594
51 Edited and commented by J. van Ess in 'Das *Kitāb al-Irğā'* des Ḥasan b. Muḥammad b. al-Ḥanafiyya', *Arabica* 21 (1975), pp. 20–5.
52 GAS, vol. 1, pp. 594 ff.
53 *Cf.* van Ess, *Anfänge*, p. 18, and M. Cook, *Early Muslim Dogma: a Source-Critical Study* (Cambridge, 1981), pp. 68 ff., 117 ff. and 124 ff.

5

The turn toward systematisation: the *taṣnīf* movement

Traditional Muslim scholars themselves noticed that in the middle of the eighth century a new method of presenting and arranging knowledge had appeared, namely *taṣnīf*. *Taṣnīf* was a method which consisted in classifying material into works systematically subdivided into chapters organised according to subject matter, works that came to be known as *muṣannafāt* (sing. *muṣannaf*). At the beginning of his voluminous commentary on the *Ṣaḥīḥ* of al-Bukhārī, Ibn Ḥajar al-ʿAsqalānī (d. 852/1449) makes the following observation about the move toward committing ḥadīths to writing:[1]

> Then, at the end of the generation of the Followers (*tābiʿūn*), (the method of) collecting traditions into a single corpus (*tadwīn al-āthār*) and of classifying reports into separate chapters (*tabwīb al-akhbār*) emerged. (This was at the time) when scholars had spread out to the large cities and when heretical Khārijī, Rāfiḍī and Qadarī innovations had become more numerous. The first individuals to produce compilations according to this model were al-Rabīʿ ibn Ḥabīb [fl. 2nd/8th], Saʿīd ibn Abī ʿArūbah [d. 156/773] and others. They classified (traditions that belonged together) into separate chapters, until there appeared, in the middle of the second [i.e. eighth] century, the Greats of the third generation [i.e. authors of *muṣannafāt*]. The latter collected legal judgments [i.e ḥadīths and *ārā'*] into a single corpus (*dawwanū al-aḥkām*). In Medina, Imām Mālik [d. 179/796] compiled (*ṣannafa*) his *Muwaṭṭa'* (in this manner) …, Abū Muḥammad ʿAbd al-Malik ibn ʿAbd al-ʿAzīz ibn Jurayj [d. 150/767] compiled (his work) (*ṣannafa*) in Mecca …, al-Awzāʿī [d. 157/774] in Syria, Abū ʿAbd Allāh Sufyān ibn Saʿīd al-Thawrī [d. 161/778] in Kufa, and Abū Salamah Ḥammād ibn Salamah ibn Dīnār [d. 167/783] in Basra …[2]

What Ibn Ḥajar describes as happening in legal Ḥadīth scholarship – the *Muwaṭṭa'* of Mālik being undoubtedly the most important work in the field of law – was also happening in several related disciplines: in exegesis, history, grammar, lexicography and theology. It might even be appropriate to consider as similar to the *muṣannafāt* the poetry collections of the learned transmitters, the *Mufaḍḍaliyyāt* (compiled by al-Mufaḍḍal al-Ḍabbī), for instance, or the *Muʿallaqāt* (possibly put together by Ḥammād al-Rāwiyah).[3] As for the Prophet's biography, Ibn Isḥāq was, according to al-Marzubānī, 'the first individual to collect the *Maghāzī* of the Messenger of God and to compose them (in a systematic way)' (*kāna awwal man jama'a Maghāzī rasūl Allāh wa-allafahā*), although al-Dhahabī is probably correct to claim that honour for Mūsā ibn 'Uqbah (d. 141/758).[4] There are many lists of such 'firsts' or *awā'il* (sing. *awwal*, 'first'), that is, 'texts identifying individuals who were the first to do such-and-such a thing'.[5] The lists are not always in agreement about who was in fact first, but they do all agree that the first works systematically subdivided into chapters appeared in the middle of the eighth century, in the late Umayyad/early 'Abbāsid period.

Oral publication

It is important to keep in mind that, as a general rule, the compilers of these *muṣannafāt* nevertheless still published them in the traditional way, through audition, by reciting themselves, by having their students recite them, or by dictating them to their students (*imlā'*) in their scholarly circles and lectures (keeping in mind that works produced under the impetus of the court were an exception). In the Iraqi centres of learning, the traditionists continued to recite ḥadīths from memory until the ninth century, refusing to rely on notes or notebooks as aides-mémoire. Sa'īd ibn Abī 'Arūbah, whom Ibn Ḥajar mentions in the list quoted above, was a Basran traditionist who, like those of subsequent generations, emphatically disapproved of the use of writing to record traditions, at least in theory.[6] Thus Sa'īd, who was the first or one of the first traditionists to undertake the systematic classification of the ḥadīths he had collected, recited from memory without using a notebook. This is how it came to be said of him:[7]

> 'Sa'īd ibn Abī 'Arūbah had no book, but kept everything in his memory.'

In his fundamental study of the development of Ḥadīth scholarship, Ignaz Goldziher concluded from the above statement that accounts reporting that *muṣannafāt* in the domain of Ḥadīth first appeared in the middle of the eighth century must be false and anachronistic.[8] In Goldziher's view, the *taṣnīf* movement did not begin until the middle of the ninth century, with the collections of al-Bukhārī and Muslim, or possibly slightly earlier that same century. One possible meaning of the statement 'Sa'īd ibn Abī 'Arūbah had no book, but kept everything in his memory' is that Sa'īd used to recite his entire *muṣannaf* from memory without using any notes or notebook as an aide-mémoire; indeed, this was Goldziher's interpretation of this report. But it does not seem likely that Sa'īd would have memorised such a collection – the *muṣannafāt* are, after all, sizeable compilations, as the earliest examples that have come down to us in later versions attest, e.g. the *Jāmi'* of Ma'mar ibn Rāshid (d. 154/770),[9] parts of the *Muṣannaf* of 'Abd Allāh ibn al-Mubārak (d. 181/797),[10] and the *Jāmi'* of 'Abd Allāh ibn Wahb (d. 197/812).[11] What, then, does the statement mean? The biographical literature tells us that Sa'īd had a scribe named 'Abd al-Wahhāb ibn 'Aṭā' who always accompanied him and who wrote his notebooks (*wa-kataba kutubahu*).[12] What appears likely, therefore, is that, before teaching, Sa'īd would retrieve the material for his lecture from a certain number of 'writings': this material would not be taken from writings belonging to him – there being no such thing – but from those in his *scribe's* possession.

In Kufa (like Basra, one of Iraq's major intellectual centres), memorisation of ḥadīths was de rigueur until at least the first half of the ninth century. One traditionist, Ibn Abī Zā'idah (d. 182/798), is said to have been the very first Kufan author of a *muṣannaf* (though, as we saw above, other names have also been advanced).[13] He recited his traditions from memory and one of his colleagues who did the same, Wakī' ibn al-Jarrāḥ (d. 197/812), is said to have used Ibn Abī Zā'idah's *Muṣannaf* as a model for his own.[14] The sources explicitly state that Wakī' 'wrote' and 'classified', which means he was in possession of 'notebooks' (*kutub*) the contents of which were systematically classified into chapters. The very same sources also tell us, however, that he recited his material from memory, e.g. the great critic Ibn Ḥibbān al-Bustī (d. 354/965), who writes:[15]

> Wakī' ibn al-Jarrāḥ ... is one of those who travelled (in search of knowledge [i.e. ḥadīths]), wrote down, collected, classified, memorised, recapitulated and reviewed (*wa-dhākara*), and disseminated.

In another place, Ibn Ḥibbān adds the following:[16]

> We never saw a book in Wakī''s hands, since he would recite his books from memory (*kāna yaqra'u kutubahu min hifẓihi*).

As for Ibn Abī Shaybah (d. 235/849), also a Kufan, and the compiler of one of the earliest extant *muṣannaf* works, he states at the beginning of many chapters of his work:[17]

> 'This is what I know by heart [or: have memorised] from the Prophet.'

This odd way of expressing oneself shows that, even at a late date, when the notes or notebooks of the traditionists had been transformed into extensive manuscripts, some Iraqi authors of systematically classified collections still felt obliged to present their compilations of traditions as writings for private use: Islam could, after all, only have one actual book, the Qur'ān.

In Medina, on the other hand, the opposition to the writing down of traditions had disappeared at the time of al-Zuhrī (d. 124/742) or soon after, i.e. by the second half of the eighth century, when the first Medinese *muṣannaf* authors emerged. Al-Bukhārī explicitly states this when describing the scandal that resulted when Ibn Isḥāq visited the wife of Hishām ibn 'Urwah ('Urwah ibn al-Zubayr's son) in search of information:[18]

> The people of Medina consider it acceptable to put (traditions) in writing (*fa-inna ahl al-Madīnah yarawna al-kitāb jā'izan*).

Unlike their Iraqi colleagues, therefore, the compilers in Medina (e.g. Ibn Isḥāq, Mūsā ibn 'Uqbah in *maghāzī*, or Mālik ibn Anas in *fiqh*), and also those in Mecca and Yemen (e.g. Ibn Jurayj and Ma'mar ibn Rāshid in the realm of Ḥadīth), did not feel the need to hide any written collections they had in their possession; and even used them in public without the least hesitation. For example, Ma'mar, a Basran who settled in Yemen, would 'care for his books and consult them' since, in that part of the Muslim world, memorisation of ḥadīths was not especially prized; whenever he had occasion to return to his home town of Basra, however, Ma'mar found himself obliged to recite the ḥadīths from memory.[19]

Ibn Isḥāq and the *Kitāb al-Maghāzī*

When it came to 'publishing' systematically classified works, oral instruction, or instruction through audition, to be precise, nevertheless remained the norm everywhere. This was accomplished by audition, by student recitation, or by dictation. This is even true of the *Kitāb al-Maghāzī* (Book of Campaigns) of Ibn Isḥāq, in spite of the fact that this *muṣannaf* work is, as we have seen, something of an exception. Information on Ibn Isḥāq's teaching and transmission practices is relatively plentiful. Yūnus ibn Bukayr (d. 199/815), one of Ibn Isḥāq's students, and a transmitter who prepared a recension of his teacher's work, says:[20]

> The whole of Ibn Isḥāq's narrative is 'supported' (*kull shay' min ḥadīth Ibn Isḥāq musnad*) [i.e. is based on Ibn Isḥāq himself], since he dictated it to me (*amlāhu*) or recited it in my presence (from a notebook?) (*qara'ahu 'alayya*) or reported it to me (from memory?) (*ḥaddathanī bihi*).[21] But what was not 'supported' is recitation (*qirā'ah*) [i.e. by a student] in the presence of Ibn Isḥāq.

Elsewhere, Ibn Bukayr says that everything he reports from his teacher about the Prophet's wives 'is word for word what Ibn Isḥāq dictated' (*kull shay' min dhikr azwāj al-nabī fa-huwa imlā' Ibn Isḥāq ḥarfan ḥarfan*).[22]

Ibn Isḥāq is said to have dictated his work twice to another student, the Kufan al-Bakkā'ī (d. 183/799).[23] According to another report, al-Bakkā'ī is said to have sold his house and accompanied Ibn Isḥāq on his journeys until he had 'heard' the *Kitāb al-Maghāzī* in its entirety.[24] This line of transmission, from Ibn Isḥāq to al-Bakkā'ī, is of critical importance – it is from al-Bakkā'ī that Ibn Hishām, the most important editor of the *Kitāb al-Maghāzī*, received the material originating with Ibn Isḥāq.[25] A third student, Salamah ibn al-Faḍl, is reported as saying: 'I heard [or: I followed] (as an auditor; *sami'tu*) the *Maghāzī* of Ibn Isḥāq twice (during academic instruction).'[26] The source reporting this adds: 'He [Salamah] used to say also, "He [Ibn Isḥāq] reported them to me (*ḥaddathanī bihi*)".' This same Salamah prepared a copy of the whole work for Ibn Isḥāq, which Ibn Isḥāq then collated against his own autograph copy.[27] Moreover, Salamah inherited all the manuscripts in Ibn Isḥāq's estate; as a result, he – and he alone – used his teacher's autograph copies in the subsequent transmission of the work.[28] This explains why it is that Salamah, on whose authority al-Ṭabarī quotes Ibn Isḥāq, is credited with having put together the 'most complete books of the *Maghāzī*'.[29]

Ibn Isḥāq compiled his *Maghāzī* work for the court, but that version, in one copy, or possibly several, and kept in the library of the 'Abbāsid caliphs, has not come down to us.[30] All that survives goes back to what Ibn Isḥāq used from it and transmitted in his own teaching to his students. To that can be added many scattered reports on the *Maghāzī* disseminated by Ibn Isḥāq outside of his great work.[31] The different versions of the *Maghāzī* accounts transmitted on the authority of Ibn Isḥāq often diverge considerably; the problem posed by such divergences is discussed further below.

Mālik Ibn Anas and the *Kitāb al-Muwaṭṭa'*

Mālik ibn Anas (d. 179/796), a Medinese like Ibn Isḥāq, was the compiler of the celebrated *Muwaṭṭa'* (The Well-Trodden [Path]), a corpus of juridical material in a systematically classified collection that brings together the basic material of *fiqh*: legal ḥadīths attributed to the Prophet or his Companions and the *ārā'* (sing. *ra'y*; i.e. juridical opinions) of a large number of Successors. It also contains reports of the *'amal* (i.e. the practice, the 'living tradition') of the people of Medina. Mālik seldom gives his own juridical opinions.[32] The *Muwaṭṭa'* is also one of the earliest systematic works in Arabic to have been given an actual title, one that goes back to the author himself and that is to be found in all recensions.[33] The titles of other compilations contemporary with the *Muwaṭṭa'* are appellatives and were not necessarily chosen by their authors: typically, one referred to the '*Muṣannaf* of so-and-so' (e.g. '*Muṣannaf* 'Abd al-Razzāq') or the '*Jāmi'* of such-and-such' (e.g. '*Jāmi'* Ma'mar ibn Rāshid'). The subdivisions of those works, called *kutub* ('books'), do, however, have titles that designate their content, thus *kitāb al-ḥajj* ('Book of pilgrimage'), for example, *kitāb al-ḥudūd* ('Book of legal punishments'), *kitāb al-ta'rīkh* ('Book of history'), and so on. This practice of giving a title based on content is also to be found in historical works of the period, the *Kitāb Ṣiffīn* (Book [of the battle] of Ṣiffīn), for instance. As for Ibn Isḥāq's *Kitāb al-Maghāzī*, it is unclear whether he himself gave the work its title, since the information in the sources is inconclusive; the existence of several different names for the work suggests that nothing was very fixed:[34] besides the title *Kitāb al-Maghāzī* (Book of Campaigns), we also find *Kitāb al-Sīrah* (Book of the [Prophet's] Life) and *al-Kitāb al-Kabīr* (The Great Book), though this last is reserved for the expanded version Ibn Isḥāq prepared for the court. Recall also that, although the title *Kitāb al-Maghāzī* was used for the whole work, it really only designated the third section, the first two sections bearing the titles *Kitāb al-Mubtada'* and *Kitāb al-Mab'ath*, respectively.[35]

To return to the *Muwaṭṭa'*, its very name ('the well-trodden (path)') is metaphorical, confirming that what Mālik had in mind was an actual book.[36] Nevertheless, Mālik did not establish a definitive edition of the work: it was his students, or his students' students, who gave the work its final form, or rather, its final forms. In the end, the publication and transmission of the *Muwaṭṭa'* by its author during teaching was not very different from the way in which the *Kitāb al-Maghāzī* was published and transmitted. Generally, Mālik preferred to have the *Muwaṭṭa'* read by one of his students while he, at least in theory, listened and monitored the recitation.[37] This is the method of transmission known as *qirā'ah* or *'arḍ*. But from time to time, the teacher read or recited the text himself in the presence of his students, thereby using audition, or *samā'*, as a method of transmission.[38] He is also said to have entrusted a copy of the work that he had himself corrected to a student and authorised that student to transmit it: this method of transmission is known as *munāwalah*.[39] Mālik also seems to have made use of the method known as *kitābah*: he is reported to have authorised a student to transmit a copy of the *Muwaṭṭa'* that the student had drawn up, without having had a look at this copy.[40] Given these diverse modes of transmission, it is understandable that the various recensions of the *Muwaṭṭa'* known to us diverge considerably.[41]

Qur'ānic exegesis

In the development of Qur'ānic exegesis (*tafsīr*) in this period, we see evidence of the same phenomenon of systematisation. We have the *Tafsīr* of Ma'mar ibn Rāshid (d. 154/770), which, like his *Jāmi'*, has survived in its entirety, or in very large part, in a recension reworked by his student, 'Abd al-Razzāq. We also have the *Tafsīr* of Muqātil ibn Sulaymān (d. 150/767) in the recension of al-Hudhayl ibn Ḥabīb al-Dandānī (d. after 190/805).[42] As for the so-called *Tafsīr Mujāhid*, it is, as we saw earlier, a compilation put together by the later scholar, Ādam ibn Abī 'Iyās.[43] The *Tafsīrs* of Ma'mar and Muqātil are both very large, especially Muqātil's, and both were transmitted in their entirety, even if their transmitters, 'Abd al-Razzāq and al-Hudhayl respectively, added material originating with other exegetes. Thanks to these two works, we can be certain that the Qur'ān commentators of that generation produced writings which reflected a high degree of organisation, and that they were able to rely on well-ordered texts in their teaching.

The history of the empire

The *taṣnīf* movement also influenced the writing of history in this period. We find monographs and compilations of historical traditions relating to specific events, in particular, episodes from the time of the Islamic conquests and the civil war, works on the latter having been composed exclusively by Shi'ites. One of the earliest authors is the Kufan Jābir ibn Yazīd al-Ju'fī (d. 128/746), to whom is attributed a *Kitāb al-Jamal* (Book [on the battle] of the Camel), a *Kitāb Ṣiffīn* (Book [on the battle] of Ṣiffīn) and other monographs of this sort;[44] works with these titles are also attested for the famous Kufan Shi'ite Abū Mikhnaf (d. 157/774).[45] Notable is the *Kitāb al-Riddah wal-futūḥ* (Book of Apostasy and Conquests) of Sayf ibn 'Umar (d. ca. 184/800), one of the most important sources for understanding the early Muslim expansion.[46]

In no case do we have the originals: all the texts that survive depend on later transmissions. But we do have extensive passages from these works, transmitted by students and compilers, and preserved by later historians such as al-Ṭabarī and Ibn A'tham al-Kūfī.[47] The only text to survive independently in its entirety is the *Kitāb Waq'at Ṣiffīn* (Book of the Battle of Ṣiffīn) of Naṣr ibn Muzāḥim (d. 212/827), a later compiler, in fact, than the ones identified above.[48] In addition, an extensive fragment of Sayf ibn 'Umar's *Kitāb al-Riddah wal-futūḥ* and a smaller fragment of his *Kitab al-Jamal* were discovered some years ago. But once again, we do not have the originals, but rather recensions of a transmitter who lived three generations after the author.

One could argue that most monographs of this type correspond more closely to chapter divisions in systematically organised works than to any of those works as a whole; in either case, traditions are organised according to topic, which then also determines the title of the *kitāb*. But in the domain of historiography, the step toward a real *muṣannaf* is taken by works such as the *Kitāb al-Riddah wal-futūḥ* of Sayf ibn 'Umar. Here, the compiler does not simply cover an isolated event, but rather a whole series of events, namely the widespread apostasy of the Arab tribes, during the caliphate of Abū Bakr specifically and during the period of the conquests generally. The fragment that has come down to us deals with the caliphate of 'Uthmān, as its successive chapter headings indicate, even if *bāb*, the usual term for chapter, does not appear:[49]

Ḥadīth al-Shūrā (Accounts relating to the Council)
Imārat 'Uthmān (The caliphate of 'Uthmān)
Maqdam Sa'īd ibn al-'Āṣ (The arrival of Sa'īd ibn al-'Āṣ)
Ḥadīth al-Baṣrah (Accounts relating to Basra)
Ḥadīth Miṣr (Accounts relating to Egypt)
Ḥadīth al-Madīnah (Accounts relating to Medina)
Ibtidā' maqtal 'Uthmān (The origins of the assassination of 'Uthmān)

Ākhir waṣiyyah awṣā bihā ʻUthmān (The final counsels offered by ʻUthmān)
Madfan ʻUthmān (The burial of ʻUthmān).

The transitional phrases between the different traditions so characteristic of Ibn Isḥāq's *Kitāb al-Maghāzī* are not to be found in Sayf's monograph, however, even if the disparate traditions are ordered to give a chronological sequence of events.

We are less well informed about the methods used to transmit these monograph compilations than about the method used for similar religious texts, *Maghāzī* works, and the like. It is almost certain that the historians also disseminated their material during sessions and scholarly circles, through audition, student recitation, or dictation.[50] But *kitābah* and *wijādah*, procedures so little esteemed by the traditionists, whereby students copied the text without having received instruction from the teacher, must also have been quite common. Al-Ṭabarī often cites the monographs of Abū Mikhnaf and Sayf ibn ʻUmar through such transmissions; for example, he introduces quotations with: 'Hishām [ibn Muḥammad al-Kalbī (d. 206/821)] said (*qāla*) …', or 'Abū Mikhnaf said …',[51] though he is exclusive in his use of the formulation 'al-Sarī wrote for me (*kataba ilayya*) on the authority of (*ʻan*) Shuʻayb (who wrote) on the authority of (*ʻan*) Sayf …' when referring to Sayf ibn ʻUmar.[52] This transmission terminology shows clearly that neither al-Ṭabarī nor his transmitters had the licence to transmit material from either Abū Mikhnaf or Sayf ibn ʻUmar and that they copied from one another without ever having 'heard' them from the mouths of their teachers. By using the expression 'wrote for me', the transmitter is frankly admitting that he was content with copying from a manuscript.

Theology

The move toward *taṣnīf* can also be seen in theological writings: classical bibliographers attribute treatises with fixed titles to theologians (mostly Muʻtazilis) in this period. According to the inventory made in the tenth century by Ibn al-Nadīm for his *Fihrist*, Ḍirār ibn ʻAmr (d. after 180/796) wrote more than thirty such treatises;[53] the following is a representative selection:

Kitāb al-Tawḥīd (Book of [belief in] the unicity of God)
Kitāb al-Makhlūq (Book of created things)
Kitāb Tanāquḍ al-ḥadīth (Book of the refutation of Tradition)
Kitāb al-Qadar (Book of destiny)
Kitāb Radd Arisṭālīs fī al-jawāhir wal-aʻrāḍ (Book of the refutation of Aristotle on [his doctrine of] substances and accidents).

To Ḍirār's teacher, Wāṣil ibn ʻAṭā' (d. 131/748), are attributed a *Kitāb al-Manzilah bayna al-manzilatayn* (Book of [the doctrine of] the intermediate position) and a

Kitāb al-Tawḥīd (Book of [belief in] the unicity of God).[54] The titles of these works certainly suggest that they were well ordered, in the manner of the *muṣannafāt* of the traditionists, but, as none survive, this can only remain speculation.

An eighth-century 'literature of the school, for the school'

Three characteristics suggest that the systematically organised works we have been discussing qualify as notes or notebooks rather than as actual books. First, none of these works has survived in its original form; second, the texts we do have are dependent on later transmissions, dating from the ninth century at the earliest; and third, whenever several recensions of one of these works exist, these recensions often show considerable textual divergence. The structured and meticulously elaborated nature of a number of these works, a characteristic that remains recognisable even after numerous and different later transmissions – this is true of the *Kitāb al-Maghāzī* of Ibn Isḥāq in particular – suggests, however, that at least some of them are actual books. It is reasonable, therefore, to posit that these *muṣannafāt* are in an intermediate category between *syngrammata* and *hypomnēmata*, one that encompasses a wide spectrum, ranging from works possessed of all the characteristics of actual books, such as Ibn Isḥāq's *Kitāb al-Maghāzī*, to works that are nothing more than well-ordered records, such as appears to have been the case with the collection of Sa'īd ibn Abī 'Arūbah.

This being the case, we are entitled to ask whether these works are examples of literature, properly speaking. We can answer this question by turning to Greek literature, which is possessed of works akin to these *muṣannafāt*. W. W. Jaeger has described Aristotle's teaching texts (*Lehrschriften*) as 'neither lecture notebooks, nor literature',[55] 'meticulously elaborated' writings to be sure, but, according to him, 'not ones intended for publication with a larger lay reading public in mind'.[56] Jaeger characterises these works (and other works of this genre too), as 'a systematic literature of the school, for the school … published … through lectures'.[57] Thus, Aristotle's book the *Topics* was neither a 'lecture notebook' nor 'a collection of drafts', but rather a *gramma*, a work 'intended to be recited to students'.[58] Jaeger's description of these teaching texts may just as easily be applied to our *muṣannafāt*: they too are *grammata*, and, in effect, examples of a literature of the school, intended solely for use by the school, and published through recitation – through audition, dictation, or recitation by a student.

Vestiges of the eighth-century '*Taṣnīf* Movement'

What remains of the *muṣannafāt*? None of them survive in their original form; at most, we have later recensions, but none dating from earlier than the ninth century, transmitted and reworked by a student or, more commonly, by a student of a student of the compiler. In the best of cases, these transmissions 'on the authority of so-and-so' either form the basis of independent works or appear as often quite lengthy quotations in later compilations. But very often, all that remains of a *muṣannaf* is isolated traditions, scattered throughout a variety of later works. Let us take a look at two of them.

Ibn Isḥāq's *Kitāb al-Maghāzī*.

Large sections of Ibn Isḥāq's *Kitāb al-Maghāzī* are preserved in the following later works:

1. The *Kitāb Sīrat Muḥammad rasūl Allāh* (Book of the biography of Muḥammad, the messenger of God) by 'Abd al-Malik ibn Hishām (d. 218/834), an Egyptian originally from Basra.[59] For his recension, Ibn Hishām relies on the material transmitted by his teacher Ziyād ibn 'Abd Allāh al-Bakkā'ī (d. 183/799), himself a student and transmitter of Ibn Isḥāq.[60] Ibn Hishām explains in the preface to his work how he has reworked Ibn Isḥāq's original:[61] the *Kitāb Sīrat Muḥammad* is an epitome, an abridged version, not of Ibn Isḥāq's whole work, but principally of the second and third parts (the 'Kitāb al-Mab'ath' [Book of the Mission (of Muḥammad)] and the 'Kitāb al-Maghāzī' [Book of Campaigns]). Ibn Hishām sometimes includes supplementary information, citing traditions he obtained from other sources, for example; on occasion, he also adds his own commentary. He states explicitly that he has suppressed the following: all reports in which the Prophet Muḥammad does not appear; selected verses; indecent passages; passages that might be injurious to certain individuals; and all traditions that his teacher, al-Bakkā'ī, had not confirmed to him. These deletions notwithstanding, Ibn Hishām's work remains the fundamental source for the life of the Prophet.
2. The slightly later book of the Kufan Aḥmad ibn 'Abd al-Jabbār al-'Uṭāridī (d. 272/886), a work without a definitive title and deriving from a transmission through Yūnus ibn Bukayr (d. 199/815), another student of Ibn Isḥāq's.[62] Yūnus's work consists primarily of material he transmits from Ibn Isḥāq, but he supplements it with numerous traditions originating with a variety of other authorities.[63] This explains why Ibn Bukayr's work is sometimes known by the title *Ziyādāt Yūnus fī Maghāzī Ibn Isḥāq* (The additions of Yūnus to the *Maghāzī* of Ibn Isḥāq).[64] The biographical literature says of him:[65] 'He used to take (the text of) Ibn Isḥāq, and then combined it with (other) traditions.' This is a case – quite common, as it happens – where the transmitter has added so many supplementary traditions he has himself collected, that we can almost think of him as an independent compiler, indeed, even as the author of a new work.[66]
3. The *Ta'rīkh* (History) and the *Tafsīr* (Qur'ān commentary) of al-Ṭabarī (d. 310/923). Al-Ṭabarī's principal source on the life of the Prophet is Ibn Isḥāq's

work, cited most often through Salamah ibn al-Faḍl, but also through Yūnus ibn Bukayr and others.[67] In the *Ta'rīkh*, al-Ṭabarī includes long passages not only from the second and third parts of Ibn Isḥāq's work, but also from the first part, which, as was noted above, Ibn Hishām did not rely upon a great deal.

4. A large number of works that preserve extracts, often quite extensive, transmitted through other lines of transmission.[68] One contemporary scholar, S. M. Al-Samuk, has made a synopsis of all the transmissions from Ibn Isḥāq and has identified more than fifty individuals transmitting directly from him. Indeed, every subsequent historical work containing a biography of the Prophet inevitably draws on Ibn Isḥāq. Al-Samuk has also shown – and this is one of his most interesting findings – that there are often considerable divergences between texts resulting from parallel transmissions, for example between the versions of a given account reported by Ibn Hishām on the one hand, and by al-Ṭabarī on the other.[69]

Mālik's *Kitāb al-Muwaṭṭa'*

As for the *Muwaṭṭa'* of Mālik, it survives principally in numerous later recensions all originating with students of Mālik, or students of theirs. These recensions – of which three or four are complete, one incomplete, and several fragmentary – diverge not only in terms of structure, but also in content.[70] Since most have been edited,[71] they can be compared relatively easily, but we limit ourselves here to the two most important recensions.

1. The first of these is the most widely disseminated, that of Yaḥyā ibn Yaḥyā al-Maṣmūdī (d. 234/848), generally regarded as the vulgate of the *Muwaṭṭa'*. Yaḥyā first received the text from his teacher, Ziyād ibn 'Abd al-Raḥmān al-Qurṭubī Shabṭūn, then went to Medina in 179/795 to hear it from Mālik himself; unfortunately, Mālik died that year.[72] Thus, Yaḥyā was not able to hear the entirety of the *Muwaṭṭa'* from Mālik, and had to transmit the rest of the work on the authority of Ziyād.
2. The second is the recension of, or rather the reworking by, the Ḥanafī Muḥammad ibn al-Ḥasan al-Shaybānī (d. 189/804), who was a student of Mālik's, one that distinguishes itself above all by its critical comments about Mālik and about the teaching of law in Medina. Al-Shaybani's comments appear at the end of most of the chapters and are not always in agreement with Mālik's juridical opinion, or with the ḥadīths Mālik quotes.[73] Notwithstanding the fact that he is a transmitter of Mālik, al-Shaybānī constantly has recourse to the juridical opinions of his Ḥanafī colleagues, which very often contradict those of Mālik, and to the opinion of his teacher, Abū Ḥanīfah (*qawl Abī Ḥanīfah*), with which he always agrees.

There are also countless juridical works, especially Mālikī ones, which include quotations from the *Muwaṭṭa'*.[74] Suffice to mention one, the famous *Mudawannah* of Saḥnūn (d. 240/854), a jurist who transmitted the *Muwaṭṭa'* from the recension of the Tunisian 'Alī ibn Ziyād and two other transmitters, and who cites these different sources both separately, and together.[75]

The canonical collections of traditions of the ninth century

Finally, we turn to the canonical collections of traditions compiled in the ninth century, the so-called 'Six Books', to which a seventh, the *Musnad* of Aḥmad ibn Ḥanbal, is often added. The 'Six Books' – of which the *Jāmi' al-Ṣaḥīḥ* of al-Bukhārī (d. 256/870) and the *Jāmi' al-Ṣaḥīḥ* of Muslim (d. 261/875) are the most important – are *muṣannaf*-type works; the book of Aḥmad ibn Ḥanbal (d. 241/855), on the other hand, is, as its title reveals, a *musnad* (pl. *masānid*), that is, a work in which traditions are arranged under the names of the Companions who originally transmitted them, and who in turn are frequently arranged according to the date of their conversion to Islam. The first works of the *musnad* type appear some time after the first *muṣannafāt*;[76] the earliest ones to come down to us are the *Musnad* of Abū Dāwūd al-Ṭayālisī (d. 203/818) and the *Musnad* of al-Ḥumaydī (d. 219/834).[77]

Al-Bukhārī, Muslim and the other traditionists of the ninth century, but no less so Ahmad ibn Ḥanbal, 'published' their works just as their predecessors had, by personal contact through teaching, employing familiar procedures, audition (*samā'*), recitation before the teacher (*qirā'ah*) and so on.[78] Most of these traditionists did not give their works a definitive shape; thus to the *Musnad* of Aḥmad ibn Ḥanbal, transmitted by his son, 'Abd Allāh (d. 290/903), then by the latter's student, Abū Bakr al-Qaṭī'ī (d. 368/979), the transmitters added other traditions.[79] Every person wishing to study the canonical collections in order then to transmit them himself was therefore, in theory at least, still obliged to attend the lectures of the traditionists themselves or of their authorised transmitters, and to receive the traditions through audition. In practice, however, few indeed were those who were able to 'hear' these very large works from beginning to end.

In some late sources, al-Bukhārī is reported to have dictated his *Ṣaḥīḥ* to ninety thousand students.[80] This high number is both a pious exaggeration and misleading, giving the erroneous impression that there were many transmitters of the work. It is certainly possible that the auditors who regularly, or occasionally, attended al-Bukhārī's lectures were very numerous, but Johann Fück's study of the transmission history of the *Ṣaḥīḥ* – for which he relied on the lines of transmission to be found in the great commentaries of the *Ṣaḥīḥ* composed in the fifteenth century by Ibn Ḥajar al-'Asqalānī (d. 852/1449), al-Qasṭallānī (d. 855/1451) and al-'Aynī (d. 923/1517) – has shown that only a limited number of al-Bukhārī's students (four, maybe five) were engaged in transmitting the whole work.[81] And among these few students, only one, al-Firabrī (d. 320/932), ever heard the totality of the *Ṣaḥīḥ* in the presence of his teacher; indeed, he heard it twice. The texts of the other transmitters, on the other hand, are not based from beginning to end on audition. Al-Nasafī, for example, had not heard the entire work, so al-Bukhārī granted him a licence (*ijāzah*) to transmit the remainder of the work, from the *Kitāb al-Aḥkām* (Book of Statutes) on; in other words, he authorised al-Nasafī to transmit the rest of the *Ṣaḥīḥ* without having heard it.

As Goldziher showed in his study of the development of the study of Ḥadīth as a discipline, this mode of transmission later became quite common.[82] As it was often impossible or impractical to hear a work in its entirety, or even parts of works as large as any of the 'Six Books', the earlier stipulation of actual audition was often just theoretical. We have already described the procedure known as *munāwalah*, whereby the teacher entrusted his student with his own autograph copy of a work, or a collated copy of it. Mālik ibn Anas, and his teacher before him, al-Zuhrī, both had recourse to this convenient and effective method. The method of transmission known as *ijāzah* (licence) was even more flexible than *munāwalah* since the student did not need to have had any contact with the teacher. From the tenth century on, scholars increasingly issued such licences, bringing to an end the need to undertake long journeys 'in search of knowledge' (*fī ṭalab al-'ilm*). It even became unnecessary explicitly to identify the title(s) of the work(s) which the recipient of the *ijāzah* was authorised to transmit: students were authorised, orally or in writing, with formulas such as 'I authorise you to transmit everything that I transmit,' and even 'I authorise you to transmit all the works which I have compiled and which I shall compile in the future.'

Al-Firabrī's recension is the one which played the most important role in the subsequent transmission and dissemination of al-Bukhārī's *Ṣaḥīḥ*, perhaps because al-Firabrī was the only student to have 'heard' the whole text. Moreover, the written version he used as a basis for his recension is said to have been a manuscript based on a copy made by al-Bukhārī's secretary Abū Ja'far Muḥammad ibn Abī Ḥātim;[83] al-Firabrī must, therefore, have verified this manuscript against al-Bukhārī's recitation. Al-Firabrī himself had at least ten students, all of whom had to make the long journey to Firabr, on the banks of the Oxus River, south-east of Bukhara, in order to receive the text from him directly. Modern scholars who have studied the transmission history of the *Ṣaḥīḥ* in detail have determined that in the thirteenth century the scholar al-Yunīnī (d. 701/1301) established a 'critical edition' of sorts by relying on several recensions, all of which went back to al-Firabrī's:[84] all the published texts in use today are based on that edition. There are, of course, texts that go back to recensions earlier than al-Yunīnī's, but they too derive from al-Firabrī's recension.

The *Ṣaḥīḥ* of al-Bukhārī and the other canonical 'Books' of the ninth century belong, as do their predecessors from the eighth century, to what Jaeger characterised as 'a systematic literature of the school, for the school', and were 'published' – in theory, at any rate – 'through lectures'. This is why there is considerable variation in the order of the chapters in the different recensions and manuscripts of the canonical books.[85] But we cannot speak yet of actual books, that is, books that can be considered *syngrammata*, even if some compilations do display some of their features (the *Ṣaḥīḥ* of Muslim, for example, has a preface or introduction by the author himself).[86] As it turns out, the first actual book in Islamic scholarship would not appear in the domain of the religious sciences at all – that honour would go to a book in linguistics.

Notes

1 Ibn Ḥajar, *Fatḥ al-bārī*, 'Muqaddimah', p. 5.

2 On Rabī' (correcting Ibn Ḥajar's 'Ṣaḥīḥ' to 'Ḥabīb'), see GAS, vol. 1, p. 93; on Sa'īd, see GAS, vol. 1, pp. 91 ff.; on Mālik, see GAS, vol. 1, pp. 457 ff.; on 'Abd al-Malik, see GAS, vo. 1, p. 91; on al-Awzā'ī, see GAS, vol. 1, p. 516; on Abū 'Abd Allāh, see GAS, vol. 1, p. 518; on Abū Salamah, see Ibn Ḥajar, *Tahdhīb*, vol. 3, pp. 11 ff.

3 On al-Mufaḍḍal, see GAS, vol. 2, pp. 53 ff.; on Ḥammād, see GAS, vol. 1, pp. 366 ff. and vol. 2, pp. 47 ff. On the compilation of the *Mu'allaqāt*, see M. J. Kister, 'The Seven Odes', *RSO* 44 (1970), pp. 27–36 = Kister, *Studies in Jāhiliyya and Early Islam* (London, 1980), ch. XVI.

4 al-Marzubānī, *Kitāb Nūr al-qabas = Die Gelehrtenbiographien … in der Rezension des Ḥāfiẓ al-Yaghmūrī (K. Nūr al-qabas al-mukhtaṣar min al-Muqtabas)*, ed. R. Sellheim (Wiesbaden, 1964), p. 310, quoted in Yāqūt, *Irshād al-arīb*, vol. 6, p. 399; al-Dhahabī, *Siyar*, vol. 6, p. 114; on Mūsā ibn 'Uqbah, see GAS, vol. 1, p. 286.

5 *Cf.* GAS, vol. 1, p. 58.

6 *Cf.* Schoeler, *The Oral and the Written*, pp. 114 ff.

7 Ibn Ḥajar, *Tahdhīb*, vol. 4, p. 57; al-Dhahabī, *Mīzān al-i'tidāl fī naqd al-rijāl*, 4 vols, ed. 'A. M. al-Bajāwī (Beirut, 1963), vol. 2, p. 153.

8 Goldziher, 'Ueber die Entwickelung', pp. 211 ff.

9 GAS, vol. 1, p. 291; transmitted by 'Abd al-Razzāq as a supplement to his *Muṣannaf*.

10 Ibid., vol. 1, p. 95; see M. Hartmann, 'Die arabisch-islamischen Handschriften der Universitätsbibliothek zu Leipzig und die Sammlungen Hartmann und Haupt', *Zeitschrift für Assyriologie* 23 (1909), pp. 240 ff.

11 GAS, vol. 1, p. 466; this work is edited by Muranyi: see the bibliography.

12 Ibn Sa'd, *Ṭabaqāt*, vol. VII b, p. 76; Ibn Ḥajar, *Tahdhīb*, vol. 6, p. 399: "*Abd al-Wahhāb ibn 'Aṭā' … wa-huwa min ahl al-Baṣrah wa-lazima Sa'īd ibn Abī 'Arūbah wa-'urifa bi-ṣuḥbatihi wa-kataba kutubahu*'.

13 On Ibn Abī Zā'idah, see Ibn Ḥajar, *Tahdhīb*, vol. 11, pp. 183 ff.

14 Ibn Ḥajar, *Tahdhīb*, vol. 11, pp. 183; on Wakī', see GAS, vol. 1, pp. 96 ff.

15 Ibn Ḥibbān, *Kitāb Mashāhīr 'ulamā' al-amṣār*, ed. M. Fleischhammer (Cairo and Wiesbaden, 1959), p. 173, no. 1374.

16 Ibn Ḥibbān, *Kitāb al-Thiqāt*, vol. 7, p. 562.

17 E.g. Ibn Abī Shaybah, *al-Kitāb al-Muṣannaf*, 15 vols, ed. 'A. Khān al-Afghānī et al. (Hyderabad and Bombay, 1966–1983), vol. 10, p. 154; vol. 14, pp. 388, 424, 427, 512, 539; on this work, see GAS, vol. 1, pp. 108 ff.
18 *Apud* Ibn Ḥajar, *Tahdhīb*, vol. 9, p. 37.
19 Ibid., vol. 6, p. 279.
20 *Apud* al-'Uṭāridī, *Siyar* 'Muḥammad b. Isḥāq', '*Kitāb al-Siyar wal-maghāzī*', ed. S. Zakkār (Beirut, 1978), p. 23; on Ibn Bukayr, see Ibn Ḥajar, *Tahdhīb*, vol. 11, p. 382.
21 The distinction between these last two methods is not entirely clear.
22 *Apud* al-'Uṭāridī, *Siyar*, p. 244.
23 Ibn Ḥajar, *Tahdhīb*, vol. 3, pp. 323, 324; al-Dhahabī, *Mīzān*, vol. 2, p. 91.
24 Ibid., vol. 3, p. 324.
25 *Sīrah*, vol. 1, p. 4.
26 Ibn Ḥajar, *Tahdhīb*, vol. 6, p. 135; Ibn 'Adī, *al-Kāmil*, vol. 3, p. 340.
27 Ibid.
28 al-Khaṭīb al-Baghdādī, *Ta'rīkh Baghdād*, vol. 1, pp. 220 ff.
29 Ibn Ḥajar, *Tahdhīb*, vol. 1, p. 135; al-Dhahabī, *Mīzān*, vol. 2, p. 92.
30 al-Khaṭīb al-Baghdādī, *Ta'rīkh Baghdād*, vol. 1, pp. 220 ff.; al-Dhahabī, *Siyar*, vol. 7 p. 48; Yāqūt, *Irshād al-arīb*, vol. 6, p. 399.
31 *Cf.* Schoeler, *Charakter*, pp. 44, 48, 127 ff.
32 *Cf.* Y. Dutton, *The Origins of Islamic Law. The Qur'ān, the Muwaṭṭa' and Madinan 'amal* (Surrey, 1999), p. 27; GAS, vol. 1, p. 458.
33 See J. Schacht, *EI*², s.v. Mālik b. Anas, and Dutton, *The Origins*, pp. 22 ff. The *Muṣannaf* of the Medinan jurist al-Mājishūn (d. 164/780), reportedly Mālik's model for his *Muwaṭṭa'*, did not have the title *al-Muwaṭṭa'*; *cf.* M. Muranyi, *Ein altes Fragment medinensicher Jurisprudenz aus Qairawān: Aus dem Kitāb al-Ḥağğ des 'Abd al-'Azīz b. 'Abd Allāh b. Abī Salamah al-Māğishūn* (st. 164/780–81) (Marburg, Stuttgart, 1985), pp. 33 ff.
34 *Cf.* M. Jarrar, *Die Prophetenbiographie im islamischen Spanien. Ein Beitrag zur Überlieferungs- and Redaktionsgeschichte* (Frankfurt a.M., 1989), pp. 1 ff. and 32 ff.
35 Ibn 'Adī, *al-Kāmil*, vol. 6, p. 112; Ibn Ḥajar, *Tahdhīb*, vol. 9, p. 39; *cf.* GAS, vol. 1, p. 289.
36 *EI*², s.v. Mālik b. Anas.
37 al-Khaṭīb al-Baghdādī, *Kitāb al-Kifāyah*, pp. 362 ff.; Ibn Abī Ḥātim, *Ādāb al-Shāfi'ī wa-manāqibuhu*, ed. 'A. 'Abd al-Khāliq (Cairo, 1953), p. 28; *cf.* Abbott, *Studies*, vol. 2, p. 126.
38 al-Sam'ānī, *Kitāb Adab al-imlā'* = *Die Methodik des Diktatkollegs (Adab al-imlā' wal-istimlā')*, ed. M. Weisweiler (Leiden, 1952), pp. 8 ff.; Abbott, *Studies*, vol. 2, p. 126 and nn. 45 and 46.
39 al-Khaṭīb al-Baghdādī, *Kitāb al-Kifāyah*, p. 443.
40 Ibid.
41 See below at n. 70.
42 GAS, vol. 1, pp. 36 ff.; Y. Goldfeld, 'Muqātil ibn Sulaymān', in *Arabic and Islamic Studies*, ed. J. Mansour (Ramat-Gan, 1978), vol. 2, p. 13; Cl. Gilliot, 'Muqātil, grand exegete, traditionniste et théologien maudit', *JA* 279 (1991), pp. 39–92; C. H. M. Versteegh, *Arabic Grammar and Qur'ānic Exegesis in Early Islam* (Leiden, 1993).
43 *Cf.* Leemhuis, 'MS 1075 Tafsīr', and Stauth, 'Die Überlieferung'.
44 GAS, vol. 1, p. 307.

45 Ibid., vol. 1, pp. 308–9; and see Sezgin, 'Abū Miḫnaf'.
46 GAS, vol. 1, pp. 311–12.
47 See Sezgin, 'Abū Miḫnaf'.
48 GAS, vol. 1, p. 313.
49 Sayf ibn 'Umar, *Kitāb al-Riddah*, pp. 4, 9, 42, 87, 111, 131, 182, 208.
50 For al-Madā'inī, e.g., see Ibn 'Abd Rabbihi, *al-'Iqd al-farīd*, 7 vols, ed. A. Amīn et al. (Cairo, 1949–65), vol. 4, p. 318.
51 See e.g. al-Ṭabarī, *Ta'rīkh*, vol. 2, pp. 1395 ff. and *passim*; *cf.* GAS, vol. 1, p. 308, n. 1.
52 See e.g. al-Ṭabarī, *Ta'rīkh*, vol. 1, pp. 2214 ff. and *passim*; *cf.* GAS, vol. 1, p. 312.
53 *Fihrist*², pp. 214 ff.
54 *Fihrist*², pp. 202 ff.
55 Jaeger, *Studien*, p. 137.
56 Ibid., pp. 135, 136.
57 Ibid., p. 147.
58 Ibid., p. 145.
59 GAS, vol. 1, pp. 297 ff.
60 Ibid., vol. 1, p. 289.
61 *Sīrah*, vol. 1, p. 4.
62 GAS, vol. 1, p. 146.
63 Schoeler, *Charakter*, p. 50; M. Muranyi, 'Ibn Isḥāq's K. *al-Maghāzī* in der *riwāya* von Yūnus b. Bukair. Bemerkungen zur frühen Überlieferungsgeschichte', *JSAI* 14 (1991), pp. 214–75.
64 See the references in Muranyi, 'Ibn Isḥāq's K. *al-Maghāzī*', pp. 219 ff.
65 Ibn Ḥajar, *Tahdhīb*, vol. 11, p. 383.
66 For examples, see Schoeler, *The Oral and the Written*, pp. 36 ff. and n. 145.
67 See Al-Samuk, *Die historischen Überlieferungen*, pp. 102, 138–9.
68 Ibid., pp. 81 ff.
69 Ibid., pp. 161 ff.
70 GAS, vol. 1, pp. 459 ff.; M. Muranyi, 'Fiqh', in *GAPh*, vol. 2, p. 313; Dutton, *The Origins*, pp. 22 ff. Dutton points out divergences 'in the order of the contents, the titles of the chapter-headings, and the inclusion or exclusion of small amounts of material'; nevertheless, he calls these divergences 'small editorial changes' (p. 24).
71 In addition to those of al-Maṣmūdī (d. 234/848) and al-Shaybānī (d. 189/804), discussed below, of 'Alī ibn Ziyād al-Tūnisī (d. 183/799), of al-Qa'nabī (d. 221/835), of Suwayd ibn Sa'īd al-Ḥadathānī (d. 240/854), and also fragmentary recensions. See Dutton, *The Origins*, p. 183.
72 'Iyāḍ b. Mūsā, *Tartīb al-madārik wa-taqrīb al-masālik li-ma'rifat a'lām madhhab Mālik*, 2 vols, ed. M. S. Hāshim (Beirut, 1998), vol. 2, p. 380; al-Zurqānī, *al-Sharḥ 'alā Muwaṭṭa' al-imām Mālik* (Beirut, 1411 H [= 1990]), vol. 1, p. 19; *cf.* H. Motzki, 'The Prophet and the Cat. On Dating Mālik's *Muwaṭṭa'* and Legal Traditions', *JSAI* 22 (1998), p. 18.
73 See Muranyi, 'Fiqh', pp. 310 ff.
74 In addition, many collections include ḥadīths and opinions recorded from Mālik that do not appear in the *Muwaṭṭa'*; *cf.* Dutton, The *Origins*, p. 31.
75 This gives formulations such as '*Ibn Wahb wa-'Alī (ibn Ziyād) wa-bn al-Qāsim 'an Mālik*', Saḥnūn, *al-Mudawwanah*, vol. 3, p. 112. On Saḥnūn, see GAS, vol. 1, pp. 468

ff., and M. Muranyi, *Die Rechtsbücher des Qairawāners Saḥnūn b. Sa'īd. Entstehungsgeschichte und Werküberlieferung* (Stuttgart, 1999); on 'Alī, see GAS, vol. 1, p. 465.

76 *GAS*, vol. 1, p. 55. The view of Goldziher ('Ueber die Entwickelung', p. 228) that *musnads* predate *muṣannafāt* is mistaken.

77 *GAS*, vol. 1, pp. 97, 101.

78 J. Fück, 'Beiträge zur Überlieferungsgeschichte von Buḫārīs Traditionssammlung', *ZDMG* 92 (1938), pp. 61 ff.; *GAS*, vol. 1, pp. 116 ff.

79 See H. Laoust, *EI*², s.v. Aḥmad b. Ḥanbal, and *GAL*², vol. 1, p. 193; C. Melchert, 'The *Musnad* of Aḥmad ibn Ḥanbal: How It Was Composed and What Distinguishes It from the Six Books', in *Der Islam* 82 (2005), pp. 32–51.

80 al-Khaṭīb al-Baghdādī, *Ta'rīkh Baghdād*, vol. 2, p. 9; *cf.* GAS, vol. 1, p. 116.

81 Fück, 'Beiträge', pp. 62 ff.

82 Goldziher, 'Ueber die Entwickelung', pp. 188 ff.

83 *GAS*, vol. 1, p. 117.

84 Fück, 'Beitrage'; *GAS*, vol. 1, pp. 115–134; F. Sezgin, *Buḫârî'nin Kaynakları hakkında araştırmalar* (Istanbul, 1956); R. Quiring-Zoche, 'How al-Buḫārī's *Ṣaḥīḥ* was Edited in the Middle Ages: 'Alī al-Yunīnī and his *Rumūz*', *Bulletin d'études orientales* 50 (1998), pp. 191–222, especially pp. 200 ff.

85 For an example (a recension of the *Kitāb al-Sunan* of Abū Dāwūd), see Schoeler, *Arabische Handschriften*, pp. 37 ff. (no. 30).

86 For an English translation, see G. H. A. Juynboll, 'Muslim's Introduction to his *Ṣaḥīḥ*. Translated and Annotated', *JSAI* 5 (1984), pp. 263–311.

6

The birth of linguistics and philology

The teaching of grammar and lexicography: beginnings in Kufa and Basra

The teaching of grammar and lexicography in Islam probably began in the seventh century, and then flourished in the towns of Basra and Kufa in the eighth century.[1] Both fields had very close ties to Qur'ānic exegesis and in all likelihood arose out of it. The earliest work in lexicography is most likely the *Masā'il Nāfi' ibn al-Azraq* (Questions [asked by] Nāfi' ibn al-Azraq), though its precise date of compilation is still not known.[2] In this work, organised as a series of questions and answers, Nāfi' (d. 65/685), the leader of an extremist Khārijī sect known as the Azraqīs, queries Ibn al-'Abbās, the Prophet's cousin and reputed founder of Qur'ānic exegesis, about the meaning of a number of Qur'ānic lexemes. Ibn al-'Abbās answers first by citing a synonym, then by citing a verse of Arabic poetry as a prooftext (*shāhid*, pl. *shawāhid*). As for grammar, Arabic tradition maintains that it was founded by the governor of Kufa, Abū al-Aswad al-Du'alī (d. 69/688), who, at the request of the caliph 'Alī ibn Abī Ṭālib, is said to have developed its basic principles in order to assist with the correct recitation of the Qur'ān.[3] In an important study, C. H. M. Versteegh has shown that the linguistic terminology of the earliest Qur'ān commentaries is similar to the terminology in the grammatical tradition, in Kufa in particular, and for which it may well have laid the groundwork;[4] the terminology in Basra, on the other hand, appears to have developed independently.

The teaching of grammar, which developed principally in Basra, was quite distinct from teaching in other disciplines; of paramount importance was the study of grammatical rules. It is true that grammar, like the other disciplines in Islamic scholarship, was, in the final analysis, dependent on transmission, but grammar differed in that it subjected the transmitted material to rational study (*ma'qūl 'an al-manqūl*).[5] In this rational approach, one method in particular played a fundamental role for the Basran scholars, namely *qiyās*, a term which appears initially to have simply meant 'rule', only later acquiring, as it would in the study of law, the meaning of 'analogical deduction'.[6] The teaching of grammar, which also encompassed linguistic hypotheses that needed to be verified and a whole system of doctrines and theories that needed to be structured and implemented, developed in particular in the course of the Basran scholars' discussions.[7]

In Kufa in the same period, teaching focused less on linguistics and grammar than on philology and lexicography. The scholars of the Kufa school (the transmitters Ḥammād and al-Mufaḍḍal al-Ḍabbī, for instance) consequently directed their energies toward the philological understanding of texts and to the collection and transmission of pre-Islamic poetry – naturally, this did not prevent them from developing a grammatical terminology.[8] In Kufa, transmission of knowledge was fundamental, but teaching in the field of lexicography more closely resembled teaching in the fields of religious scholarship than it did the discussions of the Basran scholars.

Already, toward the middle of the eighth century, or maybe earlier still, one Basran scholar, 'Īsā ibn 'Umar al-Thaqafī (d. 149/766), is reported to have compiled 'books' of grammar. To this 'Īsā are attributed two titles, a *Kitāb al-Jāmi'* (The Book of Compilation) and a *Kitāb al-Mukmil* (The Book of Completion).[9] Whereas Abū al-Ṭayyib al-Lughawī, relying on the testimony of Abū Bakr al-Ṣūlī, reports that al-Mubarrad (ca. 210–86/825–900) read pages from one of these books, al-Sīrāfī (d. 368/979) reports that neither he, nor anyone else at all, had ever seen either of these two books.[10] Certainly, the title *Kitāb al-Jāmi'* suggests that it may have been a work systematically subdivided into chapters (i.e. a *muṣannaf*) similar to the *Jāmi'* of Ma'mar ibn Rāshid, but the works do not survive and, as we have seen, their existence is open to question.

Al-Khalīl ibn Aḥmad, author of a book on grammar?

The contribution of al-Khalīl ibn Aḥmad (d. ca. 160/776), a student of 'Īsā ibn 'Umar al-Thaqafī, to the systematic development of Arabic grammar can hardly be overestimated: his student, Sībawayhi, cites him more than six hundred times.[11] Wolfgang Reuschel's analysis of these citations reveals, however, that although al-Khalīl was fully acquainted with the comprehensive system described by Sībawayhi,[12] he wrote no book on grammar. On this, the Arabic tradition and Western scholarship are in complete agreement.[13] There is an explicit statement on this issue by the medieval philologist al-Zubaydī (d. 379/989), who states in the introduction to his *Mukhtaṣar Kitāb al-'Ayn* (Epitome of the Book of [the Letter] 'Ayn):[14]

> It was he [al-Khalīl] who (first) presented (the system of) grammar …, but he did not wish to write a single letter about it, nor even to sketch an outline of it … He was, in this regard, content with the knowledge he gave to Sībawayhi … Sībawayhi picked up this knowledge from him, girded himself with it, and wrote the *Kitāb* about it …

Similarly, none of al-Khalīl's biographers state that he wrote a book of grammar. What we read about him in the biographical literature are statements such as 'He was pre-eminent in solving questions of grammar';[15] about his disciples we read statements such as 'he (*sc.* Sībawayhi) took [i.e. learned] grammar from al-Khalīl',[16] or 'he took part in al-Khalīl's sessions and adopted his grammatical methods from him'.[17]

All this does not mean that al-Khalīl did not compile written works in other disciplines – we even have one of those books, namely his *Kitāb al-'Arūḍ* (Book of Prosody), not, it is true, in its original form, but in the reworked version given by Ibn 'Abd Rabbihi in his *Kitāb al-'Iqd al-farīd* (Book of the Unique Necklace).[18] It is possible that the *Kitāb al-'Arūḍ* in its earlier form was a systematically ordered collection belonging to 'the literature of the school, for the school, intended for recitation', like the other *muṣannafs* of this period.

The *Kitāb* ('Book') of Sībawayhi

It turns out that the earliest surviving book in the field of grammar is also the very first book properly speaking in all of Islamic scholarship: the *Kitāb* ('Book') of Sībawayhi (d. ca. 180/798) is a comprehensive and systematic description of Arabic grammar.[19] Muslim scholars were quick to recognise the uniqueness of the *Kitāb* as an actual book, as biographers' characterisations of Sībawayhi and his work make clear, e.g. 'he was a scholar accomplished at composing (books)', or even 'he composed his book which people called 'the Qur'ān of grammar'.[20]

The *Kitāb* is unmistakably an actual book, a *syngramma* edited by the author himself before the reading public ever laid eyes on it; it was not compiled by a student or by a student's student,[21] notwithstanding the fact that it is devoid of an introduction and (presumably) a title chosen by the author himself. Systematically subdivided into chapters, the *Kitāb* can therefore be categorised as a *muṣannaf* – the difference is that the *Kitāb* is divided much more systematically and with much greater nuance than most other ordered collections, and that the chapter titles 'are distinctive in that they are extremely technical'.[22] A glance at the first seven chapters – frequently very short, sometimes less than a page – confirms this:[23]

bāb 'ilm mā al-kalim min al-'arabiyyah ('Chapter on knowing what Arabic words are')
bāb majārī awākhir al-kalim min al-'arabiyyah ('Chapter on the behaviour of word endings in Arabic')
bāb al-musnad wal-musnad ilayhi ('Chapter on the support [topic] and what is supported on it [predicate]')
bāb al-lafẓ lil-ma'ānī ('Chapter on the relationship of form and meaning')
bāb mā yakūnu fī al-lafẓ min al-a'rāḍ ('Chapter on accidental variations in linguistic form')

bāb al-istiqāmah min al-kalim wal-iḥālah ('Chapter on [formal/grammatical] rightness and wrongness in speech')
bāb mā yaḥtamilu al-shi'r ('Chapter on what is tolerated in poetry')

Very often, Sībawayhi begins a chapter or paragraph by addressing the reader with the phrase 'know that' (*i'lam anna*) or 'do you not see?' (*a-lā tarā*).[24] Such formulas, unthinkable in a context of oral delivery, strongly support the argument in favour of the fundamentally written nature of the *Kitāb*. But the most convincing evidence has been identified by Geneviève Humbert, who has pointed out the presence of internal cross-references in the text. One such reference (she identifies two) occurs in chapter 296 of the Derenbourg edition, where Sībawayhi uses the words, 'I have already illustrated this in a more detailed fashion at the beginning of the book', to refer to a passage that indeed occurs at the beginning of the work, in chapter 2, that is 294 chapters earlier.[25] As Humbert pertinently notes, 'By all appearances, Sībawayhi conceives of his work as a written text and would seem to be addressing himself to someone who can move from one point in the text to another as necessary, namely a reader.'[26]

Sībawayhi's *Kitāb* is the first book in Islamic scholarship to have consciously been drafted with a large readership in mind (besides the special case of the *Kitāb al-'Ayn*, on which more below). Sībawayhi speaks in his own name throughout the first seven chapters, a group that has come to be known as the *Risālah* (Epistle). He quotes authorities in subsequent chapters, but when he does so his method is quite distinct from the method of the traditionists and is closer to modern methods of quotation. The authorities he most often quotes are his teachers, al-Khalīl ibn Aḥmad and Yūnus ibn Ḥabīb (d. 182/798),[27] but he rarely quotes them quoting their own teachers.[28] The formulas introducing the quotations (*alfāẓ*) only rarely correspond to the ones used by contemporary traditionists. The one Sībawayhi most often uses when referring to al-Khalīl is 'I asked him … and he responded' (*sa'altuhu … fa-qāla*). Other similar formulations in the *Kitāb* confirm the fundamentally oral nature of al-Khalīl's teaching: these include 'he claimed' (*za'ama*) and 'he said' (*qāla*), terminologically indeterminate expressions but ones that do suggest discussion or oral instruction. On the other hand, rarely does Sībawayhi use the formula 'he reported/transmitted to me/us' (*ḥaddathanī/nā*), which in the study of the Ḥadīth as a rule signals audition during which the teacher recites the traditions, frequently on the basis of written notes. All the quotations in the *Kitāb* correspond to the discussions, doctrines, theories and points of view expressed by Sībawayhi's teachers, not to any traditions and accounts transmitted by them. These quotations thus effectively record 'the discussions of the Basra school'.[29]

We noted above that the first seven chapters of the *Kitāb* are known as the *Risālah*.[30] It may very well be that this title was chosen because the *Kitāb*, or its core at any rate, was initially a *Risālah* which Sībawayhi had written at the request of a particular individual, even if we do not know the identity of the addressee. It is, in any event, very likely that the *Kitāb* is connected to the fundamentally written tradition of the *risālah*.

The Kitāb *and later grammatical studies*

Sībawayhi's *Kitāb* earned the title 'Qur'ān of grammar' and subsequently attracted the lion's share of attention of all subsequent scholarly activity in the field of grammar; these works were devoted henceforth to commenting on, extending, and supplementing the *Kitāb* – it was as if the whole tradition rested on this one text, subjecting it to a constant and continuous process of commentary and explication.[31]

The method used to transmit the *Kitāb*, i.e. the way it was studied, was to read it aloud in the presence of a teacher (*qirā'ah*). Such transmission did not occur in Sībawayhi's lifetime, however; indeed, tradition has it that Sībawayhi had no students and that he died young. The following observation by the celebrated commentator of the *Kitāb*, Abū Sa'īd al-Sīrāfī, in his *Kitāb Akhbār al-naḥwiyyīn al-Baṣriyyīn* (Book of Accounts of the Basran Grammarians), is corroborated by others in the biographical literature:[32]

> One got access to the *Kitāb* of Sībawayhi through al-Akhfash. No-one had in fact read the *Kitāb* with Sībawayhi, and Sībawayhi had not read it with anyone either. After he died, it was read with al-Akhfash.

The comments of al-Akhfash al-Awsaṭ (d. 215/830), a student and friend of Sībawayhi's, are preserved, at least in part, as marginal glosses in the *Kitāb*, and most of these have been included in the printed edition of the *Kitāb* edited by 'Abd al-Salām Muḥammad Hārūn.

It was Basran grammarians, Abū 'Uthmān al-Māzinī (d. 248/862), Abū 'Umar al-Jarmī (d. 225/839) and others, who subsequently read the *Kitāb* with al-Akhfash al-Awsaṭ.[33] Al-Mubarrad, the leader of the Basra school in the ninth century, in turn read it with al-Māzinī and al-Jarmī.[34] In this way, an uninterrupted tradition of 'reading' the *Kitāb* developed, thanks to which chains of transmitters were formed, chains which are absent in the work itself. These name the transmitters of the book, starting with the current owner of the manuscript and going back uninterruptedly to Sībawayhi; they are thus similar to the *isnāds* of the traditionists. Good manuscripts of the *Kitāb* include such introductory chains (sing. *riwāyah*, pl. *riwāyāt*), appearing before the text proper. Two of the manuscripts used by Hārūn in the preparation of his modern edition of the *Kitāb* include these, and as we would expect, given what we know of the work's transmission history, both chains ultimately lead through al-Mubarrad, al-Māzinī and al-Akhfash to Sībawayhi.[35] Thus, a procedure which originally only applied to individual traditions – acquiring a cumulative chain of authorities via the process of transmission – now applied to an entire book. In a later period, such introductory chains of transmitters would also find their way into works of Ḥadīth, philology, and even medicine and the sciences.[36] From the time of al-Akhfash al-Awsaṭ on, 'reading' the *Kitāb* and explaining it undoubtedly dominated the teaching of grammar, but the study and discussion circles that had existed long before al-Khalīl and Sībawayhi did not cease to exist; works titled *Majālis* (Sessions) and *Amālī* (Dictations) from the ninth and tenth centuries give us important glimpses into the nature of the discussions that took places in these circles.[37]

Another significant aspect of the transmission of books is the fact that once a work had been given a definitive shape, then recitation or reading of the work by a student with a teacher in the presence of other students (*qirā'ah*) became the normative mode of transmission for that text. To be sure, this did not mean that other methods of transmission, such as audition (*samā'*), were not employed.[38] But *qirā'ah* was used to transmit the Qur'ān (lit. 'recitation'), the recitation par excellence, and also the 'Qur'ān of grammar', Sībawayhi's *Kitāb*.

Al-Khalīl ibn Aḥmad, author of the *Kitāb al-'Ayn*?

The oldest work of Arabic lexicography, the *Kitāb al-'Ayn* attributed to al-Khalīl ibn Aḥmad, is also the first complete dictionary of the Arabic language in Arabic. By virtue of the specific problems posed by this book, not least of which its authorship, and by virtue of the fact that it is in all ways a special case, we shall first look in detail at the *Kitāb al-'Ayn* before turning to lexicography more generally.

Already, in the middle of the eighth century, even before Sībawayhi had conceived of his *Kitāb*, the idea of a large dictionary, in fact the idea of a complete Arabic dictionary, had taken shape, with lexemes organised not alphabetically or by content, but on the basis of phonetic criteria.[39] We cannot speak *sensu strictu* of a *muṣannaf*, though it must be said that the *Kitāb al-'Ayn*'s organisational principles certainly correspond to the ones that inspired the *taṣnīf* movement. The difficulty with the *Kitāb al-'Ayn* is its authorship.[40] The elaborate controversy that surrounds this question was first raised by the philologists of the late eighth century and continues to this day.[41] One side has it that al-Khalīl, the great grammarian and discoverer of the system of Arabic metrics, is the author; the other, represented by the majority of medieval Arabic philologists, vehemently denies his authorship. A simple glance at the work reveals the complexity of the matter. In it, that is, in the introduction and the dictionary proper, al-Khalīl is cited as an authority, but he appears as only *one* cited authority among many; and the introduction suggests that one al-Layth ibn al-Muẓaffar (d. before 200/815) – by all accounts a friend of al-Khalīl's, but not someone known to be an accomplished philologist – played a significant part in the compilation of the work.[42]

Modern Western research on the question (notably Erich Bräunlich, Stefan Wild, Rafael Talmon) tends to regard al-Khalīl as the creative genius behind the book, but does not credit him with the work of actual compilation and redaction. According to this view, the master, al-Khalīl, conceived of the idea of the dictionary; and the student, al-Layth, was responsible for compiling, supplementing and editing the work and giving it its final form, making al-Layth the real 'author' of the *Kitāb al-'Ayn*. As there is no unanimity on this position, the alternative views that have been advanced are worth taking seriously. One of these originates within the Muslim scholarly tradition. In a work about the *Kitāb al-'Ayn*, al-Zubaydī, citing his teacher al-Qālī, observes that although al-Khalīl's leading students used to transmit the knowledge they acquired from their teacher meticulously, none either knew the *Kitāb al-'Ayn* or had even heard it recited.[43] It is only long after they had died that the work found its way from Khurasan to Basra, when Abū Ḥātim al-Sijistānī became head of the school, around 250/865. If al-Khalīl had been the author, al-Zubaydī says, again relying on al-Qālī, his most prominent students would have taken it upon themselves to transmit the work and not left it to an obscure figure like al-Layth. And if the book really was al-Khalīl's, then al-Aṣma'ī, al-Yazīdī, Ibn al-A'rābī and contemporaries of theirs, as well as scholars of the following generation such as Abū Ḥātim, Abū 'Ubayd and others, would without fail have cited it and transmitted it. This last argument is certainly persuasive: as the investigations of Bräunlich and others have shown, these philologists do not, in fact, ever cite the *Kitāb al-'Ayn* in their works.[44]

There is another argument against al-Khalīl's authorship, originally advanced within the Arabic tradition, then taken up by Bräunlich, and more recently elaborated upon by Janusz Danecki, namely that although Sībawayhi, al-Khalīl's student, cites his teacher more than six hundred times in the *Kitāb*, he never mentions him in the part of the book that deals with phonetics; what is more, al-Khalīl's alleged phonetic system is, according to Danecki, more elaborate and, all in all, superior to Sībawayhi's.[45] For these reasons, the *Kitāb al-'Ayn* must, according to Danecki, be later than Sībawayhi's, which means al-Khalīl could not possibly have been its author.

The question can definitively be settled through a more careful examination of the text of the *Kitāb al-'Ayn*. The introduction to the work opens with the following chain of transmission (*riwāyah*):[46]

> Abū Mu'ādh 'Abd Allāh ibn 'Ā'idh says: al-Layth ibn al-Muẓaffar … has transmitted to me, on the authority of al-Khalīl ibn Aḥmad, everything in this book.

Immediately thereafter, we find 'Al-Layth said: al-Khalīl said: …', a formula that is repeated several times in the introduction;[47] sometimes we find simply 'Al-Khalīl said'.[48] We also encounter expressions such as 'Al-Layth said: I asked X, he then answered', 'I asked a-Khalīl, he then answered', or 'He [al-Khalīl] sometimes said ...', or even 'Al-Khalīl used to call ...'[49] However, the formula 'Al-Khalīl transmitted to me/us' (*ḥaddathanā/nī* or *akhbaranā/nī*), which would indicate transmission through al-Khalīl's instruction to his students (*samā'*, audition, or *qirā'ah*, recitation), never appears. And at the end of the introduction, we read: 'Al-Khalīl said: We shall now begin our work (*mu'allafunā*) with (the letter) *'ayn* ...'[50]

The above may at first seem confusing, but given what we know of the methods used to transmit knowledge, it is very clear that we are dealing here with three distinct phases of transmission,[51] which can be simply schematised as follows:

al-Khalīl (writing [only fragments]; but also responding to questions etc.)
> al-Layth (compiling the fragments, supplementing them with other material, editing)
> Abū Mu'ādh (disseminating)

The last phase is represented by the little-known scholar, Abū Mu'ādh 'Abd Allāh ibn 'Ā'idh: the 'introductory *isnād*' (*riwāyah*) shows that he received the *Kitāb al-'Ayn* from al-Layth as an already complete work. The preceding, intermediate stage is represented by al-Layth: he assembled his teacher's fragments, and perfected the structure of the work, especially by drawing up and elaborating, for the dictionary proper, many *lemmata* al-Khalīl had not started on or left uncompleted. In addition, he included much miscellaneous material in the dictionary, some of which consists of his recollection of the doctrines or theories al-Khalīl put forward in scholarly circles or in discussion, often obtained by questioning al-Khalīl and other authorities. What is striking is that these recollections pertain only to grammatical and metrical questions, on occasion to musical ones, but *never to lexical ones*.[52] As for the first and oldest phase, it is represented by al-Khalīl himself and his fragments, all of which open with the formula 'al-Khalīl said' (*qāla al-Khalīl*). In one of these fragments, the one appearing at the end of the introduction, al-Khalīl explicitly states that he will begin his work (*mu'allafunā*) with the letter *'ayn*. The three phonetic treatises are examples of other fragments originating with al-Khalīl – and they are fundamental to the work as a whole as it is in them that he develops his theory of phonetics, the one that dictates the order of the words in the dictionary itself.[53] The composition of these treatises suggests strongly that they are not notes taken by a student, but are rather from the pen of the teacher himself. Two of them (I and III) begin with the formula 'Al-Khalīl said: Know that ...' (*qāla al-Khalīl: i'lam anna*), a form of address we also find in the *Kitāb* of Sībawayhi. The dictionary proper also contains fragments that originate with al-Khalīl. We even find one instance of internal cross-reference, irrefutable proof of the written character of these passages:[54]

> … Al-Khalīl said: The (letters) *qāf* and the *kāf* do not go together in a word, nor the *jīm* [i.e. with the *qāf*], except in foreign words, as I explained in the first part of the second chapter on *qāf* (*qad bayyantuhā awwal al-bāb al-thānī min al-qāf*).

Al-Khalīl is referencing an earlier passage, where he had effectively pointed out the very same thing:[55]

> The letter *qāf*. Al-Khalīl said: The *qāf* and *kāf* are not joined in a word except if it is a word borrowed from another language and Arabised. This also applies to *jīm* with *qāf* …

Al-Khalīl's use of the formulation 'our work' (*mu'allafunā*) to describe his book, and his use of expressions and formulations which underscore the written character of the work (addressing the reader, and in particular, engaging in internal cross-referencing) prove that he set out to write an actual book, a dictionary intended for readers. For this time period, this was nothing short of extraordinary: no scholar had so far written a book for *readers*.

Al-Khalīl did not disseminate his phonetic theories to numerous students during public instruction, as was common practice at the time, and as he was accustomed to doing with grammar. This is the reason why, for centuries after al-Khalīl's death, Arabic tradition did not recognise al-Khalīl as a lexicographer (*lughawī*), but as a grammarian (*naḥwī*). This is also the reason why the earliest authors of lexicographical works (al-Aṣma'ī, Abū 'Amr al-Shaybānī, Abū 'Ubayd and so on), do not ever cite al-Khalīl on matters relating to lexicography and etymology in their works. When they do cite him, it is always on matters relating to grammar.

According to one account, it was in Khurasan, at the home of his friend al-Layth, that al-Khalīl – unobserved by his leading students – formulated the framework of the *Kitāb al-'Ayn*, which he conceived of as a work specifically for readers. Al-Layth, and al-Layth alone, received the fragment or fragments from his teacher and friend, who had discussed with him, and him alone, the idea of the book and its contents.[56] Like al-Khalīl, once he had completed the work, al-Layth only transmitted the work to one student, Abū Mu'ādh 'Abd Allāh ibn 'Ā'idh.[57] Sībawayhi could not, therefore, have known the book, have cited it in his *Kitāb*, or have been influenced by its ideas.

Al-Khalīl did not complete his book – according to tradition, he died before he was able to do so.[58] The *Kitāb al-'Ayn* only appeared in definitive form very much later, certainly not before the middle of the ninth century. Had he completed it, he would have been the author of the first actual book in the history of Islamic scholarship. That prestige and honour did go, however, to one of al-Khalīl's students – to Sībawayhi, whose book of grammar was dubbed *al-Kitāb* (The Book), the book par excellence.

Lexicography

Lexicography is the study of 'the words and rare expressions of the Arabs', a field completely distinct from grammar; lexicographers' efforts are therefore largely focused on poetry and unusual expressions.[59] No written work in the field of lexicography played a role comparable to that of Sībawayhi's *Kitāb* in grammar. And unlike the case of grammar, audition and transmission of knowledge were fundamental in the teaching of lexicography. What is more, in lexicography, Bedouin Arabs, whose speech was pure and correct (*fuṣaḥā' al-'Arab*), enjoyed the same authority as scholars; this explains why al-Suyūṭī gave the title, 'Listening to (or 'auditing') the Words of the Teacher or the Bedouin' (*al-samā' min lafẓ al-shaykh aw al-'arabī*) to the first section of the first chapter of his *al-Muzhir fī 'ulūm al-lughah* (The Flowering [Book] on the Linguistic Sciences), which treats the methods of acquisition and transmission of knowledge.[60] In his *Kitāb al-Shi'r wal-shu'arā'* (Book of Poetry and Poets), Ibn Qutaybah preserves an account that underscores the importance of the Bedouin Arabs as arbiters of pure speech as follows:[61]

> The following hemistich by Abū Dhu'ayb was one day recited in al-Aṣma'ī's circle:
> 'In the deep of the valley of Dhāt al-*Dayr*, her young was set aside.'
> 'Completely wrong, O reader!' exclaimed a Bedouin who was present. 'It's Dhāt al-*Dabr*, a mountain pass where we're from.'[62] Thereafter, al-Aṣma'ī adopted that reading.

The *Kitāb al-Nawādir fī al-lughah* (Book of Lexicographical Rarities) is a good example of those works in which compilers catalogue glosses on Bedouin poetry and supplement these with a vast amount of information regarding specific words or verses, but with no attempt to present the material systematically;[63] it is also a good example of a work whose shape can only be explained with reference to the specifics of philological teaching practices. The *Kitāb al-Nawādir* is attributed to Abū Zayd al-Anṣārī,[64] and the core of the work certainly originates with him, but over time the successive generations of scholars transmitting the work extended it by also contributing to it themselves. The following are examples of comments made by the redactor of the book, al-Akhfash al-Aṣghar (d. 315/927) – who contributed much material to the work, both his own opinions, as well as information taken from other scholars – about variants of little-known proper names and obscure words:[65]

> It appears thus in my book: *Salmā*; but in my memory it is *Sulmiyyun*.
>
> ... it is thus (= *Nuhayk*) in my book, but my recollection is *Nahīk*.
>
> What was transmitted (to me) by audition (*al-masmū'*) is *'ayhalun*, but in the poem it appears as *'ayhallun*.

These suffice to show that in philological teaching practices, transmission through audition functioned side by side with transmission through writing, in much the same way they did in the teaching of Ḥadīth.

Taṣnīf *in the field of lexicography*

If the various books of linguistic rarities were not systematic at all, other lexicographic works were, notably *al-gharīb al-muṣannaf* works (about uncommon words), also called *kutub al-ṣifāt* ('books on characteristics') and *kutub fī ma'rifat asmā' al-ashyā'* ('books on the knowledge of the names of things'). The use of the term *muṣannaf* in the titles in this genre indicates that the words were systematically classified into groups based on the work's contents.[66] The earliest surviving book of this type is *al-Gharīb al-muṣannaf* (The Book of Uncommon Vocabulary, Arranged Systematically) of Abū 'Ubayd (d. 224/838), an actual book, by an author who is famous for several carefully redacted works.[67] In the beginning of his notice on Abū 'Ubayd in the *Kitāb Marātib al-naḥwiyyīn* (Book on the Classes of Grammarians), Abū al-Ṭayyib al-Lughawī notes:[68]

> Abū 'Ubayd was an author skilled in the composition of (actual) books, but one who possessed (only) little transmission [i.e. he had not received many works through audition; he had not studied them with teachers] (*muṣannif ḥasan al-ta'līf illā annahu qalīl al-riwāyah*).

Toward the end of the notice, Abū al-Ṭayyib adds:[69]

> Abū 'Ubayd used to bring his books (*muṣannafāt*) immediately to the rulers,[70] who then offered him gifts in return: this is why his books are so numerous.

A large number of manuscripts of *al-Gharīb al-muṣannaf* do survive; there are also numerous supplements (*ziyādāt*) to it, commentaries on it (*sharḥ*, pl. *shurūḥ*), and epitomes of it, all of which suggests that it was widely disseminated.[71]

Personal contact with teachers and transmitting from them through audition was not of great importance to Abū 'Ubayd.[72] Modern research on Islamic scholarship has established that Abū 'Ubayd was one of the very first scholars to have written actual handbooks composed either under the impetus of the court or in close contact with it. Abū al-Ṭayyib and other biographers disapprovingly describe him as making a practice of copying the 'books' he would compile and turning them into his own books.[73] Abū al-Ṭayyib writes:

> The people of Basra have observed that the majority of what he reports on the authority of their learned scholars did not depend on audition, but came from books.

The very same kind of reproach was directed at Abū Ḥanīfah al-Dīnawarī (d. 282/895), author of the most famous Arabic book on botany, the *Kitāb al-Nabāt* (Book of Plants), similarly prepared without its author having obtained the material for it through audition.[74]

The chain of authorities of one manuscript of the *Kitāb Gharīb al-ḥadīth* reveals that the most important individual in the transmission of Abū 'Ubayd's works, namely 'Alī ibn 'Abd al-'Azīz (d. 287/900), had heard the work with his teacher:[75]

> Aḥmad ibn Ḥammād told me: 'Alī ibn 'Abd al-'Azīz said to us: I heard this book recited by a student (*qirā'atan*) several times in the presence of Abū 'Ubayd ... I asked him: 'May we transmit what was read with you?' 'Yes,' he answered, 'using (the phrase) 'Abū 'Ubayd al-Qāsim ibn Sallām al-Khuzā'ī *told* us.'

The customary method used to transmit Abū 'Ubayd's works (the *Kitāb al-Gharīb al-muṣannaf*, and also the *Kitāb Gharīb al-ḥadīth* and the *Kitāb al-Amthāl*), therefore, was recitation in the presence of a teacher (*qirā'ah*) – they were, after all, actual books.

In the ninth century, it was no longer only the court that demanded actual books, especially handbooks. The demand came also from the large, educated reading public. And scholars very soon discovered that much could be gained from handbooks, even if their content was not acquired in the traditional way, that is, through audition with a teacher or recitation in his presence. This is not to say that personal and aural instruction was no longer important, and few scholars abandoned their expectation that it be employed. But the genesis of handbook literature in the ninth century reveals very clearly the profound change in the composition of the readership interested in academic writing.

Notes

1 See GAS, vol. 8, pp. 7 ff.; vol. 9, pp. 5 ff.; Versteegh, 'Die arabische Sprachwissenschaft', pp. 150 ff.; S. Wild, 'Arabische Lexikographie', *GAPh*, vol. 2, pp. 136 ff.; G. Troupeau, *EI*², s.v. Naḥw; Reuschel, *Al-Ḫalīl.*

2 See GAS, vol. 1, p. 27; Neuwirth, 'Koran', pp. 124 ff.

3 GAS, vol. 9, p. 31; C. H. M. Versteegh, 'Die arabische Sprachwissenschaft', *GAPh*, vol. 2, pp. 150 ff.

4 Versteegh, *Arabic Grammar*.

5 *Cf.* Versteegh, 'Die arabische Sprachwissenschaft', p. 148.

6 Ibid., p. 153.

7 Ibid., pp. 156 ff.

8 GAS, vol. 9, p. 37.

9 *Fihrist*¹, p. 41 = *Fihrist*², p. 47; *cf.* GAS, vol. 9, p. 39.

10 Abū al-Ṭayyib al-Lughawī, *Marātib al-naḥwiyyīn*, ed. M. Abū al-Faḍl Ibrāhīm (Cairo, 1995), p. 33; al-Sīrāfī, *Akhbār al-naḥwiyyīn al-baṣriyyīn = Biographies des grammairiens de l'école de Basra (Akhbār al-naḥwiyyīn al-baṣriyyīn)*, ed. F. Krenkow (Paris and Beirut, 1936), pp. 31 ff.

11 *Cf.* W. Reuschel, *Al-Ḫalīl ibn Aḥmad, der Lehrer Sībawaihs, als Grammatiker* (Berlin, 1959), pp. 9–14; G. Troupeau, 'A propos des grammairiens cités par Sībawayhi dans

le *Kitāb*', *Arabica* 8 (1961), pp. 309–312. On al-Khalīl, see GAS, vol. 8, pp. 51 ff.

12 Reuschel, *Al-Ḫalīl*, p. 10.

13 Fuat Sezgin being the only scholar to have suggested otherwise: see GAS, vol. 9, pp. 44 ff.

14 *Apud* al-Suyūṭī, *al-Muzhir fī 'ulūm al-lughah wa-anwā'ihā*, 2 vols, ed. M. A. Jād al-Mawlā et al. (Cairo, n.d.), vol. 1, pp. 80–1.

15 *Fihrist*[1], p. 42 = *Fihrist*[2], p. 48; al-Sīrāfī, *Akhbār al-naḥwiyyīn*, p. 38.

16 *Fihrist*[1], p. 51 = *Fihrist*[2], p. 57; Abū al-Ṭayyib, *Marātib*, p. 66; al-Sīrāfī, *Akhbār al-naḥwiyyīn*, p. 48.

17 al-Azharī, *Tahdhīb al-lughah*, 15 vols, ed. 'A. Hārūn et al. (Cairo, 1964–7), vol. 1, p. 19.

18 Ibn 'Abd Rabbihi, *al-'Iqd al-farīd*, vol. 5, pp. 424–95.

19 GAS, vol. 9, pp. 51 ff.; M. Carter, *EI*[2], s.v. Sībawayhi.

20 al-Azharī, *Tahdhīb*, vol. 1, p. 19; Abū al-Ṭayyib, *Marātib*, p. 65.

21 G. Humbert, 'Le *Kitāb* de Sībawayhi et l'autonomie de l'écrit', *Arabica* 44 (1997), pp. 553 ff.

22 Ibid., p. 554.

23 Sībawayhi, *al-Kitāb*, vol. 1, pp. 12–15.

24 Ibid., vol. 1, pp. 22, 24 and *passim*.

25 Humbert, 'Le *Kitāb* de Sībawayhi', p. 554; Sībawayhi, *Le livre de Sībawayhi, traité de grammaire arabe*, ed. H. Derenbourg (Paris, 1881–5), vol. 2, p. 13, and vol. 1, p. 6.

26 Ibid., p. 555.

27 GAS, vol. 8, p. 57, and vol. 9, p. 49.

28 *Cf.* Reuschel, *Al-Ḫalīl*, pp. 9–14.

29 Ibid., p. 11.

30 See *EI*[2], s.v. Sībawayhi.

31 See GAS, vol. 9, pp. 58–63. *Cf.* Versteegh, 'Die arabische Sprachwissenschaft', pp. 154 ff.

32 al-Sīrāfī, *Akhbār*, p. 50; *Fihrist*[1], p. 52 = *Fihrist*[2], p. 58; Humbert, 'Le *Kitāb* de Sībawayhi', p. 555.

33 *Fihrist*[1], p. 52 = *Fihrist*[2], p. 58; al-Sīrāfī, *Akhbār*, p. 50; on al-Akhfash, see GAS, vol. 9, p. 68; On al-Māzinī, see GAS, vol. 9, p. 75; on al-Jarmī, GAS, vol. 9, p. 72

34 *Fihrist*[1], p. 59 = *Fihrist*[1], pp. 64–5; al-Zubaydī, *Ṭabaqāt al-naḥwiyyīn wal-lughawiyyīn*, ed. M. Abū al-Faḍl Ibrāhīm (Cairo, [2]1973), p. 101. See also the *riwāyah* (introductory 'isnād') at the beginning of the *Kitāb* in Hārūn's edition, pp. 3–4, 10–11.

35 Ibid.

36 See Goldziher, 'Ueber die Entwickelung', p. 192; *cf.* G. Vajda, *La transmission du savoir en Islam (VIIe–XVIIIe siècles)*, ed. N. Cottart (London, 1983), p. 1.

37 For example, the *Majālis* and *Amālī* of al-Zajjājī, the *Majālis* of Tha'lab, and the *Amālī* of al-Qālī.

38 See Schoeler, *The Oral and the Written*, pp. 57–8.

39 S. Wild, *Das* Kitāb al-'Ain *und die arabische Lexikographie* (Wiesbaden, 1965).

40 For a detailed exploration of the problem, *cf.* Schoeler, *The Oral and the Written*, pp. 142–61 (ch. 6, 'Who is the author of the *Kitāb al-'ayn*?').

41 GAS, vol. 8, p. 52. The classic study is E. Bräunlich, 'Al-Ḫalīl und das *Kitāb al-'Ain*', *Islamica* 2 (1926), pp. 58–95

42 GAS, vol. 8, p. 159.

43 al-Zubaydī, *Istidrāk al-alfāẓ al-wāqi' fī Kitāb al-'Ayn*, *apud* al-Suyūṭī, *al-Muzhir*, vol. 1, pp. 83 ff.; al-Zubaydī, *Mukhtaṣar Kitāb al-'Ayn*, vol. 1, ed. 'A. al-Fāsī and M. al-Ṭanjī (Rabat and Casablanca, n.d.), p. 8; *cf.* Bräunlich, 'Al-Ḫalīl', p. 88 (2. and 3.). These students include al-Naḍr ibn Shumayl, al-Akhfash al-Awsaṭ, and others.
44 Bräunlich, 'Al-Ḫalīl', pp. 89 ff.
45 Ibid., p. 93; J. Danecki, 'Early Arabic Phonetical Theory. Phonetics of al-Ḫalīl Ibn Aḥmad and Sībawaihi', *Rocznik Orientalistyczny* 39 (1978), p. 56.
46 al-Khalīl ibn Aḥmad al-Farāhīdī, *Kitāb al-'Ayn*, 8 vols, ed. M. Al-Makhzūmī and I. al-Sāmarrā'ī (Baghdad, 1980–5, repr. Beirut, 1988), vol. 1, p. 47.
47 Ibid., vol. 1, pp. 57, 58, 59.
48 Ibid., vol. 1, pp. 49 (twice), 50, 51, 52.
49 Ibid., vol. 1, pp. 50, 52 (twice), 58.
50 Ibid., vol. 1, p. 60.
51 *Cf.* Wild, 'Das *Kitāb al-'Ain*', p. 16.
52 *Cf.* R. Talmon, *Arabic Grammar in its Formative Age.* Kitāb al-'Ayn *and its Attribution to Ḫalīl b. Aḥmad* (Leiden, 1997), pp. 144 ff.
53 Sībawayhi, *al-Kitāb*, vol. 1, pp. 51, 57 and 59, respectively.
54 Ibid., vol. 5, p. 32.
55 Ibid., vol. 5, p. 6.
56 *Fihrist*[1], p. 42 = *Fihrist*[2], p. 48.
57 See Schoeler, *The Oral and the Written*, p. 216, nn. 1023 and 1024.
58 *Fihrist*[1], pp. 42 ff. = *Fihrist*[2], pp. 48 ff.; Abū al-Ṭayyib, *Marātib*, p. 30; al-Suyūṭī, *al-Muzhir*, pp. 78, 82.
59 al-Azharī, *Tahdhīb*, vol. 1, pp. 8, 12.
60 al-Suyūṭī, *al-Muzhir*, vol 1, p. 144.
61 Ibn Qotaiba (Ibn Qutaybah), *Introduction au Livre de la poésie et des poètes. Muqaddimatu kitābi š-ši'ri wa-š-šu'arā'*. Texte … avec introduction, traduction et commentaire par Gaudefroy-Demombynes (Paris, 1947), p. 20.
62 The words *Dayr* and *Dabr* differ only in the placement of a single dot in Arabic.
63 *Cf.* Wild, 'Arabische Lexikographie', p. 137.
64 *GAS*, vol. 8, p. 76.
65 Abū Zayd al-Anṣārī, *Kitāb al-Nawādir fī al-lughah*, ed. S. al-Khūrī al-Sharṭūnī (Beirut, [2]1967), pp. 121, 112, 53.
66 Wild, 'Arabische Lexikographie', pp. 137 ff.
67 *GAS*, vol. 8, p. 81.
68 Abū al-Ṭayyib, *Marātib*, p. 93.
69 Ibid., p. 94.
70 *Mulūk*, lit. 'kings', by which he means the Ṭāhirids, who governed Khurāsān and held high offices in Iraq in the ninth century. See C. E. Bosworth, *EI*[2], s.v. Ṭāhirids.
71 See the long list of work in *GAS*, vol. 8, pp. 83 ff.
72 See H. Gottschalk, *EI*[2], s.v. Abū 'Ubayd.
73 Abū al-Ṭayyib, *Marātib*, p. 93.
74 *Cf.* Th. Bauer, *Das Pflanzenbuch des Abū Ḥanīfa ad-Dīnawarī. Inhalt, Aufbau, Quellen* (Wiesbaden, 1988), pp. 92 ff. On al-Dīnawarī, see *GAS*, vol. 4, p. 338.
75 Abū 'Ubayd, *Gharīb al-ḥadīth*, 2 vols (Beirut, 1967), vol. 1, p. 1, n. 1. Emphasis added.

7

Books and their readership in the ninth century

The appearance of paper in the Near East in the eighth century

The principal materials for writing before the eighth century were papyrus (*qirṭās*) and parchment (*raqq*), but because both were rare and costly the production and dissemination of literature remained relatively restricted. Techniques for the manufacturing of paper had been introduced in the Near East by Chinese prisoners captured at the battle of Aṭlakh (near Tālās) and taken to Samarqand in 134/751, and in the late eighth century, paper (*kāghad*) began its triumphant spread throughout the Near East.[1] The availability of a less costly material, paper, was an important factor contributing to large-scale literary output in the Muslim world in the ninth century and after. Paper and books also had profound influences on literacy and on learned and literary culture, not only on the nature and types of literary production, but also on the nature and transmission of knowledge, on the range and scope of vocations and professional occupations available, and on the constitution of scholarly networks and alliances. The presence of books thus had far-reaching consequences for Arab-Islamic writerly culture, broadly speaking.[2]

From Ibn al-Muqaffaʿ to al-Jāḥiẓ

The book, a conscious literary product (*syngramma*) intended for a reading public, had come into existence in the eighth century among the *kuttāb* or state secretaries, the creators of Arabic artistic prose in the preceding century. The oldest such writings were in the form of letters or epistles, and were intended for courtiers, secretaries or rulers. The men of letters (*adīb*, pl. *udabā'*) or writers of the ninth century, of whom the Basran al-Jāḥiẓ (d. 255/868–9) was the most prominent, continued the literary tradition of the writer-secretaries who, at the beginning of the ninth century, were still of Iranian origin. The most famous of them, Sahl ibn Hārūn (d. 215/830), was somewhat of a successor to Ibn al-Muqaffaʿ: like him, Sahl wrote epistles, and also translated books from Persian to Arabic,[3] one of which, the *Kitāb Wāmiq wa-ʿAdhrā'* (The Book of Wāmiq and ʿAdhrā'), was a Persian romance of Hellenistic origin.[4] Sahl also composed original texts modelled on Ibn al-Muqaffa''s *Kalīlah wa-Dimnah*, of which only the *Kitāb al-Namir wal-tha'lab* (Book of the Panther and the Fox) survives.

Al-Jāḥiẓ held Sahl in high esteem;[5] early in his career he is even said to have published his own works under Sahl's name.[6] At the beginning of the *Kitāb al-Bukhalā'* (Book of Misers), al-Jāḥiẓ cites the *Risālah fī al-bukhl* (The Epistle on Miserliness) attributed to Sahl, a work that can be considered the link between the literary epistles of the eighth century and the 'Jāḥiẓian' epistles of the ninth. But al-Jāḥiẓ did not follow Sahl's example when it came to the Shu'ūbiyyah (the movement which called for the equality of Persians and Arabs), and did not give importance to Persian subjects; he preferred to focus on Arab themes. Indeed, al-Jāḥiẓ's *adab* distinguishes itself by the fact that the author exploited the indigenous literary and religious heritage.

The writings of al-Jāḥiẓ: large works and epistles

An inventory of al-Jāḥiẓ's works undertaken by Charles Pellat catalogues more than two hundred titles, thirty of which, authentic or apocryphal, survive in their entirety, and fifty of which survive in fragments; most treat literary or quasi-scientific topics.[7] All are actual books or epistles, with specific titles, often with a preface or introduction, and frequently dedicated to a minister, secretary, judge or other high-ranking person. The three most important works are the *Kitāb al-Ḥayawān* (The Book of Living Beings), which is incomplete but comes to seven volumes in the edition published by 'Abd al-Salām Hārūn; the *Kitāb al-Bayān wal-tabyīn* (The Book of Expression and Exposition), four volumes in Hārūn's edition; and the one-volume *Kitāb al-Bukhalā'* (The Book of Misers).

Given this enormous literary output, al-Jāḥiẓ understandably enlisted the service of copyists (*warrāqūn*, sing. *warrāq*) to copy his manuscripts.[8] But the dissemination of his works through copying did not prevent parts of his books from being studied and transmitted in the context of academic instruction, where they often underwent significant modifications; there are, for instance, passages in Ibn 'Abd Rabbihi's *al-'Iqd al-farīd* based on passages in al-Jāḥiẓ's *Kitāb al-Bayān wal-tabyīn*, but which do not correspond exactly to the relevant parts of that work.[9] Typically, though, the transmission and dissemination of al-Jāḥiẓ's works was accomplished through the copying of manuscripts.

A large number of al-Jāḥiẓ's treatises and shorter books are called 'letters' or 'epistles', although, even in al-Jāḥiẓ's own time, the term *risālah* (pl. *rasā'il*) had begun to lose its original meaning of 'letter' and had often come to mean 'short work', 'essay' or 'monograph';[10] Ibn al-Nadīm provides a long list of them.[11] Hārūn has edited one collection of short works under the title *Rasā'il al-Jāḥiẓ* (Epistles of al-Jāḥiẓ). A number of these *rasā'il*, such as the *Risālah fī al-jidd wal-hazl* (Epistle on Gravity and Levity),[12] are actual letters, but, as in the larger works, the addressees in these epistles are usually anonymous, and when we do learn the identity of the addressee of a specific letter, it is typically from the title itself, e.g. *Risalāh fi … ilā …* (Epistle on … to …).[13] Innumerable epistles and books of the ninth, tenth and later centuries start with the author's assertion that a client, friend or pupil has asked him to write a book or treatise on one or other subject, e.g.:[14]

> You mentioned – may God protect you from deception – that you have read my essay (*kitābī*) on... and that I made no mention of … And you also mentioned that you would like me to write for you about … Therefore, I have written for you …

It is, however, often very hard to say whether the commission or the request to which authors refer is real or fictitious; indeed, preliminary statements such as the one quoted above are used increasingly as topoi.[15]

Dedicatees, addressees, patrons

According to Ibn al-Nadīm, al-Jāḥiẓ dedicated the *Kitāb al-Ḥayawān* to the vizier Ibn al-Zayyāt (d. 233/847), and the *Kitāb al-Bayān wal-tabyīn* to the judge Ibn Abī Du'ād (d. 240/854), though no dedicatee is mentioned in the text of the work itself.[16] Typically, dedications consisted in the prince, or some other notable, being presented with the 'first fair copy of the work'.[17] It is reasonable to assume that authors dedicated their books to wealthy individuals who would find the contents of the work appealing and from whom they could accordingly expect or exact reward. Al-Jāḥiẓ says this explicitly in the *Kitāb al-Ḥayawān*, but without naming the addressee: 'Thus have I written it, specially for you, and I bring it to you counting on you for my reward.'[18]

For each of the *Kitāb al-Ḥayawān*, the *Kitāb al-Bayān wal-tabyīn* and the *al-Zar' wal-nakhl* (The Plantation and the Date Palm), al-Jāḥiẓ reports having received five thousand dinars.[19] If true, these were very high payments indeed; by comparison, a century later Abū al-Faraj al-Iṣbahānī (d. 356/967) is said to have received one thousand dinars from Sayf al-Dawlah for his monumental *Kitāb al-Aghānī* (thirty-three volumes in its printed edition).[20] Certainly, when assessing a work and deciding on the actual amount of the remuneration, the person to whom the work was dedicated would have given thought to the value of the book and to its potential reach; a superior work of widespread fame could, after all, contribute to the dedicatee's fame.[21]

The dedicatee is not usually mentioned in the text of the work itself.[22] Indeed, at times it is actually the *reader* al-Jāḥiẓ is directly addressing, as in 'I charge you, reader anxious for understanding or listener lending an attentive ear …'[23] In the first part of the extremely long introduction to the *Kitāb al-Ḥayawān* an anonymous person is consistently addressed: after the formulaic opening (the *basmalah*, the wishes, and so on), al-Jāḥiẓ presents a long list of his previous works, all of which his addressee apparently criticised. Al-Jāḥiẓ rehearses the objections of the addressee and then presents his defence. It is highly improbable that the dedicatee, namely, the vizier Ibn al-Zayyāt, is the one being directly or primarily addressed here: that would imply that Ibn al-Zayyāt had been the one to criticise practically all of al-Jāḥiẓ's books. This is unlikely as Ibn al-Zayyāt was a Mu'tazili who played an important role in implementing the general policies of the empire under the Mu'tazili caliphs al-Mu'taṣim and al-Wāthiq,[24] and the *Kitāb al-Ḥayawān* reflects strong Mu'tazili leanings. It would appear, rather, that al-Jāḥiẓ is now turning to the *reader(s)* of his books as such, and that the criticisms he describes as having been levelled against him are probably nothing more than a literary conceit. What al-Jāḥiẓ is doing here is reminding his readers about his earlier books, informing them about their content, and guarding the present book against further objections.

The difference between the person to whom a work is dedicated and the intended reader of the work is clear in Ibn Qutaybah's (d. 276/889)[25] introduction to the *Kitāb Adab al-kātib* (The State Secretary's Handbook), dedicated to the vizier Abū al-Ḥasan 'Ubayd Allāh ibn Yaḥyā ibn Khāqān (d. 263/877), according to the commentaries.[26] Ibn Qutaybah could be sure that 'Ubayd Allāh – himself formerly a secretary – had the same interest as he did in redressing the dire educational deficiencies of the secretaries. The two also shared religious convictions: both were (unlike al-Jāḥiẓ) orthodox Sunnis with an anti-Mu'tazili bent. Lecomte even thinks it probable that the *Kitāb Adab al-kātib* was a work commissioned by 'Ubayd Allāh and that, in return for having produced it, Ibn Qutaybah was appointed judge (*qāḍī*) in Dīnawar.[27] But it is clear from Ibn Qutaybah's statement to the effect in the introduction,[28] and also from the work overall, that the book is in particular addressed to the uneducated *kuttāb* (state secretaries) whose deficit in education will be helped by this (and other) books. The *kuttāb* are not, however, ever directly addressed in the introduction; when mention is made of them, it is always in the third person. Cheikh-Moussa is thus, in principle, correct when he observes that:[29]

> All of the medieval texts that have come to us with the patron-dedicatee identified are not solely directed to that individual, nor to the community at large, but to a small group, a class of privileged persons, the *Khāṣṣa*, who alone were capable of reading and understanding these written texts, texts which were often of a very high caliber.

The writings of al-Jāḥiẓ enjoyed great popularity, especially, as might be expected, during the Mu'tazili heyday (827–49); his works were coveted, and his audience extended all the way from the Islamic East to al-Andalus (Muslim Spain).[30] The caliph al-Ma'mūn, who had introduced Mu'tazilism as state dogma, held al-Jāḥiẓ in especially high esteem: having read al-Jāḥiẓ's books on the imamate, al-Ma'mūn is reported (by al-Jāḥiẓ) to have declared, 'This is a book which does not require the presence of the author (to be understood), and needs no advocate.'[31] High-ranking state administrators quickly recognised al-Jāḥiẓ's talents as a writer and consequently hoped he would disseminate the religious ideas to which they subscribed and explain these ideas to a large readership.[32] But even after the abolition of Mu'tazilism as state doctrine, al-Jāḥiẓ still had a great deal to offer patrons and the reading public. His pro-'Abbāsid and anti-Shu'ūbiyyah stance and his treatment of many subjects that were still topical continued to secure him the favour of the very highest-ranking individuals. The orthodox Sunni caliph al-Mutawakkil (ruled 232/847–247/861), for instance, who pursued an anti-Christian policy (starting in 235/850), was particularly enthusiastic about al-Jāḥiẓ's treatise *al-Radd 'alā al-Naṣārā* (Refutation of the Christians), for which he is said to have paid him a monthly pension.[33] It was probably for the likewise orthodox Sunni and anti-Mu'tazili vizier 'Ubayd Allāh ibn Yaḥyā ibn Khāqān that al-Jāḥiẓ composed his *Kitāb faṣl mā bayna al-'adāwah wal-ḥasad* (Book on distinguishing the difference between enmity and enviousness).[34] And the famous *Risālah ilā al-Fatḥ ibn Khāqān fī manāqib al-Turk* (Epistle to al-Fatḥ ibn Khāqān on the noble qualities of the Turks) is addressed to the state secretary, al-Fatḥ ibn Khāqān (d. 247/861)[35] who himself was of Turkic origin.

Al-Jāḥiẓ and Ibn Qutaybah: content and scope of their work

Adam Mez, the first European scholar to delve into the Islamic intellectual and cultural history of the ninth and tenth centuries, was rightly impressed by the thematic diversity of al-Jāḥiẓ's prose, noting that

> Jāḥiẓ writes about everything: from the school master to the Banū Hāshim, from thieves to lizards, from the attributes of God all the way to ribaldry on the wiles of women.[36]

Indeed, al-Jāḥiẓ evinced an interest in *all* social classes, and an interest not just in human beings, but also in plants, animals and the cosmos. This was something that al-Jāḥiẓ had brought to Arabic literature for the very first time, and on a large scale too.[37]

Al-Jāḥiẓ's counterpart was Ibn Qutaybah (d. 276/889).[38] Like al-Jāḥiẓ, he was not only a man of letters (*adīb*) but also a religious scholar (*'ālim*); however, unlike al-Jāḥiẓ, who was a Mu'tazili, Ibn Qutaybah was an orthodox Sunni. He was of Iranian origin, but in his literary works chose primarily to treat Arab-Islamic subjects: his comprehensive *Kitab 'Uyūn al-akhbār* (Book of the Wellsprings of Reports) and *Kitāb al-Ma'ārif* (Book of Knowledge) and his *Kitāb al-Shi'r wal-shu'arā'* (Book of Poetry and Poets) all perfectly illustrate this. All three are actual books and include detailed introductions. In the introduction to the *Kitāb al-Shi'r wal-shu'arā'*, Ibn Qutaybah characterises the work as follows for the reader:[39]

> This is a book I have composed about poets. I have spoken in it about them, about their time, their merits, the circumstances that occasioned their verses, their tribes, the names of their ancestors …

Ibn Qutaybah was not, it is true, as many-sided as al-Jāḥiẓ, and he did not write about quite as many subjects, but this is not to say that he was narrow. In the ten chapters of his encyclopaedic *Kitāb 'Uyūn al-akhbār*, he covers government, war, sovereignty, character, knowledge and eloquence, asceticism, friendship, polite requests, food, and women. But he writes about these from a perspective different from al-Jāḥiẓ's, and with a different orientation: as he says in the introductions to both the *Kitāb 'Uyūn al-akhbār* and the *Kitāb al-Ma'ārif*, he wants to impart to the people knowledge which will be useful for them, and to inform them about correct behaviour.[40] With Ibn Qutaybah the moral aspect comes clearly to the fore. At the beginning of the *Kitāb 'Uyūn al-akhbār* he writes:

> This book, though it does not deal with the Qur'ān, Sunna, religious laws, and the science of the permissible and the prohibited, does indeed point out lofty things, guides to noble morals, discourages baseness, [and] guards against ugliness ...[41]

Audience

Al-Jāḥiẓ's ecumenical interest was a function not solely of his limitless curiosity, but also of his awareness of the interests of his readership. During his lifetime, the intellectual horizons of the educated classes had expanded enormously, thanks, among other things, to translations of the classical (Hellenistic) heritage, to the rise of mysticism and, notably, to the circulation of such ideas as Mu'tazilism. In the ninth century there arose a broad and growing readership with diverse interests and commitments. While Ibn al-Muqaffa' had written exclusively for courtiers and secretaries, and Ibn Qutaybah would write mainly for the *khāṣṣah* (the elite), al-Jāḥiẓ expressly states several times that in addition to the *khāṣṣah*, his target audience includes the *'āmmah* (lit. 'the common folk'). This can be seen most clearly in the *Kitāb al-Bayān wal-tabyīn*, where he attributes to the caliph al-Ma'mūn the following statement about his book on the imamate: '(its appeal is) both to common people and kings (i.e. caliphs), to the masses and the elite (*sūqī mulūkī 'āmmī khāṣṣī*)'.[42] The term *'āmmah* here cannot mean the uneducated populace; al-Jāḥiẓ himself offers a clarification:[43]

> When you hear me refer to the common folk (*'awāmm*), I do not mean the peasants, the rabble, the artisans, and the sellers (of goods), nor do I mean the mountain Kurds ... The common folk from among our people ... are a class whose intellectual faculties and personal qualities are superior to those of other peoples, even if they do not attain the level of our own elite (*khāṣṣah*).

This stratum has been described by Shawkat M. Toorawa as a 'sub-elite',[44] a group that 'would include, but would not be limited to, merchants, lawyers, aspiring littérateurs, the wealthy, and foreign and visiting scholars: in short, the literate, or would-be literate, bourgeoisie, and the intellectuals'.[45]

'Adab of the Jāḥiẓian type'

Al-Jāḥiẓ wrote, then, for a wide audience extending from the caliph to merchants, from the upper class to the sub-elite. He accommodated their needs and expectations in his politico-religious writings as well as in various genres of *adab* (literature for refined learning), two of which he himself created. Pellat termed these genres 'literary *adab* of the Jāḥiẓian type' and 'quasi-scientific *adab* of the Jāḥiẓian type'[46] though he admitted that the borders between the two were fluid. The aim of the new genre of literary *adab*, like earlier *adab*, was not only to inform, but also to entertain. Unlike earlier *adab*, however, al-Jāḥiẓ's drew less from the Iranian heritage – from which his predecessors, Ibn al-Muqaffa' and Sahl ibn Hārūn almost exclusively derived their subject matter – than from the indigenous Arab heritage.

Originally from Basra, al-Jāḥiẓ had heard the itinerant Bedouin who imparted tribal traditions, stories and rare words to the inquisitive scholars at the Mirbad.[47] He had also listened to the *masjidiyyūn*, those dalliers at the mosques who discussed and had explanations for everything under the sun.[48] And he had attended the lectures of the philologists in his home town, al-Aṣma'ī and Abū 'Ubaydah, and the lectures of the learned transmitters of Basra and Kufa, and later Baghdad.[49] Al-Jāḥiẓ was thus very familiar with the Arab tradition – what it lacked was its own literature; the tradition had hitherto only been cultivated and transmitted in gatherings and in academic circles, in talks, in lectures and in discussions. This is not to suggest that no part of the tradition would not otherwise have been committed to writing, but that what was written was only to be found in the lecture notebooks of the philologists and in the notes taken by their students, all only intended for private use.[50]

What interested al-Jāḥiẓ, and what he supposed would fascinate his readers, were less the special grammatical and lexical questions discussed in detail by his teachers than those aspects of the tradition that had literary and artistic value.[51] From the material that al-Jāḥiẓ collected and voraciously read, he selected the most interesting reports and the most amusing anecdotes in order to fit them into his works. He gave this material new shape, putting it into a suitable framework, commenting on it with his signature wit and irony, and, above all, presenting it in a brilliant style.[52] In short, he prepared it *for a reading public*. The most important and most representative work of this type of Jāḥiẓian *adab* is the *Kitāb al-Bayān wal-tabyīn*.

Al-Jāḥiẓ also accommodated the scientific interests of his audience. As we pointed out above, the intellectual horizons of the educated classes expanded enormously during al-Jāḥiẓ's lifetime, thanks, among other things, to translations of the classical (Hellenistic) heritage, to the rise of mysticism and, especially, to the circulation of such ideas as Mu'tazilism. The Mu'tazilis were not only interested in theological and political problems, but also in the entire cosmos, the real world and the laws of nature.[53] They formulated 'a substantial system for explaining the world and mankind', a system that included *inter alia* the conception of bodies as agglomerates of atoms, the distinction between substance and accidence, the nature of fire, and reflection on how to define humanity.[54] Literary and rhetorical questions were taken up as well.

Al-Jāḥiẓ treated all these themes, not in a dry or dull academic way, but in his characteristically entertaining, playful, never tedious style, and often with mordant wit. This he did in the other genre of *adab* he created, one that has been described by Pellat as 'scholarly' or 'quasi-scientific', the most important and most representative work of which is the *Kitāb al-Ḥayawān*.

Earlier Mu'tazili 'literature' and the works of al-Jāḥiẓ

As was the case with other Muslim scholars, for a long time the Mu'tazilis did not write books for a reading public; their only 'books' (*kutub*) and booklets (*ṣuḥuf*) were 'literature of the school, for the school', intended for oral recitation, not for written publication. This is why there is hardly a Mu'tazili work extant in its original form before al-Jāḥiẓ.[55] Al-Jāḥiẓ's works do, however, contain many quotations from lost works by earlier Mu'tazili authors, such as al-Jāḥiẓ's celebrated teacher, al-Naẓẓām (d. 220/835 or later), who is said to have written thirty-eight 'books'.[56] Only a few fragments of his works remain, most of them from his *Kitāb al-Nakth* (Book of the Breach), and al-Jāḥiẓ is the earliest author to quote from it, in his *Kitāb al-Futyā* (Book of Legal Verdicts).[57]

The Mu'tazili Bishr ibn al-Mu'tamir (d. 210/825 or later)[58] is said to have written over twenty 'books', of which not one independent work has survived. Only a few fragments have come to us, among which the text of a *ṣaḥīfah* (i.e. a booklet or aide-mémoire) on rhetoric.[59] It is cited in different works of later authors in versions sometimes greatly divergent from one another; once again, the earliest author to cite it is al-Jāḥiẓ.[60] The following quotation from the *Kitāb al-Bayān* shows that al-Jāḥiẓ does not simply string together excerpts and quotes from earlier works but, rather, puts them in their context, interrupting the quoted account with commentary. Furthermore – and importantly – it provides us with a glimpse of what the 'publication' of books and booklets in the generations *before* al-Jāḥiẓ was like:

> Bishr ibn al-Mu'tamir passed by the *khaṭīb* [Friday sermon-giver] Ibrāhīm ibn Jabalah … while he was instructing the young people in rhetoric. Bishr stopped, and Ibrāhīm thought he had done so to learn (from his lecture), or that he was a spy … whereupon Bishr gave them a booklet (*ṣaḥīfah*) he had himself composed and put together. The beginning of this treatise was: [*A part of the text follows*]. Bishr reported: 'When it (the booklet) was read to Ibrāhīm, he said to me: 'I need this (what you said) more than these young fellows!'' [*A commentary by al-Jāḥiẓ follows*.][61]

The 'publishing' of a written work in this generation consisted in its having been presented in the *study circle*, usually – as was probably the case here too – by a student. Al-Jāḥiẓ, and others besides, would have written down the text during the lecture or borrowed either the author's or a student's manuscript in order to copy it. By including this treatise (and many others besides) in his *Kitāb al-Bayān*, al-Jāḥiẓ made it accessible to a wide reading public. Indeed, one important reason for the success of al-Jāḥiẓ's books may well have been the fact that he made many topics and ideas – aesthetic, theological and quasi-scientific – hitherto exclusively available in academic and study circles as lectures and discussions, now accessible *for the first time* to a wide reading public, *khāṣṣah* and *'āmmah* alike.

The ninth century was an era of bibliophiles. That this phenomenon would arise in the ninth century is no coincidence: this was the century when large numbers of actual books came into existence and in which a broad readership arose. Two of the greatest and most famous lovers of books at this time were al-Jāḥiẓ and the state secretary al-Fatḥ ibn Khāqān (to whom al-Jāḥiẓ dedicated his 'Epistle on the noble qualities of the Turks').[62]

It is reported that al-Fatḥ would always have a book on him, in his sleeve or boot, and that he would read even when he was in the company of the caliph, or when he went to the latrine.[63] Al-Jāḥiẓ was not all that different; Ibn al-Nadīm reports:[64]

> Al-Jāḥiẓ never let a book pass through his hands without reading it from cover to cover, no matter what it was. He would even rent the shops of the booksellers (*warrāqūn*) and spend his nights there, poring over them.

And at the beginning of the *Kitāb al-Ḥayawān*, al-Jāḥiẓ spends pages and pages singing the praises of books,[65] averring that one of their virtues is that 'You will get more knowledge out of one (book) in a month than you could acquire from men's mouths in an age'.[66] In the ninth century, in the field of *adab* at least, 'the transition from a predominantly oral and aural culture to an increasingly textual, book-based, writerly one' had definitively taken place.[67]

Notes

1 See Cl. Huart-A. Grohmann, *EI*², s.v. Kāghad; J. Pedersen, *The Arabic Book*, tr. G. French, ed. R. Hillenbrand (Princeton, 1984), pp. 60 ff.; J. Bloom, *Paper before Print: the History and Impact of Paper in the Islamic World* (New Haven, 2001), pp. 1–45; and see further below.

2 See Toorawa, *Ibn Abī Ṭāhir Ṭayfūr*, *passim*, and esp. pp. 1–19, 123–4, 128–9.

3 *Fihrist*², pp. 133 ff.; M. Zakeri, *EI*², s.v. Sahl b. Hārūn.

4 This subject matter was reworked and versified in the eleventh century by the Persian poet 'Unṣurī; see J. T. P. de Bruijn, *EI*², s.v. 'Unṣurī.

5 al-Jāḥiẓ, *al-Bayān wal-tabyīn*, vol. 1, p. 52.

6 al-Jāḥiẓ, *Rasā'il*, vol. 1, p. 351 (where Salm should read Sahl) = al-Mas'ūdī, *Kitāb al-Tanbīh wal-ishrāf*, ed. M. J. De Goeje (Leiden, 1893–4), p. 76; *cf. EI*², s.v. Sahl b. Hārūn.

7 See Ch. Pellat, 'Ǧāḥiẓiana III. Essai d'inventaire de l'oeuvre Ǧāḥizienne', *Arabica* 3 (1956), pp. 147–80; Pellat, 'Nouvel essai d'inventaire de l'oeuvre Ǧāḥizienne', *Arabica* 31 (1984), pp. 117–64. Al-Jāḥiẓ was also a Mu'tazili theologian and the author of important politico-religious works, for the most part lost. See below; see also Viktūr Shalḥat, *al-Naz'ah al-kalāmiyyah fī uslūb al-Jāḥiẓ* (Cairo, 1964).

8 Two of al-Jāḥiẓ's copyists are known by name. For Abū Yaḥyā Zakariyyā' ibn Yaḥyā ibn Sulaymān, see *Fihrist*², p. 209; for Abū al-Qāsim 'Abd al-Wahhāb ibn 'Īsā ibn Abī Ḥayyah, see al-Sam'ānī, *Kitāb al-Ansāb*, 13 vols, ed. A. Mu'īd Khān (Hyderabad, Deccan, 1962–1982), vol. 13, pp. 303 ff., and van Ess, *Theologie und Gesellschaft*, vol. 4, p. 225.

9 Werkmeister, *Quellenuntersuchungen*, pp. 78 ff.

10 A. Arazi and H. Ben-Shammay, *EI*², s.v. Risāla.

11 *Fihrist*², p. 211.

12 Al-Jāḥiẓ, *Rasā'il*, vol. 1, pp. 231–278.

13 *Cf.* A. Cheikh-Moussa, 'La négation d'Eros, ou Le *'ishq* d'après deux épitres d'al-Ǧâḥiẓ', *Studia Islamica* 72 (1990), p. 83.

14 See P. Freimark, 'Das Vorwort als literarische Form in der arabischen Literatur', doctoral thesis, Münster, 1967, pp. 36 ff., 115; al-Jāḥiẓ, *Rasā'il*, vol. 1, p. 177; *cf.* Khalidi, "The Boasts", p. 3. Similar formulations are also to be found in the *Kitāb al-Bukhalā'* (The Book of Misers).

15 See e.g. Ibn Qutaybah's introduction to his *Kitāb Ta'wīl mukhtalif al-ḥadīth*: 'You have written to inform me how you noticed the attacks carried out by the theologians (*ahl al-kalām*) against the traditionists (*ahl al-ḥadīth*) … You have requested that I undertake this task …, and I have thus proceeded to do so to the extent of my knowledge and ability'. G. Lecomte, *Le Traité des Divergences du Ḥadīth d'Ibn Qutayba*. Traduction du *Kitāb Ta'wīl mukhtalif al-ḥadīth* (Damascus, 1962), pp. 1, 12. *Cf.* Freimark, *Das Vorwort*, pp. 36 ff.

16 *Fihrist*², p. 210; D. Sourdel, *EI*², s.v. Ibn al-Zayyāt; Ch. Pellat, *EI*², s.v. Aḥmad b. Abī Du'ād.

17 Pedersen, *The Arabic Book*, p. 40.

18 al-Jāḥiẓ, *Kitāb al-Ḥayawān*, vol. 5, p. 156; *cf.* Pellat, *Life and Works*, p. 165.

19 *Fihrist*², p. 210.

20 Yāqūt, *Irshād al-arīb*, vol. 5, p. 150. The reliability of this report is, however, open to question; see H. Kilpatrick, *Making the Great Book of Songs. Compilation and the author's craft in Abū l-Faraj al-Iṣbahānī's Kitāb al-aghānī* (London, New York, 2003), pp. 19 ff. Abū al-Faraj says in the introduction that the impetus to write the book was the order of an unnamed, high-ranking personality (*ra'īs*): see *Aghānī*, vol. 1, p. 4; *cf.* Kilpatrick, *Making the Great Book of Songs*, p. 28.

21 Cheikh-Moussa, 'La négation', p. 84.

22 *Cf. ibid.*, p. 83.

23 al-Jāḥiẓ, *Kitāb al-Ḥayawān*, vol. 3, p. 298; *cf.* Pellat, *Life and Works*, p. 152.

24 D. Sourdel, *EI*², s.v. Ibn al- Zayyāt.

25 G. Lecomte, *EI*², s.v. Ibn Ḳutayba; Lecomte, *Ibn Qutayba. L'homme, son oeuvre, ses idées* (Damascus, 1965).

26 An Abū al-Ḥasan is indeed addressed early in the work: see Ibn Qutaybah, *Kitāb Adab al-kātib*, ed. M. Grünert (Leiden, 1900), p. 6, note *b*.
27 Lecomte, *Ibn Qutayba*, pp. 32 ff.
28 Ibn Qutaybah, *Kitāb Adab al-kātib*, pp. 2–3.
29 Cheikh-Moussa, 'La négation', p. 84.
30 Yāqūt, *Irshād al-arīb*, vol. 6, pp. 72, 75.
31 al-Jāḥiẓ, *al-Bayān wal-tabyīn*, vol. 3, p. 375; *cf*. Pellat, *Life and Works*, pp. 108–9.
32 See Pellat, *Life and Works*, p. 5, and Montgomery, 'al-Jahiz', pp. 237–9.
33 See the letter of al-Fatḥ, quoted in Pellat, *Life and Works*, pp. 7–8.
34 al-Jāḥiẓ, *Rasā'il*, vol. 1, p. 335.
35 Ibid., vol. 1, pp. 5–86; O. Pinto, *EI*², s.v. al-Fatḥ b. Khāḳān; Pellat, *Life and Works*, pp. 7–8.
36 A. Mez, *Die Renaissance des Islam* (Heidelberg, 1922), p. 229 = *The Renaissance of Islam*, tr. S. Khuda Bakhsh and D. S. Margoliouth (London, 1937), p. 240.
37 Another prolific writer was Ibn Abī al-Dunyā (d. 281/894) sixty of whose works survive: see R. Weipert and St. Weninger, 'Die erhaltenen Werke des Ibn Abī d-Dunyā', *ZDMG* 146 (1996), pp. 415–55.
38 G. Lecomte, *EI*², s.v. Ibn Ḳutayba; Lecomte, *Ibn Qutayba*.
39 Ibn Qotaiba, *Introduction*, pp. 1–2.
40 Ibn Qutaybah, *'Uyūn al-akhbār*, 4 vols (Cairo, 1925–30), vol. 1, pp. ix and ff.; Ibn Qutaybah, *Kitāb al-Ma'ārif*, ed. T. 'Ukāshah (Cairo, ²1969), pp. 1 ff.
41 Ibn Qutaybah, *'Uyūn al-akhbār*, vol. 1, p. x.
42 al-Jāḥiẓ, *al-Bayān wal-tabyīn*, vol. 3, p. 375; *cf*. Pellat, *Life and Works*, p. 109; *Fihrist*², p. 209.
43 al-Jāḥiẓ, *al-Bayān wal-tabyīn*, vol. 1, p. 137.
44 Toorawa, *Ibn Abī Ṭāhir Ṭayfūr*, p. 54. See R. P. Mottahedeh, *Loyalty and Leadership in Early Islamic Society* (Princeton, 1980), for a discussion of the notion of sub-elite.
45 *Cf*. Toorawa, *Ibn Abī Ṭāhir Ṭayfūr*, pp. 1–2: 'The new readership expanded to include landlords and landowners, merchants and entrepreneurs, judges and jurists, physicians, poets and littérateurs, teachers, and of course, other scholars.'
46 Pellat, *Life and Works*, pp. 18 ff.
47 For the Mirbad, the celebrated caravan stopover and market outside town, see Pellat, *Le milieu basrien*, pp. 244 ff.
48 For the *masjidiyyūn* in Basra, see *ibid*.
49 al-Jāḥiẓ, *Kitāb al-Bayān wal-tabyīn*, vol. 4, pp. 23 ff.; *cf*. Pellat, *Life and Works*, p. 109.
50 *Cf*. Schoeler, *The Oral and the Written*, pp. 45–61, esp. pp. 45, 53–4.
51 al-Jāḥiẓ, *al-Bayān wal-tabyīn*, vol. 4, p. 24; *cf*. Pellat, *Life and Works*, p. 110.
52 *Cf*. Pellat, *Life and Works*, p. 19.
53 'The author is continually at pains to demonstrate that everything in nature has its uses and is evidence of the existence and wisdom of God': see al-Jāḥiẓ, *Kitāb al-Ḥayawān*, vol. 2, pp. 109–10; *cf*. Pellat, *Life and Works*, pp. 141–2.
54 *Cf*. D. Gimaret, *EI*², s.v. 'Mu'tazila'.
55 I am grateful to Professor Josef van Ess for kindly informing me that one work by Ḍirār ibn 'Amr (d. ca. 180/795), the *Kitāb al-Tahrīsh*, appears to have survived in a Yemeni collection copied in 540/1145–6, and for having brought H. A. Qummī's article, 'Kitābī kalāmī az Ḍirār ibn 'Amr', in *Kitāb-i māh-i din* 89 (1383–4 H Shamsiyyah), pp. 4–13, to my attention.

56 *Fihrist*², p. 206; van Ess, *Theologie*, vol. 3, pp. 296–418; van Ess, *EI*², s.v. al-Naẓẓām.
57 J. van Ess, *EI*², s.v. 'al-Naẓẓām'; van Ess, *Das Kitāb an-Nakṯ des Naẓẓām und seine Rezeption im Kitāb al-Futyā des Ǧāḥiẓ* (Göttingen, 1972).
58 *Fihrist*², pp. 184–5 and 205; *cf.* van Ess, *Theologie*, vol. 3, pp. 107–31.
59 van Ess, *Theologie*, vol. 3, pp. 112–14.
60 Ibid., vol. 3, p. 113; al-Jāḥiẓ, *al-Bayān wal-tabyīn*, vol. 1, pp. 135, 136.
61 al-Jāḥiẓ, *al-Bayān wal-tabyīn*, vol. 1, p. 135.
62 For the following, *cf.* Toorawa, *Ibn Abī Ṭāhir Ṭayfūr*, p. 25.
63 *Fihrist*², pp. 130, 208.
64 Ibid., pp. 130, 208. *Cf.* Toorawa, *Ibn Abī Ṭāhir Ṭayfūr*, p. 25.
65 al-Jāḥiẓ, *Kitāb al-Ḥayawān*, vol. 1, p. 48 ff. See S. Günther, 'Praise to the Books! Al-Jāḥiẓ and Ibn Qutayba on the Excellence of the Written Word in Medieval Islam', *JSAI* 32 (2006), pp. 125–43.
66 al-Jāḥiẓ, *Kitāb al-Ḥayawān*, vol. 1, p. 51; *cf.* Pellat, *Life and Works*, p. 132.
67 Toorawa, *Ibn Abī Ṭāhir Ṭayfūr*, p. 1.

8

Listening to books, or reading them?

In the ninth century, it was not only men of letters (*adīb*, pl. *udabā'*) who were writing actual books. Increasingly, many scholars also took it upon themselves to continue the pioneering work of Sībawayhi, giving their material a definitive shape, and with a readership in mind, just as the men of letters did; in this way, they too produced actual books. To be sure, many still followed the traditional method, reciting or dictating in the scholarly sessions and teaching circles, sometimes without even using notes, and redacting no works intended for 'public release'. The philologist Ibn al-A'rābī was one such scholar, so too the lexicographer Ibn Durayd (d. 321/933), who continued to 'publish' his *Jamharah* (The Great Collection) by dictating it to his students;[1] of it, Ibn al-Nadīm reports:[2]

> The manuscripts of the *Kitāb al-Jamharah fī 'ilm al-lughah* (The Great Collection in the Science of Language) all differ, and the book has numerous additions and omissions because (the author) dictated it from memory, in Fars, then in Baghdad.

The antiquarian and historian al-Madā'inī appears to have dictated his books too; in any event, he published them in the context of his teaching.[3] This was therefore an example of 'literature of the school, for the school, intended for recitation'. Recall how al-Mas'ūdī characterised this scholar's methods:[4]

> It is true that Abū al-Ḥasan al-Madā'inī was a prolific writer, but it was his practice to transmit what he had heard [to auditors, students] but … al-Jāḥiẓ (on the other hand) composed books according to the best arrangement.

Al-Madā'inī's principal transmitter, the historian 'Umar ibn Shabbah (d. 264/877), used the same method as his teacher.[5] We owe the survival of one of 'Umar ibn Shabbah's numerous works, the voluminous *Ta'rīkh al-Madinah al-munawwarah* (History of Medina the Luminous), to the zealousness of one of his students, who took notes during his teacher's instruction. This student writes:[6]

> Abū Zayd ('Umar ibn Shabbah) transmitted to us, saying: This [i.e. what follows] is not from what is in my notebook: 'X transmitted to us …'

What 'Umar ibn Shabbah's disciple was writing down – that is to say, the text of 'Umar's book as we have it in its published form today – included not only the written text of the teacher, but also supplementary material that he had added orally.

In the field of Ḥadīth in particular, most books remained 'literature of the school, for the school', and were not intended to be published for a wide readership. This was the case for the *Musnad* of Aḥmad ibn Ḥanbal, which was not given its final shape until two generations after the death of its compiler.[7] It was also the case for the *Muṣannaf* of Ibn Abī Shaybah, who says at the beginning of several of the work's chapters, 'This is what I know by heart [or: have memorised] from the Prophet.'[8] The compiler is thus characterising his magnum opus as a *hypomnēma*.

Historiography

Other scholars, on the other hand, recognised the advantages of actual books. As we have seen, the historian Ibn Hishām reworked and edited the material of Ibn Isḥāq transmitted to him by al-Bakkā'ī relating to the life of the Prophet. His biography of Muḥammad, the *Kitāb Sīrat rasūl Allāh*, is the fruit of these efforts. But the most eminent historian to have given his compilation a definitive shape is without a doubt al-Ṭabarī (d. 310/923).[9] His *Ta'rīkh al-rusul wal-mulūk* (History of Prophets and Rulers) is one of the most important universal histories of Islam. Its detailed introduction is followed by an account of the creation of the world, the history of the patriarchs and prophets of ancient Israel, the rulers of Israel and of the ancient Persians up to the history of the Sasanids. For its sections dealing with the career of Muḥammad, al-Ṭabarī most often relies on the reports of Ibn Isḥāq, principally those transmitted by his own teacher, Ibn Ḥumayd, who in turn reports from Salamah ibn al-Faḍl.[10] After Muḥammad's emigration to Medina in 622 (*Hijrah*), the chronicle is organised in the form of annals, which provides a framework into which al-Ṭabarī is then able to insert corresponding traditions, almost always with their chain of authorities. The work then covers the epoch of the caliphs, with very great detail on the period of conquests, and ends in al-Ṭabarī's own time. Occasionally, al-Ṭabarī adds personal observations, or else points out divergences in the transmissions he cites for a given event. After identifying the year in question, he typically provides an overview of the events about which he will be reporting.

With Ibn Hishām, al-Ṭabarī and other historians of the ninth and tenth centuries, historiography – which up to this point had been confined to instruction dispensed by teachers, to these teachers' private notebooks, to the notes taken by their students or, at best, to a 'literature of the school, for the school' – became real *literature*. From now on, the publication of books was no longer exclusively the outcome of recitation in a scholarly context; it spread by means of standard written transmission, making books accessible to a large and receptive readership.

Literary history and poetry

It was also at this time, in the ninth and tenth centuries, that poetic texts on the one hand, and narrative materials and historico-biographical information on the other, were definitively edited. Poems were edited in specialised collections (*dīwān*, pl. *dawāwīn*) or in anthologies such as the *Ḥamāsah* ([Poetry of] Bravery) of Abū Tammām (d. 231/845).[11] And historical and biographical material (including poetic texts) was definitively redacted in major works such as the *Kitāb al-Aghānī* (Book of Songs) of Abū al-Faraj al-Iṣbahānī (d. 356/967).[12]

The problem of the *Kitāb al-Aghānī*'s sources in general, and those sources' sources in particular, has garnered a lot of scholarly attention. Since Abū al-Faraj frequently declares that he is copying what follows from the book of so-and-so (*nasakhtu min kitāb fulān*), without specifying the book's title, the possibility of a historico-biographical 'literature' dating from before Abū al-Faraj – i.e. earlier books containing the biographies of poets – has been raised and has been of great interest to researchers.

This question can best be addressed by turning to the observations of three scholars who have taken it up: Régis Blachère, Leon Zolondek and Manfred Fleischhammer.[13] The major written sources of the *Kitāb al-Aghānī* have been identified by these scholars; they have been called 'collector sources' by Zolondek, and date from the end of the eighth century up to about the middle of the ninth century. The authors of these 'collector sources' include 'Umar ibn Shabbah, al-Madā'inī, Ibn Mihrawayhi and Ibn al-Marzubān.

The point that appears to have escaped the attention of scholars researching this question is that the majority of these works form part of 'literature of the school, for the school' – they were not composed as *syngrammata*, but were 'intended for recitation' during teaching. For this reason, none survived as an independent work. These 'books' were transmitted to Abū al-Faraj by his informants in one of two ways, either through audition, or – and this occurred very often – through written transmission (*kitābah*, *wijādah*). This is why Abū al-Faraj often says, 'I found/read in the book of so-and-so (*wajadtu/qara'tu fī kitāb fulān*), …', or 'I copied from the book of so-and-so' (*nasakhtu min kitāb fulān*) …', and so on, and why Abū al-Faraj rarely gives titles of works.

The merit of Abū al-Faraj is comparable to that of Ibn Hishām and al-Ṭabarī, in that he gave definitive form to his material and that he edited it with a public readership in mind. In the introduction to the *Kitāb al-Aghānī*, he speaks explicitly about his reader and describes, among other things, the method he intends to use to make the reading experience pleasant for the reader.[14] The impact on Abū al-Faraj of the methods of the men of letters, al-Jāḥiẓ in particular, is obvious.

As for the definitive recension of ancient and Umayyad poetry into *dīwāns*, this was undertaken by 'editor-transmitters', of whom the most important is al-Sukkarī (d. 257/888).[15] His *dīwāns* of Imru' al-Qays, Ḥassān ibn Thābit, al-Ḥuṭay'ah, al-Akhṭal and others survive and are available in printed editions. Al-Sukkarī is also the 'editor' of the only tribal *dīwān* to have come down to us, that of the Banū Hudhayl. The chain of transmitters of this *dīwān* appears at the beginning of the manuscript as shown below.[16]

The transmitters of the generations before al-Sukkarī did not generally give definitive shape to the *dīwāns* they worked on. Their copies of collections of poems were intended, rather, to be recited, studied and commented upon in the context of teaching. This was even the case for al-Sukkarī's most important teacher, Muḥammad ibn Ḥabīb (d. 245/860),[17] who left to posterity no *dīwān* that he himself edited. Ibn al-Sikkīt (d. 244/858), also of the generation before al-Sukkarī, is an exception, however, not only from the point of view of chronology, but also from the point of view of his methodology in redacting poetic material: he effectively occupies 'an intermediate position between on the one hand al-Aṣma'ī, Abū 'Ubaydah and some others who initiated the first work of methodical arrangement, and on the other hand al-Sukkarī, who completed the process'.[18] A few *dīwāns* edited by Ibn al-Sikkīt survive.

It is interesting to note that the verb *ṣana'a*, in the meaning 'to edit, to make an edition', is used by Ibn al-Nadīm in the *Fihrist*, his comprehensive catalogue

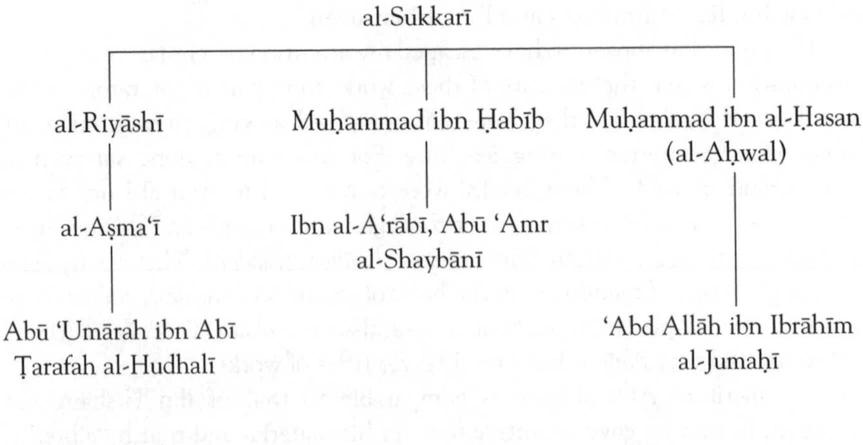

The chain of transmitters of the tribal *dīwān* of the Banū Hudhayl

of all written works in Arabic, only to characterise the work of al-Sukkarī and later editor-transmitters. The technical term used to describe the activities of al-Sukkarī's predecessors – sometimes also applied, it is true, to al-Sukkarī himself – is *'amila*, in the meaning 'to arrange'. Thus Ibn al-Nadīm writes:[19]

> Abū 'Amr (ibn al-'Alā'), al-Aṣma'ī, Khālid ibn Kulthūm and Muḥammad ibn Ḥabīb *transmitted* them (*sc.* Imru' al-Qays's poems) (*rawāhu*). Abū Sa'īd al-Sukkarī made an excellent edition (*ṣana'ahu … fa-jawwada*) based on the ensemble of the transmitted versions (*riwāyāt*); Abū al-'Abbās al-Aḥwal did not complete his edition (*ṣana'ahu wa-lam yatimmahu*). As for Ibn al-Sikkīt, he arranged these poems (*'amilahu*).

The recension of the *dīwāns* of contemporary poets, the *muḥdathūn* (sing. *muḥdath*, 'modern'), also began in the ninth century, and continued in earnest in the tenth century. It is important to note that in this period poets usually did not edit their own *dīwāns*;[20] that move did not became normative until the first half of the eleventh century when Abū al-'Alā' al-Ma'arrī (d. 449/1058) and, somewhat later, al-Ḥarīrī (d. 516/1122), to name just two, edited their own works of poetry and prose with a view to publishing them.[21] Most of the ninth and tenth century 'modern' poets still continued to entrust their poems to their transmitters or to leave them to posterity in some other way: Ḥamzah al-Iṣfahānī, one of the redactors of Abū Nuwās's *dīwān*, notes:[22]

> The Banū Naybakht report that the mother of Abū Nuwās, Jullabān, had in her possession her son's inheritance … and that among the things he left behind was a repository containing notebooks (*dafātir*), bundles of writings (*adābir*) and (rolls of) papyrus (*qarāṭīs*) on which were copies of his poems.

Ḥamzah al-Iṣfahānī, relying on a chain of authorities, informs us that a certain Ibrāhīm ibn Maḥbūb had in his possession a notebook (*daftar*) that contained hunting poems (*ṭardiyyāt*) of Abū Nuwās, dictated and signed by the poet himself.[23] It was the editor-transmitters of the ninth century and the men of letters of the tenth century who gave the poetry of Abū Nuwās its definitive form. Ibn al-Sikkīt is reported to have arranged the *dīwān* and al-Sukkarī is said to have done the same but not to have finished it:[24]

> Among the scholars (who formalised the *dīwān* of Abū Nuwās in written form) is Abū Yūsuf Ya'qūb ibn al-Sikkīt. He commented on the poems (*fassarahu*) in about 800 sheets and arranged them according to 10 genres. Abu Sa'īd al-Sukkarī also arranged them, but did not complete his work.

Today, we actually have recensions of Abū Nuwās's *dīwān* produced by *littérateurs* (*ahl al-adab*) of the tenth century, notably those of Abū Bakr al-Ṣūlī (d. 335/946) and Ḥamzah al-Iṣfahānī (d. 360/970).[25]

Ḥadīth collections and handbooks

In the domain of Ḥadīth too, compilers could no longer ignore the fact that books, often of quite considerable length, were increasingly being copied and disseminated through writing. Like al-Jāḥiẓ, the traditionist al-Bukhārī engaged a scribe by the name of Abū Ja'far Muḥammad ibn Abī Ḥātim to copy the *Ṣaḥīḥ*;[26] and Muslim ibn al-Ḥajjāj, aware of the fact that his *Ṣaḥīḥ* would have a readership, wrote an 'Introduction' to his collection.[27] Little by little, the Ḥadīth scholars themselves ceased to oppose the written dissemination of their Ḥadīth collections – as long as the text had been read and verified in the presence of the author or in the presence of an authorised transmitter.

The first handbooks of Arabic literature appeared in the ninth century. We mentioned in Chapter 6 that Abū 'Ubayd had written two handbooks in the field of lexicography, the *Gharīb al-muṣannaf* and the *Gharīb al-ḥadīth*; another work of this type, by the same author, was the *Kitāb al-Amthāl* (Book of Proverbs).[28] These three books inspired commentaries, supplements, epitomes and more, which clearly shows the fundamentally written character of these works; the 'Book' of Sībawayhi, it will be remembered, had a similar history. The *Kitāb al-Nabāt* (Book of Plants) of Abū Ḥanīfah al-Dīnawarī is also a handbook,[29] as is Ibn Qutaybah's celebrated *Kitāb Adab al-kātib* (The State Secretary's Handbook). The genesis of books of this type is also a reflection of the needs of a public readership.

The proliferation of handbooks – and of books generally – accessible to anyone resulted in people becoming less and less concerned with requiring transmission through audition. If there were enough books, why attend the scholars' lectures? But many authors, including Abū 'Ubayd, were reproached for having abandoned the 'search of knowledge' through audition. Abū al-Ṭayyib al-Lughawī describes Abū 'Ubayd as 'an author skilled in the composition of (actual) books, but one who possessed (only) little transmission'. Later in the same notice on Abū 'Ubayd, Abū al-Ṭayyib writes:[30]

> The people of Basra have noted that the majority of what he [Abū 'Ubayd] reported from their scholars is not through audition (*samā'*), but comes from 'books' (*kutub*). He was given copies of his book, *al-Gharīb al-muṣannaf*, and he did not have the slightest idea about (how to apply) the desinential inflection!

The point of the reproach (which may, admittedly, simply be a malicious accusation) is this: because Abū 'Ubayd hadn't 'heard' the texts compiled in his book from the mouths of teachers but was 'content' simply to copy from circulating notebooks, he was consequently incapable of correctly reading the texts in his own book.

The reaction to the abandoning of transmission through audition

It was inevitable that a negative reaction would develop regarding the abandoning of transmission through audition. Ibn Qutaybah, himself the author of a large number of actual books including at least one manual, gave great importance to audition. In his *Kitāb al-Shiʿr wal-shuʿarāʾ* (Book of Poetry and Poets), he writes:[31]

> Every science must be transmitted through audition (*muḥtāj ilā al-samāʿ*) and this need is nowhere greater than in the religious sciences, followed by poetry, because of its unusual expressions, dialectal varieties, unfamiliar language, names of trees, plants, places and waterholes. If you have not heard them pronounced by someone, you will be incapable of distinguishing between the place names *shābah* and *sāyah* in the poetry of the Hudhayl tribe.

Ibn Qutyaybah cites many other examples to show that 'people who misplace the diacritic points and who derive their knowledge from notebooks' (*al-muṣaḥḥifūn wal-ākhidhūn ʿan al-dafātir*) commit such serious mistakes because they have not benefited from transmission through audition.[32] This is a perfectly reasonable argument, given the fact that Arabic was habitually written without vowels and often without diacritic points, and was therefore ambiguous. The coexistence of transmissions through audition and transmissions through writing therefore became indispensable.

Al-Azharī (d. 370/980), author of the voluminous dictionary of the Arabic language, the *Tahdhīb al-lughah* (The Refinement of Language), was also a strong advocate of transmission through audition.[33] In the introduction to his work, he has the following to say about a *ṣaḥafī*, i.e. someone who gets his knowledge solely from books:[34]

> The *ṣaḥafī*, when his (only) wealth is the books (*ṣuḥuf*) he has read, makes many mistakes misplacing the diacritical points. This is because he transmits information on the basis of 'books' he has not heard (*yukhbiru ʿan kutub lam yasmaʿhā*), and on the basis of notebooks (*dafātir*) without knowing whether what is written in them is correct or not. Most of what we have read in books (*ṣuḥuf*) which did not have the correct punctuation and which experts have not corrected is weak and only relied upon by the ignorant.

Transmission through audition in the teaching of medicine

By the ninth century, the books that were essential for the study and practice of medicine, and other sciences, were mostly either translations of works from antiquity (especially Galen and Hippocrates), or Arabic commentaries, paraphrases, abridgements or adaptations of these same works. Indeed, most of the knowledge which the Arabs had of medicine was thanks to the great translation movement that began some time in the middle of the eighth century under the early 'Abbāsids. Most of the translators were Christians, usually Nestorian, of whom the most important was the philologist, physician and humanist Ḥunayn ibn Isḥāq (d. 260/873).[35] Original medical works in Arabic began to be written in this period, but did not reach their apogee until the tenth and eleventh centuries.

Even though medicine was one of the so-called 'ancient sciences' (*'ulūm qadīmah*) which owed their existence in Islam to the translation movement, thus to a written tradition, the ideal of transmitting learning through audition became important in this science. This method had already been in use before Islam in the context of medical instruction in Alexandria. Ḥunayn ibn Isḥāq himself informs us how the tenets of medicine in Alexandria were taught:[36]

> They would gather every day for the reading (*qirā'ah*) and interpretation of a fundamental work from among them [i.e., the books of Galen], in the way that our Christian colleagues gather in our own day to read a fundamental work … in those places of learning known as *uskūl* [Greek *scholē*].

We also have very precise information on the way medicine was taught in the eleventh century. A student recited the book being studied with the teacher, one passage at a time; and the teacher provided his commentary on the recited passages by dictating it to the other students. This is how the physician, philosopher and Nestorian priest Abū al-Faraj 'Abd Allāh ibn al-Ṭayyib (d. 435/1043) studied Galen's book *To Glaucon* with his students in the 'Aḍudī Hospital in Baghdad.[37] From the teacher's dictated explanations, taken down by a student, a new book, a commentary, could arise. It is said that most of 'Abd Allāh ibn al-Ṭayyib's books 'used to be transmitted on his authority through dictation based on his own words (*kānat tunqalu 'anhu imlā'an min lafẓihi*)'.[38]

The medico-philosophical controversy between Ibn Buṭlān and Ibn Riḍwān

In the eleventh century, the question of transmission through audition in the field of medicine was the subject of some disagreement and became the centrepiece of the famous medico-philosophical controversy between two physicians, Ibn Buṭlān (d. after 485/1066) and Ibn Riḍwān (d. 453/1061). The great Christian physician Ibn Buṭlān read many books with his teacher, the 'Abd Allāh ibn al-Ṭayyib mentioned above.[39] Ibn al-Ṭayyib had learned from (*akhadha 'an*) al-Ḥasan ibn Suwār (Ibn al-Khammār, d. 411/1020), who had in turn studied with (*qara'a 'alā*) Yaḥyā ibn 'Adī (d. 363/974); Yaḥyā had studied with (*qara'a 'alā*) Abū Bishr Mattā ibn Yūnus (d. 328/940) and al-Farābī (d. 339/950), the former having studied with, among others, the monks Rūfīl (?) and Binyamīn.[40] In his Third Epistle, entitled *al-Maqālah al-miṣriyyah* ('The Egyptian Discourse', so called because he composed it in Old Cairo), Ibn Buṭlān gives 'The Causes why Something Learnt from Oral Instruction by Teachers Is Better and More Easily to Understand than Something Learnt from Books, Given that the

Receptive Faculty of Both of Them be the Same'.[41] Ibn Buṭlān supports this proposition by giving seven reasons, which can be summarised as follows:[42]

1. The transfer from homogeneous to homogeneous, i.e. from teacher to student, is easier than from heterogeneous to heterogeneous, i.e. from book to student.
2. Unlike a book, a teacher can replace a word the student does not understand with a synonym.
3. Teaching and learning have a natural reciprocal relationship; for this reason, learning from a teacher is more appropriate to a student than learning from a book.
4. The spoken word is less removed from knowledge than is the written word.
5. The student receives knowledge in two ways through recitation, by hearing and by seeing.
6. In books, many things complicate understanding: ambiguous words, incorrect punctuation, limited knowledge of desinential inflection, absence or loss of vowels, and so on. To this can be added the difficulties associated with technical terminology, individual authors' styles of presentation, the terrible condition of manuscripts, bad transmission, and in particular untranslated Greek words.
7. Commentators agree that in the case of at least one specific passage by Aristotle, we would never have been able to understand it were it not for the fact that his students Theophrastus and Eudemus had heard it from the Master himself, their elucidation having become the accepted interpretation. Ibn Buṭlān also mentions the pejorative term *ṣaḥafī* as a designation for 'someone who derives his knowledge from books'. Lastly, he points out that it is customary to avoid books that do not have certificates of audition.

We know full well the reasons for Ibn Buṭlān's inclusion of these views in his correspondence with Ibn Riḍwān: the latter, who was Muslim, was an autodidact who had composed a book in which he maintained that it was more useful to study medicine from books than from teachers. Ibn Buṭlān, who was Christian, and who had studied with such teachers as ʿAbd Allāh ibn al-Ṭayyib, must have taken special pleasure in presenting his Muslim adversary with the kinds of arguments Muslim scholars had always advanced in favour of the superiority of transmission by audition to transmission based only on writings.

One reason audition was favoured was the potential for error and doubt, given the ambiguity of the Arabic script (which has similar forms for different letters and which was habitually written without vowels and often without diacritic points). Indeed, the inadequacy of the Arabic script appears to have presented real difficulties and dangers when it came to the correct reading of medical and pharmacological terms. Here is one (of several) examples given by another Christian physician, Ṣāʿid ibn al-Ḥasan, who wrote in 464/1072:[43]

> One physician found 'two dirhams of *anīsūn*' (anis) in a prescription, but the orthography was unclear – he thought the reading was *afyūn* (opium). This is why he wrote 'two dirhams of opium' in his own prescription. He gave it to his patient, and caused his death.

The real motivation for underscoring the importance of transmission from person to person and through audition (justified by pointing out the deficiencies and particularities of the Arabic script), though, may well have been the conviction that the knowledge to be preserved and transmitted needed to be in the exclusive care and control of individuals qualified to do so; dissemination through written copies, which would take place without any supervision whatsoever, meant running the risk of that information being altered or losing its substantive meaning.

The arguments of Ibn Qutaybah, al-Azharī and Ibn Buṭlān in favour of aural transmission, valid as they may have been, cannot alter the fact, however, that transfer and transmission of knowledge in their respective disciplines had shifted from the aural to the read. In the ninth and tenth centuries audition no longer played a primary role in poetry, in *adab* or in medicine: its function was secondary at best. Just as Plato's criticisms of writing more than a thousand years earlier had been made when literacy had already won the day in Hellenic culture, so too were Ibn Buṭlān's criticisms made when literacy had already won the day in Arab-Islamic culture. The shift from the aural to the read was here to stay.

Notes

1 GAS, vol. 8, p. 101.
2 *Fihrist*[1], p. 61 = *Fihrist*[2], p. 67.
3 Ibn 'Abd Rabbihi, *al-'Iqd al-farīd*, vol. 4, p. 318: 'And 'Alī ibn Muḥammad [al-Madā'inī] dictated to me on the authority of …'
4 al-Mas'ūdī, *Murūj al-dhahab*, vol. 5, p. 104 (= VIII, 34).
5 GAS, vol. 1, p. 345.
6 'Umar ibn Shabbah, *Ta'rīkh al-Madīnah al-munawwarah (Akhbār al-Madīnah al-nabawiyyah)*, 4 vols, ed. F. M. Shaltūt (Qom, 1368 H [= 1991]), vol. 1, p. 133.
7 See H. Laoust, *EI*[2], s.v. Aḥmad b. Ḥanbal; *GAL Supplement*, vol. 1, pp. 309 ff.; and GAS, vol. 1, pp. 503 ff.
8 Ibn Abī Shaybah, *al-Muṣannaf*, vol. 10, p. 154; vol. 14, pp. 388, 424, 427, 512, 539.
9 For the following *cf.* GAS, vol. 1, p. 323; C. E. Bosworth, *EI*[2], s.v. al-Ṭabarī; Gilliot, *Exégèse*.
10 Al-Samuk, *Die historischen Überlieferungen*, pp. 102, 138–9.
11 GAS, vol. 2, pp. 551 and 66 ff.
12 Ibid., vol. 1, p. 378.
13 Blachère, *Histoire*, pp. 134 ff.; L. Zolondek, 'An Approach to the Problem of the Sources of the Kitāb al-Aghānī', *JNES* 19 (1960), pp. 217–34; Fleischhammer, *Die Quellen*.

14 *Aghānī*, vol. 1, p. 4.
15 See Asad, *Maṣādir*, pp. 471 ff.; Blachère, *Histoire*, pp. 112 ff.; Wagner, *Grundzüge*, vol. 1, pp. 12–15; GAS, vol. 2, pp. 24 ff.; S. Leder, *EI²*, s.v. al-Sukkarī.
16 *Kitāb Sharḥ ash'ār al-Hudhaliyyīn*, recens. Abū Sa'īd al-Sukkarī, 2 vols, ed. 'A. A. Farrāj and M. M. Shākir (Cairo, n.d.), vol. 1, p. 3; *cf.* Asad, *Maṣādir*, p. 569; GAS, vol. 2, p. 45.
17 I. Lichtenstädter, *EI²*, s.v. Muḥammad b. Ḥabīb.
18 See *EI²*, s.v. Ibn al-Sikkīt.
19 *Fihrist¹*, p. 157 = *Fihrist²*, pp. 177 ff.
20 But Abū al-Ṭayyib al-Mutanabbī might be an exception; he himself seems to have prepared or at least overseen a recension of his poems: see A. Hamori, 'Al-Mutanabbī', in *'Abbāsid Belles-Lettres*, ed. J. Ashtiany et al. (Cambridge, 1990), pp. 314.
21 Wagner, *Die Überlieferung*, p. 308; P. Smoor, *EI²*, s.v. al-Ma'arrī; L. Massignon, *EI²*, s.v. al-Ḥarīrī.
22 Abū Nuwās, *Dīwān*, vol. 5, p. 335; *cf.* Wagner, *Die Überlieferung*, pp. 310 ff.
23 Abū Nuwās, *Dīwān*, vol. 2, pp. 176 ff.; *cf.* Wagner, *Die Überlieferung*, pp. 310 ff.
24 *Fihrist¹*, p. 160 = *Fihrist²*, p. 182.
25 GAS, vol. 1, p. 330; vol. 2, pp. 546 ff. The edition of Ewald Wagner and Gregor Schoeler is based on the two above-mentioned recensions as well as a third that appears to be by Ibrāhīm ibn Aḥmad al-Ṭabarī Tūzūn (d. 355/966; ibid., vol. 2, p. 548).
26 Ibid., vol. 1, p. 117.
27 For an English translation, see Juynboll, 'Muslim's Introduction'.
28 GAS, vol. 8, p. 84.
29 See Bauer, *Das Pflanzenbuch*, pp. 92 ff.
30 Abū al-Ṭayyib al-Lughawī, *Marātib*, pp. 93–4.
31 Ibn Qotaiba, *Introduction*, p. 20.
32 Ibid., p. 21.
33 GAS, vol. 8, p. 201.
34 al-Azharī, *Tahdhīb al-lughah*, vol. 1, p. 33.
35 GAS, vol. 3, p. 247.
36 G. Bergsträsser, *Ḥunain Ibn Isḥāq über die syrischen und arabischen Galenübersetzungen* (Leipzig, 1925), p. 18.
37 Ibn Abī Uṣaybi'ah, *'Uyūn al-anbā' fī ṭabaqāt al-aṭibbā'*, ed. N. Riḍā (Beirut, 1965), p. 323.
38 Ibid.
39 Ibid., pp. 325; *cf.* J. Schacht, *EI²*, s.v. Ibn Buṭlān.
40 Ibn Abī Uṣaybi'ah, *'Uyūn al-anbā'*, pp. 324, 428, 318, 317, and *Fihrist¹*, p. 263 = *Fihrist²*, p. 322. See GAS, vol. 3, pp. 322, 303; G. Endress, *EI²*, s.v. Mattā b. Yūnus; R. Walzer, *EI²*, s.v. al-Farābī.
41 J. Schacht and M. Meyerhof, *The Medico-Philosophical Controversy between Ibn Buṭlān of Baghdad and Ibn Riḍwān of Cairo* (Cairo, 1937), p. 83 (English), *cf.* p. 50 (Arabic).
42 Ibid., pp. 50–3 (Arabic); *cf.* pp. 83–6 (English).
43 Ṣā'id ibn al-Ḥasan, *Kitāb al-Tashwīq al-ṭibbī* = G. Bergsträsser, *Das Buch at-Tašwīq aṭ-ṭibbī des Ṣā'id ibn al-Ḥasan* (Bonn, 1968), p. 33a.

Concluding remarks: from the aural to the read

In their procedures for teaching and for transmitting knowledge, the disciplines of Islamic scholarship in the early and classical periods, from the late seventh century to the tenth century, are characterised by the coexistence of oral dissemination on the one hand, and dissemination based on writing on the other,[1] with a shift in practice, over the course of time, from the former, the *aural*, to the latter, the *read*. Did such a coexistence characterise the eleventh and later centuries, when the *madrasah*, or college of law, came to dominate formal academic instruction? It is reasonable to wonder whether transmission through personal contact and audition could survive when actual books were circulating on a very large scale.

Aural transmission in fact persisted, not only as an ideal, but also in practice: reading books under study out loud (i.e. *samāʿ*, audition proper) survived, and dictated lectures (i.e. *imlāʾ*, another kind of audition) survived. Audition continued to be practised and held in high esteem, primarily in the field of Ḥadīth, but also in other traditional disciplines, such as law, exegesis, history, grammar, poetry, *adab*,[2] even medicine and (though later, and more rarely) natural sciences and philosophy.[3] The difference was that audition in the age of the *madrasah* always relied on a *written* text, a manuscript of the work under study. It is true that explanations of the text could be provided by the professor from memory, without notes, but very often these comments were written down by the students and included in their own copies, as marginal notes, glosses, or even formed the basis of a new work, a commentary, or sub-commentary, compiled by the student and published under his own name. Audition (*samāʿ*) even generated a new document (and procedure), namely the appearance of a large number of certificates of audition (*ijāzāt al-samāʿ*, or just *samāʿāt*) in numerous manuscripts; these first appeared at the beginning of the eleventh century and proliferated in the twelfth and thirteenth centuries.[4] The names cited in these certificates include those of the teacher in whose presence the reading was done (*al-shaykh al-musmiʿ*, often abbreviated to *al-musmiʿ*), of the one doing the reading (*al-qāriʾ*), sometimes identical with the teacher, and of the auditors (*al-mustamiʿūn*). It was not ownership of a manuscript that authorised transmission of a given work, but participation in audition that did so; thus it often happened that auditors did not make a personal written copy of a given work until they wanted to make use of their authorisation to transmit it further.[5] The session during which a Ḥadīth collection was read out loud was even considered a ceremony by the auditors, one in which they saw themselves – through the uninterrupted chain of authorised transmitters – as directly and personally linked to the Prophet Muḥammad, the originator of the traditions they recited.[6]

The value accorded to the spoken word would remain a feature of the Islamic Middle Ages, not only in the transmission of knowledge and of poetry but also in other areas of intellectual and artistic culture.[7] One example is the liturgical recitation of the Qur'ān and the overwhelming effect it provoked in its listeners;[8] another is the recognition by Muslim jurists of the probative value of written texts only when the contents were orally corroborated by trustworthy witnesses.[9]

And yet, books, writing and literacy had long since carried the day. In most of the *'ulūm qadīmah* (the so-called 'ancient sciences'), in the natural sciences, in philosophy and in dialectical theology (*kalām*), literacy and written transmission had been predominant from the outset, i.e. around the end of the eighth century. Instruction and learning in these sciences were essentially private in nature and conducted on the basis of written texts,[10] though, in the age of the *madrasah*, under the influence of the teaching system in the traditional disciplines, audition was occasionally also practised in philosophical and scientific instruction.[11] In *adab*, or belles-lettres, the 'turn' to literacy had taken place in the ninth century at the latest; al-Jāḥiẓ, Ibn Abī al-Dunyā and others had produced actual books in large numbers and for a broad readership, one occasioned by the very availability of paper and books. The fact that al-Jāḥiẓ preferred books to oral and aural communication when instructing his audience is clear from his statement: 'You will get more knowledge out of one (book) in a month than you could acquire from men's mouths in an age.'[12] The same stance, seen from the perspective of al-Jāḥiẓ's readership, was expressed by the caliph al-Ma'mūn who is reported to have declared about one of al-Jāḥiẓ's works, 'This is a book which does not require the presence of the author (to be understood), and needs no advocate'.[13]

Another sign of the impact of literacy was the emergence and spread of the *ijāzah* ('licence'), a method in which the student did not need to have (had) any contact with the teacher, but was nevertheless authorised to transmit everything that the latter had compiled. We have seen that even al-Bukhārī had already given students such licences in the ninth century, and that from the tenth century on, scholars increasingly issued *ijāzahs*. The fact that the practice of dictation sessions fell time and again out of use and that the traditionists and jurists consequently had to insist on maintaining it, or reviving it, was a sign of the decline of aural transmission.[14]

There is another development that shows that the main emphasis in the transmission procedures in the traditional disciplines had shifted, namely the urgently felt need – in the thirteenth century, at the latest – for something akin to critical editions of authoritative texts in Ḥadīth, the oral and aural discipline *par excellence* in Islamic scholarship. As Johann Fück pointed out in an important article, the eminent scholar Ibn al-Ṣalāḥ (d. 643/1245), author of the standard work in the field of Ḥadīth science, had to admit that in his time, and for generations before him, the uninterrupted chain of transmitters (*isnād*) was no longer a guarantee that one was in the presence of reliable texts; Ibn al-Ṣalāḥ expressed the view that scholars were holding on to the *isnād* for the sole reason that they regarded it as a characteristic and exclusively Islamic feature of scholarship.[15] From this Ibn al-Ṣalāḥ concluded that the only way to have (and recover) an authentic and reliable text was to collate as many correct manuscripts of the different extant recensions of a work as possible.

Ibn al-Ṣalāḥ's call was answered by the traditionist al-Yunīnī (d. 701/1301), who prepared a 'critical edition' of al-Bukhārī's *Ṣaḥīḥ*. As Rosemarie Quiring-Zoche has pointed out in a detailed study of al-Yunīnī and his *Rumūz 'alā Ṣaḥīḥ al-Bukhārī*, 'collating various manuscripts, al-Yunīnī left a copy of the *Ṣaḥīḥ* [the so-called *Yunīniyyah*] which was probably very close to the original … Containing variants with notes and signs in a critical apparatus, it was less suited for transmission by reading and listening.'[16] All the texts of the *Ṣaḥīḥ* available today are likely based on the *Yunīniyyah*. The most eminent traditionists of the fifteenth and sixteenth centuries, Ibn Ḥajar al-'Asqalānī, al-'Aynī and al-Qasṭallānī, followed in al-Yunīnī's footsteps, each producing a recension of al-Bukhārī's work on the basis of different manuscripts.[17] What is more, they wrote lengthy commentaries on the *Ṣaḥīḥ*, showing that they were cognizant of the written character of the work, just as the commentators of the *Kitāb* of Sībawayhi and the *Kitāb al-Amthāl* of Abū 'Ubayd had done.

The growing awareness of the need to establish correct texts was felt in other fields too. It is true that the correction of texts often took place in teaching sessions, during the process of audition and recitation, when students checked their own copies against the text being recited. Far more often, however, the scribe or owner of a manuscript simply collated his copy with one or two other copies; he would then write the variants in the margins of his own copy. Consequently, many manuscripts include such notes of collation (*mu'āraḍah*, *muqābalah*);[18] an *ijāzah* to transmit a book further could also be given through such a *muqābalah*.[19]

Very few cultures in the world have literatures that can compare with the vastness of Arabic literature. So much was written in Arabic that in spite of periodic attempts to catalogue this phenomenal output – Ibn al-Nadīm in the tenth century, for example, Ḥājjī Khalīfah in the seventeenth century and, in recent times, Carl Brockelmann and Fuat Sezgin[20] – we still do not have an inventory of everything that was written. All in all, only a tiny part of this enormous literature was ever transmitted personally and by audition. In practice, as this book has tried to show, Islamic scholarship and Arabic literature both transitioned, irrevocably and irreversibly, from the oral to the written – from the aural to the read.

Notes

1 For remarks on the origins of this Islamic system of transmission (indigenous development and/or aspects borrowed from an other tradition), see Schoeler, *The Oral and the Written*, pp. 42 ff.

2 See P. A. MacKay, 'Certificates of Transmission on a Manuscript of the *Maqāmāt* of Ḥarīrī (Ms. *Cairo, Adab* 105)', *Transactions of the American Philosophical Society* N.S. 61/4 (1971), pp. 1–81.

3 Vajda, *Les Certificats de lectures et transmissions dans les manuscrits arabes de la Bibliothèque Nationale* (Paris, 1956), p. v; Endress, 'Handschriftenkunde', pp. 288 ff.

4 See Vajda, *La transmission*, articles I and XV; Endress, 'Handschriftenkunde', pp. 288 ff.; F. Déroche et al., *Manuel de codicologie des manuscripts en écriture arabe* (Paris, 2000), p. 352; S. Leder, Y. M. al-Sawwās and M. al-Ṣāgharjī, *Mu'jam al-Samā'āt al-Dimashqiyya. Les certificats d'audition à Damas 550–750 h./1155–1349* (Damascus, 1996), pp. 7 ff.

5 See Chapter 3 above.

6 See S. Leder, 'Dokumente zum Ḥadīṯ in Schrifttum und Unterricht aus Damaskus im 6./12. Jhdt.', *Oriens* 34 (1994), pp. 57–75.

7 For Plato's defence of the spoken word, see Phaidros [Stephanus] 275a–276a; for an English translation, see Plato, *Phaedros*, tr. C. J. Rowe, rev. edn (Warminster, 2000), pp. 123 ff.; *cf.* Schoeler, *The Oral and the Written*, pp. 83–5.

8 See S. Wild, '«Die schauerliche Öde des heiligen Buches». Westliche Wertungen des koranischen Stils', in *Gott ist schön und Er liebt die Schönheit. Festschrift für Annemarie Schimmel*, ed. A. Giese and J. Chr. Bürgel (Bern, 1994), pp. 429–47, especially pp. 438 ff.; and N. Kermani, *Gott ist schön. Das ästhetische Erleben des Koran* (Munich, [2]2000).

9 *Cf.* E. Tyan, 'Le notariat et le régime de la preuve par écrit dans la pratique du droit musulman', *Annales de l'Ecole française de droit de Beyrouth* 2 (1945), pp. 3–99; J. A. Wakin, *The Function of Documents in Islamic Law. The Chapter on Sales from Ṭaḥāwī's* Kitāb al-Shurūṭ al-kabīr (New York, 1972); Schoeler, *The Oral and the Written*, pp. 82–3.

10 *Cf.* F. E. Peters, *Aristotle and the Arabs: The Aristotelian Tradition in Islam* (New York, 1968), pp. 71 ff., especially 72 and 74. But see Schoeler, *The Oral and the Written*, p. 186, n. 225.

11 See Endress, 'Handschriftenkunde', pp. 288 ff.; Vajda, *Les Certificats*, p. v.
12 al-Jāḥiẓ, *Kitāb al-Ḥayawān*, p. 51; *cf.* Pellat, *Life and Works*, p. 132.
13 al-Jāḥiẓ, *al-Bayān wal-tabyīn*, vol. 3, p. 375; *cf.* Pellat, *Life and Works*, pp. 108–9.
14 'The practice of dictation … underwent a hiatus after the death of Ibn al-Ṣalāḥ (d. 643 [= 1245–6]). It was resumed by Abū al-Faḍl al-'Irāqī in 796 [= 1394], but was again abandoned after the death of Ibn Ḥajar (in 852 [= 1449]). Twenty years later, al-Suyūṭī revived it anew …' (W. Marçais, 'Le Taqrīb de en-Nawawī, traduit et annoté', *JA* 18 [1901], p. 86, n. 4).
15 Fück, 'Beiträge zur Überlieferungsgeschichte', pp. 60–87, esp. pp. 79 ff.
16 R. Quiring-Zoche, 'How al-Buḫārī's Ṣaḥīḥ was Edited in the Middle Ages: 'Alī al-Yunīnī and his *Rumūz*', *Bulletin d'études orientales* 50 (1998), pp. 191–222, *cf.* pp. 192 and 212.
17 Fück, 'Beiträge zur Überlieferungsgeschichte', pp. 81 ff. and Quiring-Zoche, 'How al-Buḫārī's Ṣaḥīḥ was Edited?', pp. 192 ff.
18 An illustrative example is the following notice in the colophon of a manuscript of al-Suyūṭī's *al-Itqān fī 'ulūm al-Qur'ān*: *qūbilat 'alā nuskhah ṣaḥīḥah qūbilat 'alā nuskhah qūbilat 'alā nuskhat al-mu'allif* ('[this copy] was collated with a correct copy that was collated with a copy that was collated with the copy of the author'). See T. Seidensticker, *Arabische Handschriften*, vol. 4 (= Verzeichnis der orientalischen Handschriften in Deutschland, vol. XVIIB, 4) (Stuttgart, 2005), p. 71.
19 Endress, 'Handschriftenkunde,' p. 290; *cf.* F. Rosenthal, *EI*², s.v. Mukābala, sect. 2.
20 Ibn al-Nadīm, *Fihrist*; Ḥājjī Khalīfah, *Kashf al-ẓunūn*; Brockelmann, GAL; Sezgin, GAS.

Glossary

adab General culture and refinement; belles-lettres; writerly culture. Also, more generally, conduct; good manners; professional knowledge.

adīb, pl. *udabā'* A cultured man of letters; a practitioner of writerly culture.

Anṣār Lit. 'Helpers'; the Medinan followers and supporters of the Prophet Muḥammad.

'arabiyyah 'Pure' Arabic, notably the language of ancient poetry and the Qur'ān.

'ard see qirā'ah

Companion Someone who knew or met the Prophet Muḥammad (Ar. *ṣaḥābī*, pl. *ṣaḥābā*).

dīwān, pl. *dawāwīn* The collected poetic works of a poet, or tribe; a chancery.

fiqh Systematic study of Divine Law, or Sharī'ah.

ḥadīth Lit. 'saying', a tradition about the words or deeds of the Prophet Muḥammad or one of his companions; also, the whole corpus or genre of such traditions; report.

ḥalqah (or ḥalaqah), pl. *ḥalaqāt* Study circle; teaching circle.

hypomnēma, pl. *hypomnēmata* (Gk) Notes, notebook, aide-mémoire.

ijāzah Authorisation to transmit, sometimes granted by a letter in which case the student need not read or have read the authorised work with the teacher granting the authorisation.

'ilm Lit. 'knowledge, science'; frequently refers to knowledge of the Ḥadīth corpus.

imlā' Dictation; dictation session.

isnād A chain of transmitters who transmit a report or account, especially in the field of Ḥadīth.

kitāb Any piece of writing, e.g. a note, letter, contract, inscription, book.

kitābah A method of transmission dependent on the authorised written copy of a work.

maghāzī Lit. 'campaigns', but in fact more generally, life of the Prophet.

majlis, pl. *majālis* Lit. 'a place of sitting'; a scholarly session for discussion or instruction; a literary gathering.

mudhākarah Recitation from memory by a student; a session during which students repeat and review ḥadīths.

munāwalah A method of transmission in which the teacher entrusts his student with his autograph manuscript or with a collated copy.

muqābalah Collation, i.e. textual comparison of a manuscript with another of the same work.

muṣannaf, pl. *muṣannafāt* A work systematically subdivided into thematic chapters.

muṣannif, pl. *muṣannifūn* A compiler of a *muṣannaf*.

muṣḥaf, pl. *maṣāḥif* A copy or 'codex' of the Qur'ān.

musnad, pl. *masānid* A work in which traditions or ḥadīths are organised according to the names of the Companions of the Prophet Muḥammad who initially transmitted them; the Companions are often arranged chronologically by date of conversion to Islam.

qāri', pl. *qurrā'* Reciter (Lit. 'reader') of the Qur'ānic text.

qirā'ah (later also called *'arḍ*) A method of transmission in which the student recites or reads the text with (i.e. in the presence of) a teacher.

qiyās In grammar, rule; later, analogical deduction.

rāwī, pl. *ruwāt* A transmitter, a person entrusted with the recitation and transmission of a poet's works.

rāwiyah A learned transmitter of poetry; often synonymous with *rāwī*.

ra'y, pl. *ārā'* A personal juridical opinion (lit. 'view').

risālah, pl. *rasā'il* Letter, epistle.

riwāyah Transmission of knowledge; a chain of transmission at the beginning of a manuscript.

riwāyah bil-lafẓ Lit. 'transmission through words', i.e. transmission in which the exact wording is scrupulously followed; verbatim transmission.

riwāyah bil-ma'nā Lit. 'transmission through meaning', i.e. transmission in which only the sense of the text is preserved.

ṣaḥafī (or *ṣuḥufī*), pl. *ṣaḥafiyyūn* (or *ṣuḥufiyyūn*) A person whose knowledge derives solely from books or notebooks.

samā' Audition. A method of transmission in which the student ('auditor') listens to ('audits') the text recited by the teacher. Also a certificate or endorsement of 'audition', attesting to this.

sharḥ, pl. *shurūḥ* Commentary.

shaykh, pl. *ashyākh* (or *shuyūkh*) Elder, tribal chief, teacher.

shu'ūbiyyah The belief that Arabs are not superior to other Muslim peoples.

syngramma, pl. *syngrammata* (Gk) A consciously literary work, an actual book.

tadwīn Large-scale collection, or recension, of materials such as poetry, or reports.

tafsīr Exegesis, Qur'ān commentary.

taṣnīf A method of presenting knowledge consisting of classifying items systematically in books (*kutub*) subdivided into chapters.

'ulūm islāmiyyah The 'Islamic sciences', those disciplines that arose within Islamic scholarship.

'ulūm qadīmah The 'ancient sciences', those dsiciplines of Hellenistic origin.

wijādah A method of transmission restricted to the use of a copy of a given text.

Bibliography

Abbreviations

Aghānī	Abū al-Faraj al-Iṣbahānī, *Kitāb al-Aghānī*, 20 vols (Būlāq, 1285 H [= 1868])
AKM	*Abhandlungen für die Kunde des Morgenlandes*
BSOAS	*Bulletin of the School of Oriental and African Studies*
EI^{1}	*Encyclopaedia of Islam* (Leiden and London, 1913–38)
EI^{2}	*Encyclopaedia of Islam*, new edn (Leiden and London, 1954–2006)
Fihrist^{1}	Ibn al-Nadīm, *Kitāb al-Fihrist*, 2 vols, ed. G. Flügel (Leipzig, 1871–2)
Fihrist^{2}	*Kitāb al-Fihrist lil-Nadīm*, ed. R. Tajaddod (Teheran, n.d. [^{2}1393 H = 1973])
GAL	C. Brockelmann, *Geschichte der arabischen Litteratur*, 2 vols, 3 suppls (Leiden, ^{2}1943–9, 1937–42)
GAPh	*Grundriss der arabischen Philologie*, I, *Sprachwissenschaft*, ed. W. Fischer (Wiesbaden, 1982); II, *Literaturwissenschaft*, ed. H. Gätje (Wiesbaden, 1987); III, *Supplement*, ed. W. Fischer (Wiesbaden, 1992)
GAS	F. Sezgin, *Geschichte des arabischen Schrifttums*, 13 vols (Leiden, 1967–2007)
GdQ	Th. Nöldeke, *Geschichte des Qorâns*, 3 vols, vols 1–2, ed. F. Schwally, vol. 3, ed. G. Bergsträsser and O. Pretzl (Leipzig, 1919–38, repr. Hildesheim, 1981)
JA	*Journal asiatique*
JAL	*Journal of Arabic Literature*
JAOS	*Journal of the American Oriental Society*
JNES	*Journal of Near Eastern Studies*
JRAS	*Journal of the Royal Asiatic Society*
JSAI	*Jerusalem Studies in Arabic and Islam*
RSO	*Rivista degli Studi Orientali*
Sīrah	Ibn Hishām, *al-Sīrah al-nabawiyyah*, 2 vols, ed. M. al-Saqqā, I. al-Ibyārī and ʻA. Shalabī (Cairo, ^{2}1955).
WKAS	*Wörterbuch der klassischen arabischen Sprache*, ed. M. Ullmann (Wiesbaden, 1970–).

WZKM *Wiener Zeitschrift für die Kunde des Morgenlandes*
ZDMG *Zeitschrift der Deutschen Morgenländischen Gesellschaft*

Primary sources

'Abd Allah ibn Wahb, *Al-Ǧāmi': Die Koranwissenschaften*, ed. M. Muranyi (Wiesbaden, 1992).
— *al-Ǧāmi': Tafsīr al-Qur'ān: Die Koranexegese*, ed. M. Muranyi (Wiesbaden, 1993).
— *al-Muwaṭṭa'. Kitāb al-muḥāraba*, ed. M. Muranyi (Wiesbaden, 1992).
'Abd al-Razzāq ibn Hammām al-Ṣan'ānī, *al-Muṣannaf*, ed. H. al-A'ẓamī, 10 vols (Beirut, 1970–2).
Abū al-Faraj al-Iṣbahānī, *Kitāb al-Aghānī*, 20 vols (Būlāq, 1285 H [= 1868]).
Abū Ḥātim al-Sijistānī, *Kitāb al-Mu'ammarīn = Das Kitāb al-Mu'ammarīn des Abū Ḥātim al-Siǧistānī*, ed. I. Goldziher (Leiden, 1899).
Abū Nu'aym al-Iṣbahānī, *Ḥilyat al-awliyā' wa-ṭabaqāt al-aṣfiyā'*, 10 vols (Cairo, 1932–8).
Abū Nuwās, *Dīwān*, 6 vols, ed. E. Wagner and G. Schoeler (Wiesbaden, 1958–2006).
Abū al-Ṭayyib al-Lughawī, *Marātib al-naḥwiyyīn*, ed. M. Abū al-Faḍl Ibrāhīm (Cairo, 1995).
Abū 'Ubayd al-Qāsim ibn Sallām, *Gharīb al-ḥadīth*, 2 vols (Beirut, 1967).
Abū 'Ubaydah Ma'mar ibn al-Muthannā, *Majāz al-Qur'ān*, 2 vols, ed. F. Sezgin (Cairo, 1954–62).
Abū Yūsuf, *Kitāb al-Kharāj* (Būlāq, 1302 H [= 1884–5]).
Abū Zayd al-Anṣārī, *Kitāb al-Nawādir fī al-lughah*, ed. S. al-Khūrī al-Sharṭūnī (Beirut, ²1967).
al-'Askarī, Abū Aḥmad, *Sharḥ mā yaqa'u fīhi al-taṣḥīf wal-taḥrīf*, vol. 1, ed. S. M. Yūsuf and A. R. al-Naffākh (Cairo, 1975).
al-Azharī, Abū Manṣūr, *Tahdhīb al-lughah*, 15 vols, ed. 'A. Hārūn et al. (Cairo, 1964–7).
al-Balādhurī, *Anonyme arabische Chronik* (= *Ansāb al-ashrāf*, vol. 11), ed. W. Ahlwardt (Greifswald, 1883).
al-Bukhārī, *(al-Jāmi') al-Ṣaḥīḥ*: see Ibn Ḥajar al-'Asqalānī, *Fatḥ al-bārī*.
al-Dānī, *Kitāb al-Muqni' fī rasm maṣāḥif al-amṣār* (*Orthographie und Punktierung des Koran*), ed. O. Pretzl (Istanbul and Leipzig, 1932).
al-Dārimī, *al-Sunan*, 2 vols, ed. 'A. H. Yamānī al-Madanī (Medina, 1966).
al-Dhahabī, *Siyar a'lām al-nubalā'*, 23 vols, ed. S. al-Arna'ūṭ et al. (Beirut, ³1985).
— *Mīzān al-i'tidāl fī naqd al-rijāl*, 4 vols, ed. 'A. M. Al-Bajāwī (Beirut, 1963).
al-Farrā', *Ma'ānī al-Qur'ān*, vol. 1 (Cairo, ²1980); vol. 2 (Cairo, n.d.); vol. 3 (Cairo, 1972), ed. A. Y. Najātī and M. 'A. al-Najjār.
al-Fasawī, Abū Yūsuf, *Kitāb al-Ma'rifah wal-ta'rīkh*, 3 vols, ed. A. Ḍ. al-'Umarī (Beirut, ²1981).

Ḥājjī Khalīfah, Muṣṭafā ibn 'Abd Allāh Kātib Čelebī, *Kashf al-ẓunūn 'an asāmī al-kutub wal-funūn*, 2 vols, ed. S. Yaltakaya and K. R. Bilge (Istanbul, 1941–3, repr. Baghdad, n.d. [ca. 1970]).
Ḥassān ibn Thābit, *Dīwān*, 2 vols, ed. W. N. 'Arafāt (London, 1971).
al-Hudhaliyyīn: see *Sharḥ ash'ār al-Hudhaliyyīn*.
Ḥunayn ibn Isḥāq, *Risālah*: see Bergsträsser, *Ḥunain b. Isḥāq*.
al-Ḥuṭay'ah, Jarwal ibn Aws, 'Der Dīwān' (ed. I. Goldziher), *ZDMG* 46 (1892), pp. 1–53.
— *Der Dīwān* (Leipzig, 1893).
Ibn 'Abd al-Barr, *Jāmi' bayān al-'ilm wa-faḍlihi wa-mā yanbaghī fī riwāyatihi wa-ḥamalatihi*, 2 vols (Cairo, n.d.).
Ibn 'Abd Rabbihi, *al-'Iqd al-farīd*, 7 vols, ed. A. Amīn et al. (Cairo, 1949–65).
Ibn Abī Dāwūd, *Kitāb al-Maṣāḥif*: see Jeffery, *Materials*.
Ibn Abī Ḥātim, *Ādāb al-Shāfi'ī wa-manāqibuhu*, ed. 'A. 'Abd al-Khāliq (Cairo, 1953).
Ibn Abī Shaybah, *al-Kitāb al-Muṣannaf*, 15 vols, ed. 'A. Khān al-Afghānī et al. (Hyderabad and Bombay, 1966–83).
Ibn Abī Uṣaybi'ah, *'Uyūn al-anbā' fī ṭabaqāt al-aṭibbā'*, ed. N. Riḍā (Beirut, 1965).
Ibn 'Adī, Abū Aḥmad, *al-Kāmil fī ḍu'afā' al-rijāl*, 8 vols, ed. S. Zakkār (Beirut, ^{3}1988).
Ibn 'Asākir, *Ta'rīkh madīnat Dimashq: al-Zuhrī...*, ed. Sh. Ibn N. Qawchānī (Beirut, 1982).
Ibn Ḥabīb, Muḥammad, *Kitāb al-Munammaq fī akhbār Quraysh* (Hyderabad, Deccan, 1964).
Ibn Ḥajar al-'Asqalānī, *Fatḥ al-bārī bi-sharḥ Ṣaḥīḥ al-Bukhārī*, 28 vols, *Muqaddimah*, ed. Ṭ. 'A. Sa'd and M. M. al-Hawārī (Cairo, 1978).
— *Tahdhīb al-tahdhīb*, 14 vols (Beirut, 1984–5).
Ibn Ḥibbān al-Bustī, *Kitāb Mashāhīr 'ulamā' al-amṣār*, ed. M. Fleischhammer (Cairo and Wiesbaden, 1959).
— *Kitāb al-Thiqāt*, 9 vols (Hyderabad, Deccan, 1973–83, repr. Beirut, 1988).
Ibn Hishām, *al-Sīrah al-nabawiyyah*, 2 vols (4 parts), ed. M. al-Saqqā, I. al-Abyārī and 'A. Shalabī (Cairo, ^{2}1955).
— *Sīrat Sayyidinā Muḥammad rasūl Allāh. Das Leben Muhammed's nach M. Ibn Isḥāq*, 2 vols, ed. F. Wüstenfeld (Göttingen, 1858–1860).
'Ibn Isḥāq, Muḥammad', *'Kitāb al-Siyar wal-maghāzī'*: see al-'Uṭāridī.
Ibn al-Jazarī, Shams al-dīn, *Ghāyat al-nihāyah fī ṭabaqāt al-qurrā'* (*Das biographische Lexikon der Koranleser*), 3 vols, ed. G. Bergsträsser (Cairo, Leipzig, 1932–5).
Ibn Kathīr, *al-Bidāyah wal-nihāyah*, 14 vols (Cairo, 1932–9).
Ibn al-Muqaffa', 'Abd Allāh, *al-Manṭiq, wa-Ḥudūd al-manṭiq li-Ibn Bihrīz*, ed. M. T. Dānishpajūh (Teheran, 1357 H [= 1978]).
Ibn al-Nadīm, *Kitāb al-Fihrist*, 2 vols, ed. G. Flügel (Leipzig, 1871–2).
— *Kitāb al-Fihrist lil-Nadīm*, ed. R. Tajaddod (Teheran, ^{2}1393 H = 1973).
Ibn Qotaiba (= Ibn Qutaybah) *Introduction au Livre de la poésie et des poètes*.

Muqaddimatu kitābi š-ši'ri wa-š-šu'arā'. Texte... avec introduction, traduction et commentaire par Gaudefroy-Demombynes (Paris, 1947)
Ibn Qutaybah, *Kitāb Adab al-kātib*, ed. M. Grünert (Leiden, 1900).
— *Kitāb al-Ma'ārif*, ed. Th. 'Ukāshah (Cairo, ²1969).
— *al-Shi'r wal-shu'arā'*, 2 vols, ed. A. M. Shākir (Cairo, 1966–7).
— *'Uyūn al-akhbār*, 4 vols (Cairo, 1925–30).
Ibn Sa'd, *Kitāb aṭ-Ṭabaqāt al-kabīr. Biographien Muhammeds, seiner Gefährten und der späteren Träger des Islams bis zum Jahre 230*, 9 vols, ed. E. Sachau, C. Brockelmann et al. (Leiden, 1904–40).
— *al-Ṭabaqāt al-kubrā, al-qism al-mutammim*, ed. Z. M. Manṣūr (Medina, 1308 H [= 1987]).
'Iyāḍ ibn Mūsā, *Tartīb al-madārik wa-taqrīb al-masālik li-ma'rifat a'lām madhhab Mālik*, 2 vols, ed. M. S. Hāshim (Beirut, 1998).
al-Jāḥiẓ, *al-Bayān wal-tabyīn*, 4 vols, ed. 'A. M. Hārūn (²Cairo, n.d).
— *Kitāb al-Ḥayawān*, 7 vols, ed. 'A. M. Hārūn (Cairo, ²1965).
— *Rasā'il*, 2 vols, ed. 'A. M. Hārūn (Cairo, 1964–5).
al-Kattānī, Muḥammad ibn Ja'far, *al-Risālah al-mustaṭrafah li-bayān mashhūr kutub al-sunnah al-musharrafah* (Damascus, ³1964).
al-Khalīl ibn Aḥmad al-Farāhīdī, *Kitāb al-'Ayn*, 8 vols, ed. M. al-Makhzūmī and I. al-Sāmarrā'ī (Baghdad, 1980–5, repr. Beirut, 1988).
— *Kitāb al-'Ayn*, vol. 1, ed. A. Darwīsh (Baghdad, 1967).
al-Khaṭīb al-Baghdādī, *Kitāb al-Kifāyah fī 'ilm al-riwāyah* (Hyderabad, Deccan, ²1970).
— *Ta'rīkh Baghdād*, 14 vols (Cairo, 1931).
— *Taqyīd al-'ilm*, ed. Y. al-'Ishsh (n.p., ²1975).
Mālik ibn Anas, *al-Muwaṭṭa'*, recens. Yaḥyā ibn Yaḥyā, ed. M. F. 'Abd al-Bāqī (Cairo, 1951).
— *al-Muwaṭṭa'*, recens. al-Shaybānī, ed. 'A. 'Abd al-Laṭīf (Cairo, 1967).
al-Marzubānī, *al-Muwashshaḥ*, ed. 'A. M. al-Bajāwī (Cairo, 1965).
— *K. Nūr al-qabas al-mukhtaṣar min al-Muqtabas = Die Gelehrtenbiographien... in der Rezension des Ḥāfiẓ al-Yaghmūrī*, ed. R. Sellheim (Wiesbaden, 1964).
al-Mas'ūdī, *Murūj al-dhahab wa-ma'ādin al-jawhar*, 7 vols, ed. Ch. Pellat (Beirut, 1965–1979).
— *Kitāb al-Tanbīh wal-ishrāf*, ed. M. J. De Goeje (Leiden, 1893–4).
al-Mufaḍḍal al-Ḍabbī, *al-Mufaḍḍaliyyāt = The Mufaḍḍaliyāt. An Anthology of Ancient Arabic Odes Compiled by al-Mufaḍḍal Son of Muḥammad*, ed. Ch. J. Lyall (Oxford, 1921).
Mujāhid ibn Jabr, *Tafsīr*, ed. M. 'A. Abū al-Nīl (Cairo, 1989).
al-Naqā'iḍ = The Naḳā'iḍ of Jarīr and al-Farazdaq, 3 vols, ed. A. A. Bevan (Leiden, 1905–12).
Nawādir al-makhṭūṭāt, 2 vols, ed. 'A. M. Hārūn (Cairo, 1951).
Plato, *Phaedros*, tr. C. J. Rowe, rev. edn (Warminster, 2000).
al-Qālī, Abū 'Alī, *Kitāb Dhayl al-Amālī wal-nawādir* (Cairo, 1344 H [= 1926]).

Qays ibn al-Khaṭīm, *Dīwān*, ed. N. al-Asad (Cairo, 1962).
al-Qur'ān: al-Muṣḥaf al-sharīf (Cairo, 1344 H [= 1926]).
Saḥnūn ibn Sa'īd, *al-Mudawwanah al-kubrā*, 6 vols (Cairo, 1323 H [= 1905]).
Ṣā'id ibn al-Ḥasan, *al-Tashwīq al-ṭibbī*: see Spies, *Das Buch at-Tašwīq aṭ-ṭibbī*.
al-Sam'ānī, 'Abd al-Karīm, *Adab al-imlā' wal-istimlā' = Die Methodik des Diktatkollegs*, ed. M. Weisweiler (Leiden, 1952).
— *Kitāb al-Ansāb*, 13 vols, ed. A. Mu'īd Khān (Hyderabad, Deccan, 1962–82).
Sayf ibn 'Umar, *Kitāb al-Riddah wal-futūḥ, wa-Kitāb al-Jamal wa-sayr 'Ā'ishah wa-'Alī*, ed. Q. al-Sāmarrā'ī (Leiden, 1995).
K. *Sharḥ ash'ār al-Hudhaliyyīn*, recens. Abū Sa'īd al-Sukkarī, 2 vols, ed. 'A. A. Farrāj and M. M. Shākir (Cairo, n.d.).
Sībawayhi, *al-Kitāb*, 5 vols, ed. 'A. M. Hārūn (Cairo, 1966–77).
— *(al-Kitāb =) Le livre de Sībawaihi, traité de grammaire arabe*, 2 vols, ed. H. Derenbourg (Paris, 1881–9; repr. Hildesheim, 1970).
al-Sīrāfī, *Biographies des grammairiens de l'école de Basra (Akhbār al-naḥwiyyīn al-baṣriyyīn)*, ed. F. Krenkow (Paris and Beirut, 1936).
al-Suyūṭī, *al-Muzhir fī 'ulūm al-lughah wa-anwā'ihā*, 2 vols, ed. M. A. Jād al-Mawlā et al. (Cairo, n.d.).
al-Ṭabarī, *al-Tafsīr (= Jāmi' al-bayān fī tafsīr al-Qur'ān)*, vol. 1 (Būlāq, 1322 H [= 1904]).
— *Ta'rīkh al-rusul wal-mulūk (Annales)*, Series 1–3, ed. M. J. de Goeje et al. (Leiden, 1879–1901).
Tha'lab, Abū al-'Abbās, *Majālis*, ed. 'A. M. Hārūn (Cairo, ²1957).
'Umar ibn Shabbah, *Ta'rīkh al-Madīnah al-munawwarah (Akhbār al-Madīnah al-nabawiyyah)*, 4 vols, ed. F. M. Shaltūt (Qom, 1368 H [= 1991]).
'Urwah ibn al-Zubayr, *Maghāzī rasūl Allāh bi-riwāyat Abī al-Aswad 'anhu*, ed. M. M. al-A'ẓamī (Riyadh, 1981).
al-'Uṭāridī, Aḥmad ibn 'Abd al-Jabbār, *al-Siyar* = 'Muḥammad b. Isḥāq', '*Kitāb al-Siyar wal-maghāzī*', ed. S. Zakkār (Beirut, 1978) [actually a recension of the *Kitāb Ziyādat Yūnus ibn Bukayr fī Maghāzī Ibn Isḥāq*, transmitted by al-'Uṭāridī].
Yāqūt al-Ḥamawī, *Irshād al-arīb ilā ma'rifat al-adīb*, 7 vols, ed. D. S. Margoliouth (²Cairo, 1923–30).
al-Zubaydī, Abū Bakr Muḥammad, *Mukhtaṣar Kitāb al-'Ayn*, vol. 1, ed. 'A. al-Fāsī and M. al-Ṭanjī (Rabat and Casablanca, n.d.).
— *Ṭabaqāt al-naḥwiyyīn wal-lughawiyyīn*, ed. M. Abū al-Faḍl Ibrāhīm (Cairo, ²1973).
al-Zubayr ibn Bakkār, *al-Akhbār al-Muwaffaqiyyāt*, ed. S. M. al-'Ānī (Baghdad, 1972).
(Pseudo-) al-Zuhrī, Muḥammad ibn Muslim, '*al-Maghāzī al-nabawiyyah*', ed. S. Zakkār (Damascus, 1980) [actually the *Kitāb al-Maghāzī* of 'Abd al-Razzāq ibn Hammām, part of his *al-Muṣannaf*].
al-Zurqānī, Muḥammad ibn 'Abd al-Bāqī, *al-Sharḥ 'alā Muwaṭṭa' al-imām Mālik* (Beirut, 1411 H [= 1990]).

Secondary literature

Abbott, N., *Studies in Arabic Literary Papyri*, 3 vols (Chicago, 1957–72).

Abdel-Tawab, R., *Das Kitāb al-Ġarīb al-Muṣannaf von Abū 'Ubaid und seine Bedeutung für die nationalarabische Lexikographie* (Heppenheim, 1962).

Abdul Rauf, M., '*Ḥadīth* Literature – I: The Development of the Science of *Ḥadīth*', in Beeston et al., *Arabic Literature to the End of the Umayyad Period*, pp. 271–88.

Ahmed, M., 'The Institution of al-Mudhākara', ZDMG *Suppl.* I, part 2 (1969), pp. 595–603.

Al-Samuk, S. M., 'Die historischen Überlieferungen nach Ibn Iṣḥāq', doctoral thesis, Frankfurt a.M., 1978.

Arnim, H. von, *Leben und Werke des Dio von Prusa* (Berlin, 1898).

al-Asad, N., *Maṣādir al-shi'r al-jāhilī wa-qīmatuhā al-ta'rīkhiyyah* (Cairo, ⁵1978).

Ashtiany, J. et al., *'Abbāsid Belles-Lettres* (Cambridge, 1990).

Bauer, Th., *Das Pflanzenbuch des Abū Ḥanīfa ad-Dīnawarī. Inhalt, Aufbau, Quellen* (Wiesbaden, 1988).

Baumstark, A., 'Das Problem eines vorislamischen christlich-arabischen Schrifttums in arabischer Sprache', *Islamica* 4 (1931), pp. 562–75.

Beck, E., "Arabiyya, Sunna und 'Āmma in der Koranlesung des zweiten Jahrhunderts', *Orientalia* N.S. 15 (1946), pp. 180–244.

– 'Die Kodizesvarianten der Amṣār', *Orientalia* N.S. 16 (1947), pp. 353–76.

– 'Der 'uṯmānische Kodex in der Koranlesung des zweiten Jahrhunderts', *Orientalia* N.S. 14 (1945), pp. 355–373.

Becker, C. H., 'Islam', *Archiv für Religionswissenschaft* 15 (1912), pp. 530–602.

– 'Prinzipielles zu Lammens' *Sīra*studien', *Der Islam* 4 (1913), pp. 263–9.

Beeston, A. F. L. et al. (eds), *Arabic Literature to the End of the Umayyad Period* (Cambridge, 1983).

Bellamy, J., 'The Mysterious Letters of the Koran: Old Abbreviations of the Basmalah', *JAOS* 93 (1973), pp. 267–85.

Bergsträsser, G., 'Die Koranlesung des Ḥasan von Basra', *Islamica* 2 (1926), pp. 11–57.

— (ed. and tr.), *Ḥunain Ibn Isḥāq über die syrischen und arabischen Galenübersetzungen* (Leipzig, 1925).

Blachère, R., *Histoire de la littérature arabe*, 3 vols (Paris, 1952–66).

— *Introduction au Coran* (Paris, ²1959).

— *Le problème de Mahomet. Essai de biographie critique du fondateur de l'Islam* (Paris, 1952).

Bloom, J., *Paper before Print: the History and Impact of Paper in the Islamic World* (New Haven, 2001).

Bothmer, H.-C. von, et al., 'Neue Wege der Koranforschung', *Magazin Forschung, Universität des Saarlandes* 1 (1999), pp. 33–46.

Bräu, H. H. 'Die alte Einteilung der arabischen Dichter und das 'Amr-Buch des Ibn al-Jarrāḥ' (= supplement to) R. Geyer, *Die Mukāṯara von aṭ-Ṭayālisī* (Vienna and Leipzig, 1927).

Bräunlich, E., 'Al-Ḫalīl und das *Kitāb al-'Ain*', *Islamica* 2 (1926), pp. 58–95.

Buhl, F., *Das Leben Muhammeds*, tr. H. H. Schaeder (Leipzig, 1930).

Burton, J., *The Collection of the Qur'ān* (Cambridge, 1977).

Caetani, L., *Annali dell' Islam*, 2 vols (Milan, 1905–7).

Cheikh-Moussa, A., 'La négation d'Eros, ou Le *'ishq* d'après deux épitres d'al-Ǧâḥiẓ', *Studia Islamica* 72 (1990), pp. 71–119.

Cook, M., *Early Muslim Dogma: a Source-Critical Study* (Cambridge, 1981).

— *Muhammad* (Oxford, 1983).

Cooperson, M. and S. M. Toorawa (eds), *Arabic Literary Culture*, 500–925 (Detroit, 2004).

Crone, P., *Meccan Trade and the Rise of Islam* (Princeton, 1987).

Crone, P. and M. Cook, *Hagarism. The Making of the Islamic World* (Cambridge, 1977).

Danecki, J., 'Early Arabic Phonetical Theory. Phonetics of al-Ḫalīl Ibn Aḥmad and Sībawaihi', *Rocznik Orientalistyczny* 39 (1978), pp. 51–6.

Déroche, F., *La transmission écrite du Coran dans les débuts de l'Islam. Le codex Parisino-Petropolitanus* (Leiden, in press).

Déroche, F. et al., *Manuel de codicologie des manuscrits en écriture arabe* (Paris, 2000).

Duri, A. A., *The Rise of Historical Writing among the Arabs*, ed. and tr. L. I. Conrad, introd. F. M. Donner (Princeton, 1983).

— 'Al-Zuhrī. A Study on the Beginnings of History Writing in Islam', *BSOAS* 19 (1957), pp. 1–12.

Dutton, Y., *The Origins of Islamic Law. The Qur'ān, the Muwaṭṭa' and Madinan 'amal* (Surrey, 1999).

Eche, Y., *Les bibliothèques arabes publiques et sémi-publiques en Mésopotamie, en Syrie et en Egypte au Moyen Age* (Damascus, 1967).

Endress, G., 'Handschriftenkunde', *GAPh*, vol. 1, pp. 271–302.

— 'Wissenschaftliche Literatur', *GAPh*, vol. 2, pp. 400–506, vol. 3, pp. 3–152.

Ess, J. van, *Anfänge muslimischer Theologie. Zwei antiqadaritische Traktate aus dem ersten Jahrhundert der Hiǧra* (Beirut, 1977).

— 'Das *Kitāb al-Irǧā'* des Ḥasan b. Muḥammad b. al-Ḥanafiyya', *Arabica* 21 (1975), pp. 20–52.

— *Das Kitāb an-Nakṯ des Naẓẓām und seine Rezeption im Kitāb al-Futyā des Ǧāḥiẓ* (Göttingen, 1972).

— *Theologie und Gesellschaft im 2. und 3. Jahrhundert Hidschra. Eine Geschichte des religiösen Denkens im frühen Islam*, 6 vols (Berlin, 1991–5).

— *Zwischen Ḥadīṯ und Theologie* (Berlin, 1975).

Fischer, A., *Biographien von Gewährsmännern des Ibn Isḥāq, hauptsächlich aus aḏ-Ḏahabī* (Leiden, 1980).

Fleischhammer, M. *Die Quellen des* Kitāb al-Aġānī (Wiesbaden, 2004).

Freimark, P., 'Das Vorwort als literarische Form in der arabischen Literatur', doctoral thesis, Münster, 1967.

Fück, J., 'Beiträge zur Überlieferungsgeschichte von Buḫārīs Traditionssammlung', *ZDMG* 92 (1938), pp. 60–87.

— 'Muḥammad Ibn Isḥāq. Literaturhistorische Untersuchungen', doctoral thesis, Frankurt a.M., 1925.

— 'Die Rolle des Traditionalismus im Islam', *ZDMG* 93 (1939), pp. 1–32.

Gibb, H. A. R., 'The Social Significance of the Shuubiyya', in *idem*, *Studies on the Civilization of Islam*, ed. S. J. Shaw and W. R. Polk (London, 1962).

Gilliot, Cl., 'Les débuts de l'exégèse coranique', *Revue du monde musulman et de la Méditerranée* 58 (1990), pp. 82–100.

— *Exégèse, langue et théologie en Islam. L'exégèse coranique de Tabari (m. 311/923)* (Paris, 1990).

— 'Les «informateurs» juifs et chrétiens de Muḥammad. Reprise d'un problème traité par Aloys Sprenger et Theodor Nöldeke', *JSAI* 22 (1998), pp. 84–126.

— 'Muḥammad, le Coran et les «contraintes de l'histoire»', in S. Wild (ed.), *The Qur'ān as Text* (Leiden, 1996), pp. 3–26.

— 'Muqātil, grand exégète, traditionniste et théologien maudit', *JA* 279 (1991), pp. 39–92.

— 'Portrait «mythique» d'Ibn 'Abbās', *Arabica* 32 (1985), pp. 127–84.

Goldfeld, Y., 'Muqātil Ibn Sulaymān', in *Arabic and Islamic Studies*, ed. J. Mansour (Ramat-Gan, 1978), vol. 2, pp. 1–18.

Goldziher, I., 'Kämpfe um die Stellung des Ḥadīth', *ZDMG* 61 (1907), pp. 860–72 = 'Disputes over the Status of *Ḥadīth* in Islam', tr. G. Goldbloom, in H. Motzki (ed.), *Ḥadīth: Origins and Developments* (Aldershot; Burlington, VT, 2004), pp. 55–66.

— 'Neue Materialen zur Literatur des Ueberlieferungswesens bei den Muhammedanern', *ZDMG* 50 (1896), pp. 465–506.

— 'Some Notes on the Dīwāns of the Arabic Tribes', *JRAS* (1897), pp. 233–40.

— 'Ueber die Entwickelung des Ḥadīth', in *Muhammedanische Studien*, vol. 2 (Halle, 1890), pp. 1–274 = 'On the Development of the Ḥadīth', in *Muslim Studies*, ed. S. M. Stern, tr. C. R. Barber and S. M. Stern (London, 1971), vol. 2, pp. 17–251.

Görke, A. and G. Schoeler, *Die ältesten Berichte über das Leben Muḥammads. Das Korpus 'Urwa ibn az-Zubair* (Princeton, 2008).

— 'Reconstructing the Earliest *sīra* Texts: the Hiğra in the Corpus of 'Urwa b. al-Zubayr', *Der Islam* 82 (2005), pp. 209–20.

Graf, S., *Geschichte der christlichen arabischen Literatur*, vol. 1, *Die Übersetzungen* (Vatican City, 1944).

Günther, S., *Quellenuntersuchungen zu den «Maqātil aṭ-Ṭālibiyyīn» des Abū l-Farağ al-Iṣfahānī (gest. 356/967)* (Hildesheim, 1991).

— 'Maqātil Literature in Medieval Islam', *JAL* 25 (1994), pp. 192–212.

— 'New Results in the Theory of Source-Criticism in Medieval Arabic Literature', *al-Abḥāth* 42 (1994), pp. 4–15.

— 'Praise to the Books! Al-Jāḥiẓ and Ibn Qutayba on the Excellence of the Written Word in Medieval Islam', *JSAI* 32 (2006), pp. 125–43.

Gutas, D., *Greek Thought, Arabic Culture. The Graeco-Arabic Translation Movement in Baghdad and Early 'Abbāsid Society (2nd–4th/8th–10th centuries)* (London, 1998).

Hamori, A., 'Al-Mutanabbī', in Ashtiany et al., *'Abbāsid Belles-Lettres*, pp. 300–14.

Hartmann, M., 'Die arabisch-islamischen Handschriften der Universitätsbibliothek zu Leipzig und die Sammlungen Hartmann und Haupt', *Zeitschrift für Assyriologie* 23 (1909), pp. 235–66.

Haywood, J. A., *Arabic Lexicography – Its History and its Place in the General History of Lexicography* (Leiden, 1960).

Heinrichs, W., *Arabische Dichtung und grieschische Poetik* (Beirut, 1969).

Horovitz, J., 'Alter und Ursprung des Isnād', *Der Islam* 8 (1918), pp. 39–47 = 'The Antiquity and Origin of the Isnād', tr. G. Goldbloom, in H. Motzki (ed.), *Ḥadīth: Origins and Development* (Aldershot; Burlington, VT, 2004), pp. 151–61.

— *The Earliest Biographies of the Prophet and their Authors*, ed. L. I. Conrad (Princeton, 2002).

Horst, H., 'Zur Überlieferung im Korankommentar aṭ-Ṭabarīs', *ZDMG* 103 (1953), pp. 290–307.

Humbert, G., 'Le *Kitāb* de Sībawayhi et l'autonomie de l'écrit', *Arabica* 44 (1997), pp. 553–67.

Jaeger, W. W., *Studien zur Entstehungsgeschichte der Metaphysik des Aristoteles* (Berlin, 1912).

Jarrar, M., *Die Prophetenbiographie im islamischen Spanien. Ein Beitrag zur Überlieferungs- and Redaktionsgeschichte* (Frankfurt a.M., 1989).

Jeffery, A., *Materials for the History of the Text of the Qur'ān. The Old Codices. The Kitāb al-Maṣāḥif of Ibn Abī Dāwūd …* (Cairo, 1936, Leiden, 1937).

Juynboll, G. H. A., *Muslim Tradition* (Cambridge, 1983).

— 'Muslim's Introduction to his *Ṣaḥīḥ*. Translated and Annotated', *JSAI* 5 (1984), pp. 263–311.

Kaplan, J., *The Redaction of the Babylonian Talmud* (New York, 1933).

Kermani, N., *Gott ist schön. Das ästhetische Erleben des Koran* (Munich, ²2000).

Khalidi, T. (tr.), "The Boasts of the Blacks over the Whites' (Jahiz)', *Islamic Quarterly* 25(1&2) (1981), pp. 3–52.

Kilpatrick, H., *Making the Great Book of Songs. Compilation and the author's craft in Abū l-Faraj al-Iṣbahānī's* Kitāb al-aghānī (London, New York, 2003).

Kister, M. J., 'Lā taqra'ū l-qur'āna …', *JSAI* 22 (1988), pp. 127–62.

— 'The Seven Odes', *RSO* 44 (1970), pp. 27–36 = Kister, *Studies in Jāhiliyya and Early Islam* (London, 1980), ch. XVI.

Kraus, P., 'Zu Ibn al-Muqaffa'. I. Die angeblichen Aristoteles-Übersetzungen des Ibn al-Muqaffa'', *RSO* 14 (1933), pp. 1–14.

Kunitzsch, P., 'Über das Frühstadium der arabischen Aneignung antiken Gutes', *Saeculum* 26 (1975), pp. 268–282.

Lammens, H., 'Qoran et tradition. Comment fut composée la vie de Mahomet?', *Recherches des sciences religieuses* 1 (1910), pp. 27–51.

Latham, D., 'The Beginnings of Arabic Prose Literature: The Epistolary Genre', in A. F. Beeston et al., *Arabic Literature to the End of the Umayyad Period* (Cambridge, 1983), pp. 154–79.

— 'Ibn al-Muqaffa' and Early 'Abbāsid Prose', in A. F. Beeston et al., *Arabic Literature to the End of the Umayyad Period* (Cambridge, 1983), pp. 48–77.

Lecker, M., *The 'Constitution of Medina': Muḥammad's First Legal Document* (Princeton, 2004).

— 'The Death of the Prophet Muḥammad's Father: Did Wāqidī Invent some of the Evidence?', *ZDMG* 145 (1995), pp. 9–27.

— 'Zayd b. Thābit: 'A Jew with Two Sidelocks': Judaism and Literacy in Pre-Islamic Medina (Yathrib)', *Journal of Near Eastern Studies*, vol. 56/4 (1997), pp. 259–73.

Lecomte, G., *Ibn Qutayba. L'homme, son oeuvre, ses idées* (Damascus, 1965).

— *Le Traité des Divergences du Ḥadīth d'Ibn Qutayba. Traduction du Kitāb Ta'wīl mukhtalif al-ḥadīth* (Damascus, 1962).

Leder, S., *Das Korpus al-Haiṯam ibn 'Adī (st. 207/822). Herkunft, Überlieferung, Gestalt früher Texte der aḫbār Literatur* (Frankfurt, 1991).

— 'Dokumente zum Ḥadīṯ in Schrifttum und Unterricht aus Damaskus im 6./12. Jhdt.', *Oriens* 34 (1994), pp. 57–75.

Leder, S., Y. M. al-Sawwās and M. al-Ṣāgharjī, *Mu'jam al-Samā'āt al-Dimashqiyya. Les certificats d'audition à Damas 550–750 h./1155–1349* (Damascus, 1996).

Leemhuis, F., 'Ms. 1075 Tafsīr of the Cairene Dār al-kutub and Muǧāhid's Tafsīr', in *Proceedings of the Ninth Congress of the Union européenne des arabisants et islamisants* (Amsterdam, 1978), ed. R. Peters (Leiden, 1981), pp. 169–180.

Lieberman, S., *Hellenism in Jewish Palestine* (New York, 1950).

Loth, O., *Das Classenbuch des Ibn Sa'd. Einleitende Untersuchungen über Authentie und Inhalt* (Leipzig, 1869).

MacKay, P. A., 'Certificates of Transmission on a Manuscript of the Maqāmāt of Ḥarīrī (Ms. *Cairo, Adab* 105)', *Transactions of the American Philosophical Society* N.S. 61/4 (1971), pp. 1–81.

Madigan, D., *The Qur'ān's Self-Image: Writing and Authority in Islam's Scripture* (Princeton, 2001).

Marçais, W., 'Le Taqrīb de en-Nawawī, traduit et annoté', *JA* 16 (1900), pp. 315–46, 478–531; 17 (1901), pp. 101–49, 193–232, 524–40; 18 (1901), pp. 61–146.

Melchert, C., 'The *Musnad* of Aḥmad ibn Ḥanbal: How It was Composed and What Distinguishes It from the Six Books', *Der Islam* 82 (2005), pp. 32–51.

Mez, A., *Die Renaissance des Islams* (Heidelberg, 1922) = *The Renaissance of Islam*, tr. S. Khuda Bakhsh and D. S. Margoliouth (London, 1937).

Monroe, J. T., 'Oral Composition in Pre-Islamic Poetry', *JAL* 3 (1972), pp. 1–53.

Montgomery, J. E., 'al-Jahiz,' in *Arabic Literary Culture*, 500–925, ed. M. Cooperson and S. M. Toorawa (Detroit, 2004), pp. 231–42.

Mottahedeh, R. P., *Loyalty and Leadership in Early Islamic Society* (Princeton, 1980).

Motzki, H., *Die Anfänge der islamischen Jurisprudenz. Ihre Entwicklung in Mekka bis zur Mitte des 2./8. Jahrhunderts* (Stuttgart, 1991) = *The Origins of Islamic Jurisprudence: Meccan Fiqh before the Classical Schools*, tr. M. Katz (Leiden, Boston, 2002).

— 'Der Fiqh des -Zuhrī: Die Quellenproblematik', *Der Islam* 68 (1991), pp. 1–44.

— 'The *Muṣannaf* of 'Abd al-Razzāq al-Ṣan'ānī as a Source of Authentic *Aḥādīth* of the First Century A.H.', *JNES* 50 (1991), pp. 1–21.

— 'The Prophet and the Cat. On Dating Mālik's *Muwaṭṭa'* and Legal Traditions', *JSAI* 22 (1998), pp. 18–83.

Muranyi, M., *Ein altes Fragment medinensischer Jurisprudenz aus Qairawān: Aus dem Kitāb al-Ḥağğ des 'Abd al-'Azīz b. 'Abd Allāh b. Abī Salamah al-Māğishūn* (st. 164/780–81) (Stuttgart, 1985).

— *Die Rechtsbücher des Qairawāners Saḥnūn b. Sa'īd. Entstehungsgeschichte und Werküberlieferung* (Stuttgart, 1999).

— 'Fiqh', in *GAPh*, vol. 2, pp. 299–325.

— 'Ibn Isḥāq's *K. al-Maghāzī* in der *riwāya* von Yūnus b. Bukair. Bemerkungen zur frühen Überlieferungsgeschichte', *JSAI* 14 (1991), pp. 214–75.

Nagel, T., 'Vom «Qur'ān» zur «Schrift». Bells Hypothese aus religionsgeschichtlicher Sicht', *Der Islam* 60 (1983), pp. 143–65.

Neuwirth, A., 'Koran', in *GAPh*, vol. 2, pp. 96–135.

Nöldeke, Th., *Geschichte des Qorāns*, 3 vols, vols 1–2, ed. F. Schwally, vol. 3, ed. G. Bergsträsser and O. Pretzl (Leipzig, 1919–38, repr. Hildesheim, 1981).

— 'Die Tradition über das Leben Muhammeds', *Der Islam* 5 (1914), pp. 160–70.

— Review of Leone Caetani, *Annali dell'Islam*, *WZKM* 21 (1907), pp. 297– 312.

Nyberg, H. S., *Die Religionen des alten Iran* (Leipzig, 1939).

— 'Bemerkungen zum «Buch der Götzen» von Ibn al-Kalbī', in *Dragma. Martino P. Nilsson… dedicatum* (Lund, 1939), pp. 347–66.

Paret, R. (tr.), *Der Koran, Kommentar und Konkordanz* (Stuttgart, [2]1980).

Pedersen, J., *The Arabic Book*, tr. G. French, ed. R. Hillenbrand (Princeton, 1984).

Pellat, Ch., *The Life and Works of Jahiz: Translations of Selected Texts*, tr. D. M. Hawke (Berkeley, 1969).

— *Le milieu baṣrien et la formation de Ğāḥiẓ* (Paris, 1953).

— 'Ğāḥiẓiana III. Essai d'inventaire de l'oeuvre ğāḥiẓienne', *Arabica* 3 (1956), pp. 147–80.

— 'Nouvel essai d'inventaire de l'oeuvre ğāḥiẓienne', *Arabica* 31 (1984), pp. 117–64.

Peters, F. E., *Aristotle and the Arabs: The Aristotelian Tradition in Islam* (New York, 1968).

— 'The Quest of the Historical Muhammad', *International Journal of Middle East Studies* 23 (1991), pp. 291–315.

Peterson, E., *Heis Theos* (Göttingen, 1926).

Pöhlmann, E., 'Zur Überlieferung griechischer Literatur vom 8. bis 4. Jh', in *Der Übergang von der Mündlichkeit zur Literatur bei den Griechen*, ed. W. Kullmann and M. Reichel (Tübingen, 1990) [= *Scriptoralia* 30], pp. 11–30.

Praechter, K., 'Die griechischen Aristoteleskommentare', *Byzantinische Zeitschrift* 18 (1909), pp. 516–38.

Puin, G.-R., 'Der Dīwān von 'Umar Ibn al-Ḫaṭṭāb', doctoral thesis, Bonn, 1970.

al-Qāḍī, W., 'Early Islamic State Letters: The Question of Authenticity', in *The Byzantine and Early Islamic Near East*, vol. 1, *Problems in the Literary Source Material*, ed. A. Cameron and L. I. Conrad (Princeton, 1992), pp. 215–75.

Quiring-Zoche, R., 'How al-Buḫārī's *Ṣaḥīḥ* was Edited in the Middle Ages: 'Alī al-Yunīnī and his *Rumūz*', *Bulletin d'études orientales* 50 (1998), pp. 191–222.

Qummī, Ḥ., 'Kitābī kalāmī az Ḍirār ibn 'Amr', in *Kitāb-i māh-i dīn* 89 (1383–4 H Shamsiyyah), pp. 4–13.

Reuschel, W., *Al-Ḫalīl ibn-Aḥmad, der Lehrer Sībawaihs, als Grammatiker* (Berlin, 1959).

Ritter, H., 'Studien zur Geschichte der islamischen Frömmigkeit I: Ḥasan al-Baṣrī', *Der Islam* 21 (1933), pp. 67–82.

Rosenthal, F., *A History of Muslim Historiography* (Leiden, ²1968).

Rubin, U. 'The 'Constitution of Medina', Some Notes', *Studia Islamica* 62 (1985), pp. 5–23.

Saliba, G., *al-Fikr al-'ilmī al-'arabī: nash'atuhu wa-taṭawwuruhu* (Beirut, 1998).

Sauvaget, J., *Introduction à l'histoire de l'Orient musulman. Eléments de bibliographie*, rev. edn Cl. Cahen (Paris, 1961).

Sayed, R., *Die Revolte des Ibn al-Aš'aṯ und die Koranleser* (Freiburg i.Br., 1977).

Schacht, J., *The Origins of Muhammadan Jurisprudence* (Oxford, 1950).

— 'On Mūsā ibn 'Uqba's *Kitāb al-Maghāzī*', *Acta Orientalia* 21 (1953), pp. 288–300.

— 'A Revaluation of Islamic Traditions', *JRAS* (1949), pp. 143–54.

Schacht, J. and M. Meyerhof, *The Medico-Philosophical Controversy between Ibn Buṭlān of Baghdad and Ibn Riḍwān of Cairo* (Cairo, 1937).

Schoeler, G., *Arabische Handschriften*, vol. 2 (= *Verzeichnis der orientalischen Handschriften in Deutschland*, XVIIB, 2) (Stuttgart, 1990).

— *Charakter und Authentie der muslimischen Überlieferung über das Leben Mohammeds* (Berlin, New York, 1996).

— *The Oral and the Written in Early Islam*, tr. U. Vagelpohl, ed. J. E. Montgomery (London, New York, 2006).

— 'Die Anwendung der oral poetry-Theorie auf die arabische Literatur', *Der Islam* 66 (1989), pp. 205–36 = 'Oral Poetry Theory and Arabic Literature', in Schoeler, *The Oral and the Written*, ch. 4, pp. 87–110.

— 'Die Frage der schriftlichen oder mündlichen Überlieferung der Wissenschaften im frühen Islam', *Der Islam* 62 (1985), pp. 201–30 = 'The Transmission of the Sciences in Early Islam: Oral or Written', in Schoeler, *The Oral and the Written*, ch. 1, pp. 28–44.

— 'Mündliche Thora und Ḥadīṯ: Überlieferung, Schreibverbot, Redaktion', *Der Islam* 66 (1989), pp. 213–51 = 'Oral Torah and *Ḥadīṯ*: Transmission, Prohibition of Writing, Redaction', in Schoeler, *The Oral and the Written*, ch. 5, pp. 111–41.

— 'Schreiben und Veröffentlichen. Zu Verwendung und Funktion der Schrift in den ersten islamischen Jahrhunderten', *Der Islam* 69 (1992), pp. 1–43 = 'Writing and Publishing: On the Use and Function of Writing in Early Islam', in Schoeler, *The Oral and the Written*, ch. 3, pp. 62–86.

— 'Weiteres zur Frage der schriftlichen oder mündlichen Überlieferung der Wissenschaften im Islam', *Der Islam* 66 (1989), pp. 38–67 = 'The Transmission of the Sciences in Early Islam Revisited', in Schoeler, *The Oral and the Written*, ch. 2, pp. 45–61.

— 'Wer ist der Verfasser des *Kitāb al-'Ain?*', *Zeitschrift für Arabische Linguistik* 38 (2000), pp. 15–45 = 'Who is the Author of the *Kitāb al-'ayn?*', in Schoeler, *The Oral and the Written*, ch. 6, pp. 142–63.

— 'Writing and Publishing. On the Use and Function of Writing in the First Centuries of Islam', *Arabica* 44 (1997), pp. 423–35.

— Review of W. Werkmeister, *Quellenuntersuchungen*, ZDMG 136 (1986), pp. 118–28.

Seidensticker, T., *Arabische Handschriften*, vol. 4 (= *Verzeichnis der orientalischen Handschriften in Deutschland*, vol. XVIIB, 4) (Stuttgart, 2005).

Sellheim, R., *Materialien zur arabischen Literaturgeschichte*, 2 vols (Wiesbaden, Stuttgart, 1976–87).

— 'Abū 'Alī al-Qālī. Zum Problem mündlicher und schriftlicher Überlieferung am Beispiel von Sprichwörtersammlungen', in *Studien zur Geschichte und Kultur des Vorderen Orients. Festschrift für Bertold Spuler zum siebzigsten Geburtstag*, ed. H. R. Roemer and A. Noth (Leiden, 1981), pp. 362–74.

— 'Muhammeds erstes Offenbarungserlebnis. Zum Problem mündlicher und schriftlicher Überlieferung im 1./7. und 2./8. Jahrhundert', *JSAI* 10 (1987), pp. 1–16.

Sergeant, R. B., 'Early Arabic Prose', in A. F. Beeston et al., *Arabic Literature to the End of the Umayyad Period* (Cambridge, 1983), pp. 114–53.

— 'Meccan Trade and the Rise of the Islam: Misconceptions and Flawed Polemics', *JAOS* 110 (1967), pp. 472–86.

Sezgin, F., *Buḫârî'nin Kaynakları hakkında araştırmalar* (Istanbul, 1956).

— *Geschichte des arabischen Schrifttums*, 13 vols (Leiden, 1967–2007).

Sezgin, U., 'Abū Miḫnaf, Ibrāhīm b. Hilāl al-Ṯaqafī and Muḥammad b. A'ṯam al-Kūfī über *ġārāt*', ZDMG 131 (1981), pp. *1*–*3*.

Shalḥat, V., *al-Naz'ah al-kalāmiyyah fī uslūb al-Jāḥiẓ* (Cairo, 1964).

Spies, O., *Das Buch at-Tašwīq aṭ-ṭibbī des Ṣā'id ibn al-Ḥasan* (Bonn, 1968).

Spitaler, A., *al-Qalamu aḥadu l-lisānaini* (Munich, 1989).

Sprenger, A., *Das Leben und die Lehre des Mohammad* (Berlin, ²1869).

— 'Ueber das Traditionswesen bei den Arabern', ZDMG 10 (1856), pp. 1–17.

Stauth, G., 'Die Überlieferung des Korankommentars Muǧāhid b. Ǧabrs', doctoral thesis, Giessen, 1969.
Strack, H. L., *Einleitung in Talmud und Midraš* (Munich, [5]1921).
Stülpnagel, J. von, "Urwa Ibn az-Zubair. Sein Leben und seine Bedeutung als Quelle frühislamischer Überlieferung', doctoral thesis, Tübingen, 1956.
al-Ṭāhir, S. Mursī, *Bidāyat al-kitābah al-ta'rīkhiyyah 'inda al-'Arab, awwal sīrah fī al-Islām: 'Urwah ibn al-Zubayr ibn al-'Awwām* (Beirut, 1995).
Talmon, R., *Arabic Grammar in its Formative Age.* Kitāb al-'Ayn *and its Attribution to Ḫalīl b. Aḥmad* (Leiden, 1997).
Toorawa, S. M., *Ibn Abī Ṭāhir Ṭayfūr and Arabic Writerly Culture: a Ninth-Century Bookman in Baghdad* (London, New York, 2005).
— 'Defining *Adab* by (Re)defining the *Adīb*: Ibn Abī Ṭāhir and Storytelling', in *On Fiction and* Adab *in Medieval Arabic Literature*, ed. P. F. Kennedy (Wiesbaden, 2005), pp. 287–304.
— 'Ibn Abī Ṭāhir Ṭayfūr vs al-Jāḥiẓ', in *'Abbāsid Studies. Occasional Papers of the School of 'Abbāsid Studies. Cambridge, 6–10 July 2002*, ed. J. E. Montgomery (Leuven, 2004), pp. 247–61.
Troupeau, G., 'A propos des grammairiens cités par Sībawayhi dans le *Kitāb*', *Arabica* 8 (1961), pp. 309–12.
Tyan, E., 'Le notariat et le régime de la preuve par écrit dans la pratique du droit musulman', *Annales de l'Ecole française de droit de Beyrouth* 2 (1945), pp. 3–99.
Vajda, G., *Les Certificats de lectures et transmissions dans les manuscrits arabes de la Bibliothèque Nationale* (Paris, 1956).
— *La transmission du savoir en Islam (VIIe–XVIIIe siècles)*, ed. N. Cottart (London, 1983).
Versteegh, C. H. M., *Arabic Grammar and Qur'ānic Exegesis in Early Islam* (Leiden, 1993).
— 'Die arabische Sprachwissenschaft', *GAPh*, vol. 2, pp. 148–76.
Violet, B., 'Ein zweisprachiges Psalmfragment aus Damaskus', *Orientalistische Literaturzeitung* 4 (1901), pp. 384–403, 425–41, 475–88.
Wagner, E., *Grundzüge der klassischen arabischen Dichtung*, 2 vols (Darmstadt, 1987–8).
— *Die Überlieferung des Abū Nuwās Dīwān und seine Handschriften* (Mainz-Wiesbaden, 1957).
Wakin, J. A., *The Function of Documents in Islamic Law. The Chapter on Sales from Ṭaḥāwī's* Kitāb al-Shurūṭ al-kabīr (New York, 1972).
Wansbrough, J., *Quranic Studies. Sources and Methods of Scriptural Interpretation* (Oxford, 1977).
— *The Sectarian Milieu. Content and Composition of Islamic Salvation History* (Oxford, 1978).
Watt, W. M., *Bell's Introduction to the Qur'ān* (Edinburgh, 1977).
— *Muhammad at Mecca* (Oxford, 1953).
— *Muhammad at Medina* (Oxford, 1956).

— 'The Reliability of Ibn Isḥāq's Sources', in *La vie de prophète Mahomet: colloque de Strasbourg (octobre 1980)*, pref. T. Fahd (Paris, 1983), pp. 31–43.
— and M. V. McDonald (trs), *The Foundation of the Community*, The History of al-Ṭabarī, vol. 7 (Albany, 1987).
Weipert, R. and St. Weninger, 'Die erhaltenen Werke des Ibn Abī d-Dunyā', *ZDMG* 146 (1996), pp. 415–55.
Weisweiler, M., *Die Methodik des Diktatkollegs*. See: al-Samʿānī, *Adab al-imlā'*.
Wellhausen, J., 'Ibn Sa'd: Die Schreiben Muhammads und die Gesandtschaften an ihn', in *idem*, *Skizzen und Vorarbeiten*, vol. 4 (Berlin, 1899), pp. 85–194 (German), 1–78 (Arabic).
— 'Muhammads Gemeindeordnung von Medina', in *idem*, *Skizzen und Vorarbeiten*, vol. 4 (Berlin, 1899), pp. 65–83.
Werkmeister, W., *Quellenuntersuchungen zum Kitāb al-ʿIqd al-farīd des Andalusiers Ibn ʿAbdrabbih (246/860–328/940). Ein Beitrag zur arabischen Literaturgeschichte* (Berlin, 1983).
Westerink, L. G., 'Ein astrologisches Kolleg aus dem Jahre 564', *Byzantinische Zeitschrift* 64 (1971), pp. 6–21.
Wild, S., *Das* Kitāb al-ʿAin *und die arabische Lexikographie* (Wiesbaden, 1965).
— (ed.), *The Qur'ān as Text* (Leiden, 1996).
— 'Arabische Lexikographie', *GAPh*, vol. 2, pp. 136–47.
— '«Die schauerliche Öde des heiligen Buches». Westliche Wertungen des koranischen Stils', in *Gott ist schön und Er liebt die Schönheit. Festschrift für Annemarie Schimmel*, ed. A. Giese and J. Chr. Bürgel (Bern, 1994), pp. 429–47.
Zolondek, Leon, 'An Approach to the Problem of the Sources of the *Kitāb al-Aġānī*', *JNES* 19 (1960), pp. 217–234.
Zwettler, Michael, *The Oral Tradition of Classical Arabic Poetry: Its Character and Implications* (Columbus, 1978).

Index

Note: The Arabic definite article 'al-' as well as the word *Kitāb*, here abbreviated to *K.*, are ignored alphabetically.

Citations from Scripture